ALSO BY FRED MOODY

I Sing the Body Electronic

Fighting Chance

THE VISIONARY POSITION

THE
VISIONARY
POSITION

The Inside Story
of the Digital Dreamers Who Are
Making Virtual Reality a Reality

FRED MOODY

TIMES BUSINESS

RANDOM HOUSE

Copyright © 1999 by Fred Moody

All rights reserved under International and Pan-American
Copyright Conventions. Published in the United States by Times Books,
a division of Random House, Inc., New York, and simultaneously in Canada
by Random House of Canada Limited, Toronto.

Library of Congress Cataloging-in-Publication Data

Moody, Fred.
The visionary position: the inside story of the digital dreamers
who are making virtual reality a reality / Fred Moody.
p.   cm.
ISBN 0-8129-2852-0
1. Human-computer interaction—Research—History.
2. Virtual reality—Research—History.
3. Furness, Thomas A.   I. Title.
QA76.9.H85M67   1999
004′.01′9—dc21   98-22335

Random House website address: www.atrandom.com
Printed in the United States of America on acid-free paper
2   4   6   8   9   7   5   3
First Edition
Book design by Oksana Kushnir

SPECIAL SALES
Times Books are available at special discounts for bulk purchases for sales promotions
or premiums. Special editions, including personalized covers, excerpts of existing books,
and corporate imprints, can be created in large quantities for special needs. For more
information, write to Special Markets, Times Books, 201 East 50th Street, New York,
New York 10022, or call 800-800-3246.

For Don McLeod

My soul stands now planted in what once was for it
a practically unreal object, and speaks from it as
from its proper habitat and centre.

—*William James*

He related how the crazy installation had developed,
step by step, typically, from the furthest-fetched
of visions to a reality that would not function.

—*Samuel Beckett*

CONTENTS

CAST OF "CHARACTERS"

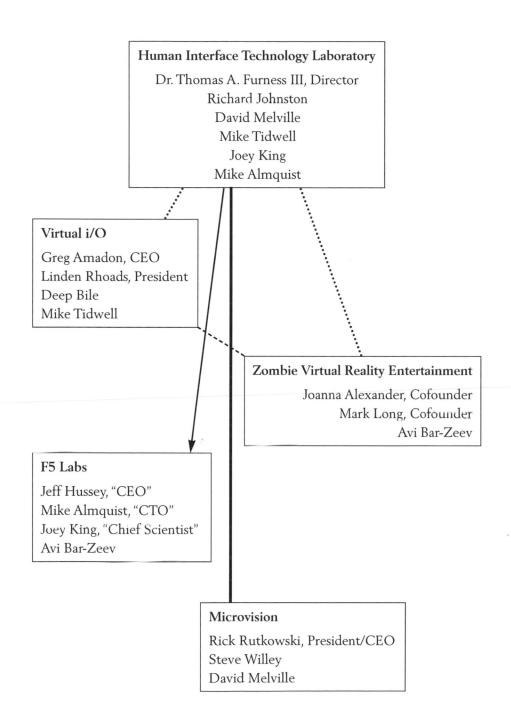

Human Interface Technology Laboratory

Dr. Thomas A. Furness III, Director
Richard Johnston
David Melville
Mike Tidwell
Joey King
Mike Almquist

Virtual i/O

Greg Amadon, CEO
Linden Rhoads, President
Deep Bile
Mike Tidwell

Zombie Virtual Reality Entertainment

Joanna Alexander, Cofounder
Mark Long, Cofounder
Avi Bar-Zeev

F5 Labs

Jeff Hussey, "CEO"
Mike Almquist, "CTO"
Joey King, "Chief Scientist"
Avi Bar-Zeev

Microvision

Rick Rutkowski, President/CEO
Steve Willey
David Melville

INTRODUCTION

This book has distant origins in two conversations I had years ago—one with Intel's Andrew Grove, the other with Microsoft's Bill Gates. I had asked each of them why he and his company had succeeded so spectacularly, and discovered that neither man seemed to feel particularly successful. Grove said, "Well, there was a certain amount of historical inevitability to it," and Gates said, "We tend to focus more on our failures here than on our successes."

I went on to discover at Microsoft—arguably the most successful company in history—a culture thoroughly steeped in feelings of anxiety and failure. And the histories of both companies eventually made it clear to me that if they had not parlayed a combination of skill, determination, luck, and timing into their positions of dominance, someone else would have. It was as if technology itself were marching forward, and the people fated to develop and profit from it were simply soft machines exploited by progress to help move things along.

Gates's disgruntlement and Grove's humility eventually led to more questions: What is success? Does real success ever feel like success to the successful person? And in industry, where does the individual leave off and the zeitgeist begin?

I had scarcely begun work on this book when I encountered a visiting Japanese engineer, the Fujitsu Research Institute's Dr. Masahiro Kawahata, here to study and meet with some of the researchers and entrepreneurs whose work I was chronicling. Kawahata is an unabashed lover of the United States, which he regards as a vibrant, turbulent, and productive dream factory. "Every day a new company is born, but every day some other company is dying, right?" he said to me. "So it is activating the U.S. economy!"

Kawahata described the essential difference between the United States and Japan as one of aptitude and level of imagination. Japanese primacy in manufacturing, he said, arose because "the U.S. engineer didn't recognize the importance of product engineering. Or quality engineering. The idea is fine, but product engineering is poor. In Japan, the idea is poor, but product engineering is very nice." Although the Japanese industrial complex built a massive economic machine out of its ability to turn American inventions into products, this disparity has caused more crises than complacency in Japan. "We in Japan now are saying that we are very poor in generating ideas. And the *idea* is very important now. So we have a lot of talk about why the U.S. is better at generating new ideas, and why Japan is poor. That's a kind of big issue in Japan in recent years. We are very well trained, but lack creativity."

There does seem to be something uniquely American in the niche we have in this country for what might be called the shamans of engineering—visionaries who struggle to realize a more distant and less immediately profitable future than the rest of us have the time or imagination to contemplate. As I went on in the course of this project to watch visionaries spin fantasies for money, and to watch young industrialists flare up and burn out in the course of trying to get their outlandish ideas off the ground, I grew thoroughly amazed at the American worship of the American dreamer. I was to learn that there is an unacknowledged and in large part accidental appreciation in this country for the restless soul who is determined to find a different, or better, or more exciting way to do things. These people are never of practical mind and often seem not to be of particularly sound mind, yet their fellow citizens indulge them again and again in their fantasies. I came to see the group in this book as exemplars of the American spirit that has engendered so many industries (automobile, aerospace, oil, cola, personal computer, entertainment . . .) that have gone on to dominate the world. I was to come away from my research convinced that I had watched an archetypal exercise: the messy, troublesome birth process of a new American industry, a process identical in its dynamic to the origins of countless previous passages from dreamy vision to multibillion-dollar enterprise.

For as long as engineers have dreamed of building faster and more powerful computers, some among them have dreamed of displaying computer-stored and -generated information in three dimensions, with users walking through information landscapes the way they walk down grocery-store aisles and city streets. Among the earliest and most persistent of these dreamers was Dr. Thomas A. Furness III, an electrical engineer who began working on such display technology in 1966 (twenty-three years before the term "virtual reality" was coined by Jaron Lanier), in a secret laboratory at Wright-Patterson Air Force Base, in Dayton, Ohio. After more than twenty years of largely classified research into what he called the "visually coupled system," or the "virtual world interface," Furness left the air force and set out on an avowed mission to turn his new interface into a powerful weapon of moral and social change for the better.

Furness's wanderings led him to Seattle, Washington, in 1989, where he set up shop on the campus of the University of Washington under the auspices of the Washington Technology Center (WTC). Established in 1983, the WTC was charged with licensing technology developed at the University of Washington to businesses headquartered and incorporated in the state as a way of hastening the transition of academic lab discoveries into the marketplace. Furness's new lab, which he dubbed the Human Interface Technology (HIT) Laboratory, commenced innumerable research projects into the development and use of VR hardware and software, with particular emphasis on "human factors"—the ways in which people assimilate and disseminate information through computer interfaces.

Although most of the work he had done for the air force was classified, Furness was well known in the worldwide VR community as one of a handful of pioneers. To the VR literate, his move to

Seattle was big news, and before long a somewhat disorganized orbit of allies, enemies, followers, collaborators, competitors, exploiters, and exploited had moved to the Northwest and taken form around him and his lab.

Furness arrived in a Seattle that was going through the second gold rush in its history. Like the Alaska gold rush that preceded it by some one hundred years, the digital gold rush of the present age sent visionaries and hallucinaries flooding into the Pacific Northwest in the late 1980s and early 1990s. By 1996—the year the technology sector officially passed the natural-resources-based sector of Washington industry as the leading employer of the state's citizens—what once had been a land of dropouts, drifters, lumberjacks, fishermen, and the occasional Boeing engineer now was almost entirely the territory of a new breed of prospector: the computer-industry entrepreneur.

There loomed in the imaginations of these prospectors a single overpowering model: the Microsoft Corporation. Ever since two local boys, Bill Gates and Paul Allen, had made good in the process of taking their tiny start-up to the pinnacle of power in the software industry, digital dreamers in Seattle and its surrounding communities have been launching new companies, large and small, that seek to emulate Microsoft in one way or another. This start-up culture spread with shocking speed: It was reliably estimated in 1996 that the number of high-tech start-ups in the Seattle area had jumped from 85 to more than 1,100 in four short years, with 200 of the new enterprises launched by young Microsoft retirees.

From little refurbished Alaska-gold-rush-era hotels in downtown Seattle's Pioneer Square, to spiffy new office suites across Lake Washington in Redmond, to tattered second-floor walk-ups in northwest Seattle's sprawling Ballard district, computer-technology ventures of every imaginable genre were sprouting up daily. There were companies producing office software, games, multimedia software, digital animation, interactive movies, Internet software and hardware, switching technologies and other services, voice-recognition software, one-handed keyboards, and goggles that were said to be on the verge of replacing computer screens. Invariably, these businesses were founded by young people who dreamed not only of mining the miniature infinitudes of silicon for fabulous wealth, but also of "making a difference," "pushing the envelope," "having an impact," or "advancing the state of the art." For many of these adventurers, the glamour of the cutting edge was as alluring as the stock options their companies constantly proffered in lieu of legal tender.

By the time Furness arrived in Seattle, the PC revolution was in full swing. The VR discipline, however, was floundering. It suffered from an image problem that stemmed partly from an exaggerated media portrayal, partly from the eccentricities of its early advocates and developers, and partly from its own overhype. Thus in the popular imagination, the VR world quite reasonably consisted of a few mad scientists or game players wearing outlandish helmets and gloves from which extended a confusing, perilous tangle of wires. The late 1980s had brought no end of predictions that virtual reality was just around the corner; when by 1993 it had not yet arrived, public interest in it subsided almost to nothing. As far as most Americans were concerned, virtual reality was the lunatic fringe of the PC revolution.

Virtual-world interface designers, headset makers, architects, entrepreneurs, and other adepts, however, kept working away at their technological designs and business plans, and the mid-1990s saw the first tentative emergence of VR technology out of the laboratory and into the mainstream marketplace. It looked as if the steady increase in microprocessor computing power and the steady decrease in price of personal computers had finally conspired to bring virtual reality to the threshold of the mass market by the end of 1995. A growing group of Seattle prospectors was hard at work trying to do for virtual reality what Microsoft had done for personal computing: to come up not only with a set of standards that would bring uniformity and ease of use to the VR arena, but also with a "killer app"—a use for virtual reality so compelling that millions of people would feel forced to buy VR hardware. Their efforts began attracting the nervous attention—and sometimes the money—of investors from the financial markets, the PC industry, and the entertainment industry.

.   .   .

From May 1996 until September 1997, I set up shop in Furness's Human Interface Technology lab, researching its history and the lives of its scientists, and watching the lab's life unfold around me. I also spent countless hours in the offices and laboratories of other companies—some working in collaboration with the lab, others working effectively in competition with it, still others apparently doing both.

Much of this book is devoted to studying the uneasy alliances, misalliances, and battles between the research lab and companies in the industrial sector. My exploration took me around among the HIT lab and four Seattle start-up companies: Microvision, F5 Labs, Zombie Virtual Reality Entertainment, and Virtual i/O. Microvision was trying to bring to market an invention of Furness's called the Virtual Retinal Display (VRD), a means of seeing images without using a screen; F5 Labs was developing and trying to market an Internet switching system that would dramatically speed the flow of data in and out of web sites, allowing for the rendering of fully three-dimensional artificial environments; Zombie, cofounded by two VR pioneers, was developing CD-ROM VR games using discoveries and technologies developed in military research labs; and Virtual i/O developed and marketed the world's first lightweight head-mounted display (HMD), to be used both for viewing video and playing games in three-dimensional virtual environments.

In addition to fighting for their own survival, all of these companies maneuvered in concert and opposition at various times with one another and with the HIT lab, everyone caught up in a high-tech soap opera that was a complex welter of ego clashes, struggles for money, Shakespearean intrigues, nurture gone wrong, overlapping and conflicting visions, disillusionment, disgust, fury, revenge, and occasional respect and reverence. The tensions, of course, were a function both of the incredible difficulty in bringing an ambitious technological vision into the marketplace and the high emotional stakes involved in betting one's life on the endeavor.

I set off on this exploration because I wanted to find out what had happened to VR technology, which a few short years ago was being hailed as the Next Big Thing. I also wanted to climb into a microcosm—a tiny, illustrative slice in space and time—in order to study its inhabitants and their struggles from up close. I have long believed that the examination of a microcosm is far more instructive, and far more interesting, than the overview of a macrocosm, and I entered this one in the hopes that I could divine the way an American turns an idea into a commercial product, an industry, a fortune, or a disaster. In this respect, the resulting book is less a study of virtual reality in particular than of the origins of American industry in general. These VR pioneers, I believe, continue an illustrious American tradition—of the first adventurers into uncharted industrial territory, trying to develop new products and processes and consumer demand all at once, in the hopes that they will launch a world-changing new venture.

As often happens on such escapades as mine, I was soon faced with an intricate array of psychological avenues to explore, and I think now of the resulting book as a look—however uncomprehending—at the mysterious combination of ambitions, circumstances, obsessions, attainments, education, policies, personalities, and personal quests that go into the making of what we call progress. Every tangible enterprise, from the single small invention to the international conglomerate, begins with an intangible notion, a tug at the heart of a dreamer. What follows here is an examination of the people and events that gathered and grew, both wittingly and unwittingly, in the wake of just such a tug at the heart.

TECHNICAL INTERLUDE

In an effort to keep this book's plot churning and its soap suds-ing mightily, a certain amount of distracting yet indispensable technical information is offered here, for the reader unfamiliar with the rudiments of VR technology. Readers conversant in the history and terminology of virtual reality should feel free to skip through this vestibule and proceed directly to the storyhouse proper.

The term *virtual reality* has been degraded in recent years to the point where it is virtually meaningless. It is currently used to de-scribe all manner of common computer interfaces, including touch-screen PCs and crude computer-aided design programs for desktop PCs. As envisioned by the characters in this book, the definition of virtual reality is quite narrow. It is a computer inter-face that appears to surround the user with an artificial environ-ment, often called an *immersive world*, or *immersive environment*. A person employing this interface most likely would wear a *head-mounted display*—a set of goggles, wraparound glasses, or a helmet with a display built inside it—that shuts out most or all of the out-side world. The head-mounted display would include a tracker that monitors movement of the user's head, a microphone for in-putting, and earphones. The most widely used tracker, manufac-tured by Polhemus, is a system comprised of a magnetic radiator, or emitter, that sends signals out to receivers worn by the user; the receivers detect where they are in the radiator's field, and con-stantly send information to the computer that is displaying the virtual world. The images then are updated to reflect the tracker-reported changes in the user's point of view.

The user also would most likely wear a *data glove* on one hand. This glove also would have a tracker built into it, so that this hand/glove could correspond to the image of a hand in the artificial environment. This "virtual hand" moves in concert with the user's gloved hand, and touches or grasps virtual objects in the artificial environment. Often, the user also carries a *data wand*. Clicks on various buttons on this wand allow the user to zoom and pan through the virtual world, and to select, as with mouse clicks, objects in the environment. The data wand most commonly used by the people in this book is the CyberMan, manufactured by Logitech.

Finally, the user might stand on some kind of treadmill or pressure-sensitive platform, or have his or her feet attached to trackers that would facilitate the illusion of movement through the virtual environment.

You often hear VR researchers, when talking about these controls and trackers, say that they offer *six degrees of freedom*. This means that they move along and rotate around an X, Y, and Z axis. X is the horizontal axis, Y the vertical axis, and Z the axis running fore to aft. A tracker or control device with six degrees of freedom, then, *rotates, pitches,* and *yaws*—moves, in other words, through and around each axis in each of three dimensions.

All of this equipment is attached by cables and wires to a high-end computer most often referred to as a *rendering engine*. The most widely used rendering engines currently are manufactured by Silicon Graphics, whose most popular engine is called the Onyx Reality Engine. They are designed to *render* virtual environments by constantly updating the display as the user moves his or her head around. Just as our view of the real world changes with even the slightest movement of our head or eyes, so is the virtual world supposed to change as we change our points of view. These *graphics accelerators*, though, are not yet powerful enough to update their graphical displays as fast as we move our heads and eyes, so virtual worlds tend to lag a little behind the movements of their inhabitants. This can sometimes cause discomfort and nausea—a condition generally known as *sim sickness,* or *simulator sickness.*

Sometimes the user might enter a *networked distributed virtual world:* a graphic environment in which various users "meet" via computers linked by a network. Each user would be represented in the virtual world by an *avatar,* a figure that the other occupants can see, and that moves and speaks in correspondence with the user. There is a good depiction of distributed virtual world interaction in Neal Stephenson's science-fiction novel *Snow Crash.* In it, avatars representing a seller and buyer negotiate in a virtual office, eventually exchanging an icon representing $25 million. As the icon passes from the hand of one avatar to that of the other, bank computers effect the actual financial transfer between the two users' real bank accounts.

Although it presently is possible for avatars to meet and interact in an immersive virtual world, all of these devices and metaphors are in a relatively early stage of development. VR researchers are working toward an interface that is as natural and intuitive as our human interface with the material world. While they argue strenuously and constantly about the details and mechanics of the interface, they all envision a day when abstract data—words, molecular structures, philosophical concepts, stock market tables, etc.—will appear in easily interpretable form in virtual worlds, and people will interact with and manipulate them as naturally as they now interact with real objects in the real world.

Probably the best-known use of virtual reality in the commercial sector to date is Disney's *Aladdin* "ride," which made a brief appearance in 1996. Users sat on a bicycle-like contraption and had a huge helmet, hung from cables, eased down over their heads. By manipulating controls on the bicycle's handles, they could make it seem as if they were cruising through the world of *Aladdin,* encountering the animated movie's characters along the way. In 1997, Sega and DreamWorks SKG opened their first GameWorks arcade, in which a variety of VR games were included. Players could hold a real fishing pole and catch big-game fish that appeared on a large curved screen in front of them; they could sit in a cockpit that rotated 360 degrees forward, backward, and sideways while exchanging fire with enemy aircraft that they could see on a video screen; they could sit in a race car that bounced and shifted as it would on a real racetrack, while they "drove" along a track that unfolded on a large screen overhead; they could swing a real baseball bat at the image of a ball coming at them on a video screen; and so on. In mid-1998, Disney opened similar arcades in eight American cities. Called DisneyQuest, these arcades included VR rides and games, one of which—a "virtual roller coaster"—was developed by characters in this book.

It is important to note that virtual reality is neither a new idea nor a radical departure from standard computer science. It is instead an evolutionary advance in computer technology, just as the desktop PC is an evolutionary advance beyond the mainframe and the minicomputer. Research in virtual reality dates back at least to the early 1960s, when a number of researchers in the computer and entertainment industries began envisioning and developing primitive VR machinery. Most notable among these was a graduate student named Ivan Sutherland. Although the television and the computer had not yet converged—computers at that time did not even have screens—Sutherland envisioned an evolutionary path along which computers would be fitted with TV screens, and the punch-card-and-printout interface would be replaced by a CRT interface; that the screen's alphanumeric display eventually would be replaced by a graphical user interface and that users would be able to interact with and manipulate data by moving images around on their screens; and that that interface in turn would be succeeded by head-mounted displays, allowing users to move through three-dimensional renditions of abstract data. Sutherland, working at the University of Utah, built the first head-mounted display in 1968—two years after Tom Furness, recently graduated from Duke University, entered the laboratory where he was to begin his life's work in virtual space.

A final word: in addition to the familiar terms *hardware* and *software*, the reader will occasionally encounter an unfamiliar one—*wetware*. An engineer's term for the human brain, it is particularly important in this book. For when all is said and done, this is essentially a book about wetware.

INCUBATION

Promises, Promises

IT WOULD SEEM at first glance that the room has been ransacked.
Packing crates have been torn open and plundered. Hundreds of
cords either lie tangled on the floor or hang in massive snarls from
hooks, racks, and pieces of plastic pipe attached at various points
to a ceiling that is missing most of its tiles. A Styrofoam head,
perched on a low table, is wearing a pair of large goggles. The lights
are turned off. There is electronic junk piled haphazardly everywhere—video cameras, keyboards, helmets, computer monitors,
computer mice, computer guts, oversized trackballs, joysticks. . . .

A second glance leads you to believe that the arrangement is
more or less deliberate. You notice that a great deal of the mess is
held together by duct tape. A large, doughnut-shaped, plywood
contraption, suspended from the ceiling by bungee cords in the far
corner of the room, has duct-taped to it a variety of electronic cables, some of which are attached to a helmet, others to gloves, others disappear into a hole in the ceiling, and still others snake their
way across the room to a computer. A bedsheet is stuck with duct
tape to one wall; another wall has been fashioned from trash bags
duct-taped to one another.

It is hardly the setting you would dream up as a treatment center for someone in severe psychological distress. Yet it is precisely this mess into which I watched two psychologists lead a visibly nervous young woman one summer evening, at the beginning of a treatment session for her crippling arachnophobia.

The woman had long, black hair, black clothes, and the deathly pale skin of someone who never ventures outdoors. She wore a pair of candy-apple-red, high-topped, leather sneakers that perversely highlighted the already conspicuous lifelessness of her skin and wardrobe. She was terribly thin, as if her nervous energy burned calories faster than she could ingest them. Her voice was so soft and quavering that I had a hard time hearing it over the deafening whine of the computers in the room.

Everything about her testified to the fragility of her mental state: darting eyes, fluttering hands, and an array of tics and twitches that made it look as if she were on the verge of disintegration.

I was never told the woman's name—a condition of my being allowed to observe her treatment—and the psychologists would refer to her in subsequent professional papers as "Miss Muffet."

The woman sat down on a chair, and one of the psychologists—a postdoctoral student named Hunter Hoffman—started fiddling with two of the computers and arranging various objects on a table set up in the center of the room. Hoffman always began these sessions with a lot of tedious and tense arrangement of his equipment—the most noticeable piece being a huge, homemade, hairy toy spider that he had hooked up to a Polhemus tracker. Once everything was in place and his computers were running properly (not a simple task, I noticed, as the infernal machines habitually went awry), Hoffman helped Miss Muffet put on a large VR helmet and data glove, then led her to where he wanted her to stand. I could see on a television monitor that she was immersed in a crude cartoonish kitchen, with a counter, a sink, some cupboards, a window, a spiderweb, and—on the wall next to a window over the kitchen sink—a huge, black spider. Miss Muffet held a Cyber-Man in her hand, which allowed her to zoom toward or away from the spider.

Hoffman had told me before that a number of universities now were doing research into the treatment of fears and phobias with VR technology. In applying virtual reality to Miss Muffet, he and the other psychologist in the room, Dr. Albert S. Carlin, were employing a regimen modeled on treatment of fear of heights undertaken at Emory University and the Georgia Institute of Technology. "What we're doing with her is both an experiment and a treatment," Hoffman said. "The experiment is to see if you can use VR as a treatment. So, to some extent, we're just basically trying to treat her for spiderphobia, and at the same time we're trying to learn from her experience whether this is an effective medium."

Hoffman sat at a keyboard, keeping the software running, while Carlin sat in a chair nearby, notepad and pen in hand. As the woman stood looking at the spider from a distance, Carlin asked, "Can you tell me zero to ten what anxiety you're experiencing?"

"An eight."

She reached out with her data-gloved hand, and I could see the virtual hand on the screen float up and touch the spider for an instant, then immediately withdraw as she drew back her gloved hand. "That's kind of creepy," she said softly, zooming away from it.

Now the spider looked quite small, and Carlin asked her again to rate her anxiety level. "About a six now . . . a six . . . ," she answered.

Moments later, she slowly zoomed in and reached out with her gloved hand again, and clicked a button on the CyberMan that allowed her virtual hand to grab the virtual spider and set it down on the counter. Then she released it and zoomed away. "Now that's much better," she said. "For some reason, when they're on the wall, that bothers me more than when they're on the counter. When they're on the wall, it's more like all the spider incidences I've had . . . where they're staring with their big eyes and everything."

For the next few minutes, she zoomed in and back, at varying speeds and distances, picking the spider up and putting it in various places, zooming back to regard it each time, saying at one moment, "Now that's about an eight," another time, "about a six–seven," yet another, "a five . . . ," then saying, in a more trembling voice, "I'm really shaky." As she zoomed back now, I could see her grimacing and licking her lips before trying to reassure Hoffman, who looked as if he were about to shut off the session. "All I am is really shaky," she said. "I mean, I'm not sweating or anything."

Hoffman had her rest for a few minutes while he hooked the toy spider up to the system. Now the image on the screen corresponded to the physical toy, and Hoffman rather than the woman could move it around. Hoffman held it suspended in the air in front of her, and the virtual spider floated in the middle of the virtual kitchen. Two minutes went by before she reached out, at his direction, and touched the physical spider with a finger and thumb. The woman's hand was shaking. "I'm about a six . . . seven . . . eight," she said.

For the next ten minutes, the woman alternately touched the spider gingerly, held it in one hand, held it in both hands, palpated its legs, put it down, picked it up, all the while delivering status reports. Near the end of the session, Hoffman asked, "Any physical symptoms?"

"Well, I'm trying not to shake," his patient said. "My hands are the only thing that's shaking. And I'm trying to keep my eyeballs open."

After she was finished and Hoffman had removed her helmet and glove, the woman sat down and told me her story. Her phobia had begun nearly twenty years ago and worsened dramatically, until her life was entirely defined by her fear. She took a night-shift job so she wouldn't have to go out during the day, believing that spiders moved around by day and slept at night. She removed all her shades and drapes so that spiders could not hide behind them. When she arrived home from work, she would put "magic towels" at the base of her doors, both inside and out, then duct-tape the doors shut and keep them that way until she went to work the next night. She kept her windows closed and sealed with duct tape even in the summer, no matter how hot it was inside her house. After she washed her laundry, she would iron all her clothing, then store each item in a separate, sealed, plastic bag. Each night just before she went to work, she would carefully sweep and wash out her pickup truck, then fumigate it with insecticides. During her commute, she would wear rubber gloves that extended past her elbows and keep a cigarette smoldering in the truck's ashtray in the belief that spiders hated cigarette smoke.

She was increasingly careful to avoid grassy areas. If cajoled into going to a park—for a picnic, say—she would wear high boots, keep her pants tucked into her socks, wear a heavy parka zipped up to her chin even in the summer, and run to the nearest picnic table and sit up on top of it, looking around vigilantly.

She began to believe that spiders had prodigious powers—that they could leap across the room to get her, that they could fly, that they could conspire against her. "It didn't make sense," she said, "it was totally untrue, but yet I would think, 'This spider has a personal vendetta against me.'" When home, she would spend her time looking constantly for spiders, even to the point of obsessively examining her walls and ceilings, inch by inch, through binoculars.

The more obsessive and fearful she grew, the more ashamed she felt. "I knew it was totally irrational, but I couldn't help it."

She also suffered from a recurring nightmare in which she would wake up to go to the bathroom in the middle of the night and find "that everywhere around my bed there were spiderwebs, that the floor was covered with spiders, and that when I finally fought my way to the bathroom this single-file line of spiders would follow me in there. I'd run back to bed, pull the blanket over my head, and make a little breathing hole."

Hoffman was unsure to what degree his VR treatments could be credited for the woman's subsequent improvement. But there was no question that Miss Muffet had made tremendous progress. While still preoccupied and vigilant, she now professed to feel almost entirely liberated. She ventured out during the day. When home, she no longer sealed herself inside with tape. She could walk through grass. She was capable of seeing spiders in her home and leaving them alone—something she hadn't been able to do in years.

Even her dream life had improved. "Now, in my dream," she said of her recurring nightmare, "I say, 'See, they're not bothering

me,' and I talk to them and they talk to me. I tell them they give
me the creeps, and they say, 'That's okay . . . we give *everyone* the
creeps.' "

The Miss Muffet experiments graphically illustrate the maddening
allure of virtual reality—a technology that seems to have been lin-
gering on the threshold of the mass market for decades. There is on
the one hand the dramatic improvement a virtual world interface
has wrought in this young woman's life, apparent proof positive of
the inherent worth of the technology. On the other hand, there is
the unreliability of the system used on Miss Muffet, the hours of
preparation required for each of her treatment sessions, the constant fear that something will go wrong with some part of the system used in her treatment, and the astronomical expense of
present-day VR equipment. For each of Miss Muffet's one-hour
sessions, Hunter Hoffman spent some three to four hours tinkering with his electronics, never really being assured that his computers would work properly. And while the turnaround Hoffman
and Carlin wrought in Miss Muffet's life inspires visions of clinics
on every street corner outfitted with helmets, gloves, computers,
and miracle-working software, in reality the equipment costs of
such treatment are prohibitive, to say the least. Hoffman estimated
that the machinery used on Miss Muffet cost close to $100,000.

The overall impression of watching people labor so mightily
and so uncertainly on something that persistently remains an unrealized promise is that of seeing a light at the end of a tunnel
designed by a sadistic engineer: The tunnel keeps lengthening
ever so slightly faster than the speed of the vehicle traveling
through it.

The room where Hoffman and Carlin experimented on Miss
Muffet (labeled the "Visual Simulation Laboratory," it is the nerve
center of the University of Washington's HIT lab, the world's leading VR research center) is a protean place whose visitors and inhabitants constantly refashion it. It is by turns an architectural
studio, a medical research center, an arcade, a psychologist's clinic,
an industrial lab, an artist's studio, a zoo inhabited by virtual di-
nosaurs, a virtual playground for bedridden children. My first few

weeks in the HIT lab were spent largely in this space, studying and cataloging an array of future uses of VR technology that will change the world in ways that are at once odd, exhilarating, disconcerting, subtle, and dramatic. Just as the personal computer has been spreading in all directions at once, taking on the roles of calculator, typewriter, file cabinet, fax machine, mailbox, appointment calendar, video-game player, television, telephone, printing press, income-tax adviser, and bookshelf, among countless other things, so is this new technology—more or less the third wave of the PC revolution—now poised to enter our lives in multifarious ways.

I saw countless examples in the Visual Simulation Laboratory of future uses for VR machinery, from architectural applications allowing users to build virtual structures from which blueprints could be extrapolated by computer, to medical applications in which remote surgeons operating on virtual bodies were controlling teleconnected robots operating on real bodies. The most dramatic—and, in the final analysis, most discouraging—of these demonstrations was one put on by Dr. Tom Riess, a California podiatrist-turned-inventor who was forced into retirement by Parkinson's disease.

Working with the HIT lab's Suzanne Weghorst and other lab researchers, Riess had devised a headset that displayed a row of vertically scrolling dots, superimposed on reality, as he walked along. This was a high-tech version of a trick Parkinson's patients use to overcome the disease's breakdown of the brain's "visual cueing" mechanism. Often, Parkinson's sufferers lay out rows of playing cards on the floors of their houses, as such evenly spaced visual aids eliminate their tremors and disorientation, and Riess wanted to build a portable system that would work wherever he went. "You can't really lay out playing cards on the floor of the supermarket," he liked to say.

When the display was turned on, it completely eliminated the tremors and twitches caused by Riess's disease. I watched him one day, twitching and flailing so violently that he could scarcely maintain his balance, get himself fitted with the headset and belt-pack-mounted computer that powered the display. Then, once the display was in place and turned on, his symptoms miraculously disappeared, and he started walking and running around the lab.

This was in mid-1993, and it looked at the time as if Riess was about to be set free from his prison. Yet three years later, he had essentially made no further progress with his invention. The display proved unreliable at high altitudes and under temperature extremes, and Riess's efforts at making the computer pack smaller and easier to use had proven futile. As has happened time and again with VR inventions, the difficulties in moving beyond the beguiling prototype to the practical and useful product had proven insurmountable.

To see a hacked-together laboratory prototype bring such dramatic deliverance to someone like Riess or Miss Muffet—someone, in other words, who otherwise would be cut off from the world—is immediately to see an almost infinite potential for technology to aid in the struggle for the mind's transcendence over the body's limits. You begin to understand the hunger and impatience that thoroughly color the lives of VR adepts; in the case of psychologist Hunter Hoffman and HIT lab director Tom Furness, the easing of human suffering had understandably become something of an obsession by the time I arrived at the lab. Furness, in particular, was marked with an intense impatience for computer technology—which seems constantly to fall short of its potential—to finally *get there*, and start bringing forth the results that VR visionaries had been promising for decades.

Tom Furness—more formally known as Dr. Thomas A. Furness III—is an exotic commodity in the Pacific Northwest. A North Carolina native with a pronounced accent, he has an arresting manner that is at once courtly and folksy. Along with his spectacles and graying hair and beard, his accent gives him the avuncular air of a Colonel Sanders. He is formal in a way not commonly seen in modern America, opening doors for women, shaking hands every time he greets a friend, and pulling chairs out from tables for his guests. Yet his speech, marked by a musical drawl, is determinedly downhome, packed with odd, strangled sounds, as if consonants keep getting swallowed in mid-expression by his sinus cavity.

"Isn't" is rendered as "idn't," "ninety" is "niney," "want" is "won't," "presented" is "bresented," "student" is "stunent," "my" is "muh," and so on. His enthusiasms are highly contagious, bewitching investors, entrepreneurs, students, fellow faculty, and journalists alike. When he talks about his hopes and dreams for virtual reality, you find yourself reflexively reaching for your wallet—whether to hand over its contents to Furness or hide them from him, you're never quite sure.

The story of the HIT lab, I was told again and again, is very much "the story of Tom." I have since learned that the same is true of the story of virtual reality in general. Accordingly, in order to properly understand the quest to connect the world's citizens with one another through the virtual world interface, it is necessary first to take a look out Mrs. Margaret Furness's kitchen window in 1946, from where we can watch with her as her three-year-old son, a dreamy American boy named Tommy Furness, is tottering toward his new tricycle.

The Road to Damascus

FROM THE BEGINNING, Margaret Furness was thinking as she watched her son at play out in the backyard, he was different from the other children. She and her husband, Tom Furness Jr., had just bought Tommy a tricycle, and she was watching him confront it for the first time by himself. Every little boy she had ever seen had put his efforts into figuring out how to step up on the little platform mounted between the two rear wheels of his new trike, wriggle up onto the seat, grip the handlebars, put his feet down on the pedals, and start wheeling around. Tommy, however, didn't bother trying to mount the new toy. Instead, he tipped it over and went to work on it, purposefully trying to take it apart.

The Furness family lived in an odd little village, called Enka, built in the shadow of the Enka rayon textile plant. Set twelve miles outside of Canton, North Carolina, in the Great Smoky Mountains, a few miles from Black Mountain—birthplace of the evangelist Billy Graham—the village was, Furness recalls, "quite a neat place to live." Akzo, the Dutch chemical and textile company that owned the plant and built the village, took a paternalistic approach in the care and feeding of its employees. Enka included a company library, store, gymnasium, swim club, medical clinic, and a host of other amenities to keep the villagers happy and on the premises.

Tommy Furness spent his boyhood playing with his dog in the woods on the fringe of the village, following his father—an inveterate tinkerer—around while he worked on his car engine and other motors and mechanical parts, and learning how to build radios. While his coevals were playing baseball and basketball, he was either studying engines with his father or learning about radios from a Furness family friend and neighbor who was a ham radio operator. By the time he entered elementary school in 1949, Furness already had extensive experience working on short-wave radios, oscilloscopes, and other electronic gadgets, and he was still in grade school when he built his first hi-fi system.

It did not take long for Furness's teachers to discover that he liked nothing better than to fiddle around with science projects. Many of his teachers let him set up a laboratory in the back of their classrooms and sit back there puttering while his classmates did their schoolwork. Once a week, his teachers would turn the class over to him for fifteen to thirty minutes of "Tommy Time," or "Tommy Furness Time," when he would bring in a science or electronics project from home and show it off to the rest of his class.

Furness was fond of adding special effects to his shows, some of which ended with spectacular explosions and showers of sparks. This penchant for mixing chemicals and subjecting them to heat ultimately led him into the main passion of his early adolescence— building rockets.

By the time he entered junior high school, Furness had grown fixated on the idea that he would someday be a space traveler. Nearly all of his free time by then was spent building rockets and experimenting with different kinds of homemade rocket fuel. His goal in these experiments was to mix a fuel that burned as fast as possible—a trick, unfortunately, that he generally pulled off all too well. His mixes tended to burn too quickly, exploding on ignition and destroying his spacecraft.

Despairing of getting him to concentrate on much of anything other than science, his junior high teachers let Furness spend the bulk of his school days either down in the school's abandoned chemistry lab or in his homemade electronics lab in the back of their classrooms.

Furness's dreams of space travel coincided nicely with the national agenda at the time, which was focused on building a space program. This mandate took on tremendous urgency in 1957—Furness was fourteen—when the Soviet Union's launch of *Sputnik* elevated the American space program to the level of a national emergency. The next year, when Furness entered high school, he began entering science fair competitions, where interest in space exploration was strongly encouraged; the nation had decided that the public education system should goad students into studying science in order to help the United States ultimately win the space race with the Russians. In 1958, Furness's first entry into his school district's science fair—an exhibit on the design of rockets and the mixing of rocket fuels—won a blue ribbon.

From then on, he spent all his time working on more sophisticated rocket designs. He wrote to the leading aerospace companies of the time, asking for pictures of rockets, books on rockets, and any other material the companies were willing to send him. By 1960, when he entered his junior year, his interest in scientific matters had shifted slightly—to telemetry systems, the electronics through which controllers on land and rockets in the air could communicate back and forth, while his interest in personal matters shifted momentously—to the woman Furness still calls, half a lifetime later, "my sweetheart, my wife."

He had gone one night with two friends to a state National Honor Society convention at Louisburg College, down in the middle of the state. At a mixer on the convention's first evening, he recalls, "We walked into this gym, and the first person I see there is this tall, good-looking lady, wearing a black, slinky dress—just *smashing.* I punched my guys and said, 'That one's mine.' So I strutted up to her and—you have lots of courage when you have other guys with you—I introduced myself, said my name. She said her name was Linda Pearce, and I looked at her and said, 'Your name oughta be Blackie!' Then I motioned to muh buds"—Furness's speech is peppered with colloquialisms like this—"to come on over, and I introduced her as Blackie."

Forty years later, no one remembers Blackie's given name.

Back in his lab, meanwhile, Furness had taken part of a discarded Navy sonic buoy—originally designed to locate submarines—and developed it into a rocket telemetry system that ultimately won the North Carolina state science fair's Navy Science Cruiser Award. The award entitled him to join fifty other winners—one from each state—for a week-long tour of the U.S. Naval Air Station in Norfolk, Virginia. An enthralled Furness spent five days aboard the U.S.S. *Independence*, the nation's largest aircraft carrier at the time, saw missile firings and dive-bombing exercises, and came home more determined than ever to be a pilot and an astronaut.

His science fair project drew the attention of the commander of the naval ROTC unit at the University of North Carolina, and Furness was invited to the campus to give a talk on his telemetry system. It proved to be the high point of his life: The *Mercury* astronauts, still preparing for America's first manned space flight, were training at the campus. Furness had avidly followed the progress of the astronauts and the space program as his nation approached its first attempt at space exploration, and he was fascinated by the pioneers who would lead the way. He was astonished when his hosts arranged for him to spend an hour with astronauts Alan Shepard, John Glenn, and Gus Grissom. "Oh, man, can you imagine?" he says. "Here I was, this high school kid, with these three astronauts! I was in hog heaven."

Afterward, the starstruck Furness saw his future laid out clearly before him: He would go to the air force academy, "because I wanted a career in space, and that's where it was going to happen. I had to go there, get this education, become a pilot, and take off from there. Because all these astronauts were pilots."

Your garden-variety dream generally ends here, where the dreamer, confronted with his first tangible hurdle, falters, gives up, and moves on to adulthood and resignation. But for Furness the hurdle in question—gaining entry to the U.S. Air Force Academy—proved surprisingly easy. He applied, turned in his record of accomplishments and letters of recommendation, was recommended by a North Carolina congressman, and was accepted.

There was, however, one catch: In order to accept his appointment, he had to pass an eye examination. This was no small matter, as his eyes had always been weak. He traveled down to Shaw Air Force Base for his physical, and did, indeed, fail the eye test. Because he was "right on the borderline," though, the air force scheduled a second test for a few weeks later.

Furness spent the interim at the family's kitchen table, where his mother forced carrots and carrot juice down him in the hopes that it would bring enough improvement to his vision to get him into the air force. But when the appointed day arrived, he failed the exam again.

It was a crushing blow. Never having considered any other future for himself, Furness had applied to no other colleges. Now, considering his options, he saw only the University of North Carolina—which had, at the time, no serious engineering department—and North Carolina State, which he considered a lackluster school leading to a dead end. The only university in the state with a decent engineering school—Duke University, whose fledgling engineering department had some of the best faculty in the country—Furness considered completely out of reach, as it was too expensive, had daunting entry requirements, and an application deadline that had already passed. It was only through the strenuous efforts of his father, who talked his son into visiting the Duke campus and eventually talked the school's registrar into letting Furness into the school, that the depressed would-be astronaut continued his education.

Once his acceptance to Duke came through, Furness was "excited again, really pumped up"—particularly since he learned he could join the air force ROTC on campus and, upon leaving college, "still be commissioned in the air force, even though I wouldn't be able to fly."

The electrical engineering curriculum at Duke turned out to be something of . . . ahem . . . a shock. The years spent in a small rural school system fooling around on his own in the back of the classroom had left Furness ill prepared to study in one of the nation's leading engineering departments. He was required to take high-level physics courses that relied on calculus, a class that had never even been offered in his high school. "I was way behind on a lot of this stuff," he recalls, "and these other kids were really good. I mean, most of them had been to prep school, and here I was a country bumpkin."

Matters were made worse by the fact that high school had been so easy for Furness. He had never learned how to study. He also was spending a great deal of time hitchhiking the thirteen miles between his school and the University of North Carolina, where Blackie was enrolled.

Thus he struggled through his first two years, barely passing his courses, until the end of his sophomore year, when he flunked two of his engineering classes.

This precipitated another identity crisis for Furness, as he was beginning to wonder if he was cut out for engineering. He spent the summer as a "cracker packer" and cookie salesman for Nabisco, mulling over his future and relishing a job that called upon him to do two things he loved. The first was packing trucks with cracker and cookie boxes of various shapes and sizes, in as efficient a manner possible, with the boxes packed in reverse order—farthest stops out on the route in the front of the truck, nearest stops in the back. It was essentially a three-dimensional puzzle, and Furness took great pride in packing the truck from top to bottom with no wasted space. He also liked driving the route, since "everyone loved the Cookie Man," and he loved nothing better than driving around the North Carolina countryside, chatting up the people working in the small grocery stores along the way.

Furness decided during the summer to return to school, but was undecided about engineering. Since he had to wait until spring semester to retake the classes he had failed, and since he couldn't take any more engineering classes until he passed those two, he took some philosophy, religion, and economics classes, and also took a battery of tests from the university counseling center. The tests were designed to "find out what I should do as a career. And it came back that I would be fit for doing one of two things: either be a preacher, or be an engineer."

Mystified, Furness settled on engineering. The next year, he "buckled down," studied harder, began getting better grades, and made the dean's list at Duke. He and Blackie—who by then had graduated from North Carolina with a major in chemistry—married, and she worked to support them both while he finished his fifth year. After graduating with a degree in electrical engineering, Furness looked back over his years at Duke with justifiable pride: Out of 120 students in his class who had started out as electrical engineering majors, only 16 had graduated with E.E. degrees.

After spending three months helping design and run a Scope mouthwash production line for Procter & Gamble, Furness received his air force commission and reported to Wright-Patterson Air Force Base in Dayton, Ohio, in September 1966. It was at the height of the Vietnam War, and researchers at Wright-Patterson were hard at work trying to improve the capabilities and performance of fighter aircraft, which were not doing well under the bizarre and unprecedented battle conditions set by the Vietnamese terrain, and by America's determined and resourceful enemy.

Furness spent three months each in four different laboratories at Wright-Patterson before settling down for good in the Armstrong Aerospace Medical Research Laboratory (AAMRL, as the lab was known), where he was put to work studying ways to make cockpits easier for fighter pilots to operate. His first project involved finding ways to superimpose information on the pilot's view of the landscape below as he flew overhead looking for enemy activity, then radioed target coordinates back to bombers and artillery batteries. The Vietnamese enemy had proven adept at moving whole bases so quickly when detected by spy aircraft that by the time pilots could do geographic calculations, radio information back to their bases, and get forces marshaled to attack the site, the intended target would have vanished.

From the beginning, though, Furness was interested in grander problems—what he calls "the human factors side of displays."

The human half of the human-machine interface was—and, in many ways, remains to this day—an almost entirely neglected facet of information display technology. The impetus in research and development—whether that of televisions, VCRs, dashboards, heavy machinery, telephones, timepieces, toasters, personal computers, or just about any other machine, device, or electronic gadget built for use by human beings—is to make people change to accommodate the needs of machines rather than to tailor machines to accommodate the needs of people.

It occurred to Furness almost immediately that nothing showed this more strikingly than the evolution of the fighter cockpit. The modern pilot, he noticed, was sealed in a tiny compartment, so cut off from the outside world that he could see virtually nothing through his helmet visor and the tiny canopy overhead. Contact with reality was furnished through interface with the instrument panel, which had proliferated around all sides of the cockpit, surrounding the pilot of the F-15A fighter jet with, in Furness's words, "Seventy-five different displays, three hundred switches, eleven switches on the control stick and nine switches on the throttle. And those switches change their function depending upon what system mode you happen to be in at the time." The history of cockpit design, he realized, had been a gradual estrangement of the pilot from the reality around him. "Good ol' technology just kept proliferating, adding another piece of avionics to the aircraft every time someone came up with a new system to install in it." The result? "You can't even see out the window anymore—and in air-to-air combat, you spend a lot of time trying to look out the window. The pilots spent a lot of time complaining about that: 'Hey, you're putting all this stuff up here, and I can't see out anymore.' "

Considering this "human factors nightmare," Furness realized that the instrument panel was designed to tell pilots what they used to take in directly from the environment, through all five senses. "It was sort of simple when you were flying those old airplanes, because it was sort of the wind and the earth. You would just tell how high you were by looking at the ground as you were flying along, and how fast you were going by the way the view would stream by. The first cockpits were ones where you gleaned the information from observing the flow field, the wind in your sideburns, and the earth and things like that. This took some practice, but it actually used the natural abilities of the human."

As the power and complexity of airplanes grew, however, such direct interaction with the environment grew less and less possible. Now, the pilot had to contend with a set of information sources so complex that learning how to read and interpret them was harder than the act of flying itself; he also had to perform this task while traveling faster than the speed of sound, while the speed of the jet was pulling Gs and taking him constantly to the brink of unconsciousness, and while someone was trying to shoot him down. The worse conditions grew for processing information, the more complex became the information he had to process. "Any time you go to coded information," Furness said, referring to the instrument panel displays, "you get into a situation where the more coding you do, the more you have to learn how to do the decoding." As a result, pilots devoted more brainpower to deciphering information than they did to reacting to the information itself. "So—especially when there's a lot of workload—you're really busy, your brains sort of ooze out of your fingertips."

Furness teaches a popular computer interface design course at the University of Washington, during which he gives a famous series of lectures on interface design history, with an emphasis on the lessons he learned while studying pilots and cockpits. He is a riveting public speaker, and his lectures—accompanied by slides showing the interior of various cockpits and by his own pantomimes, asides, gestures, and imitations of pilots under stress—are hypnotic, evocative presentations on the predicament of the human held captive by seemingly sadistic technologists. Furness always tells the story of the pilot he saw inadvertently shoot down another aircraft when, intending to activate a video camera, he instead launched a missile, not realizing that a circuit breaker behind his seat had been switched, the switch changing the function of the switch the pilot set when he tried to turn on his camera. He tells story after story of pilots not hearing loud audio warnings and not seeing video warnings projected onto the display in front of them—warnings that their landing gear was still up as they were coming in for a landing, or that they were about to run out of fuel—because they were overwhelmed with information, or because they were too fixated on getting a target in their sights. "We had this 'pull up!' command in the head-up display. This is when you are diving toward the target, we were putting up this electronically generated information on top of your view of the real world, where pilots got so involved in the target that they didn't notice that they had to pull up out of the dive—otherwise they'd crash into the ground. So the pull-up command that would come up in the display was this big X. It would come right across the display and just sit there and flash. And they didn't even see it! I mean, this was the display they were looking at because they were trying to get the sight over onto the target. We had a few accidents because of that."

Sometimes pilots didn't see or hear warnings because they were unconscious. "Whenever you really wanted to activate some of these functions," Furness says in his lecture, "usually you were pulling Gs"—fighting pressures many times the force of gravity. "And the process of pulling Gs changed everything. Your speech pattern and everything. As a matter of fact, about the only thing that you could do at six or seven Gs was just grunt—you can't talk too much when you're pulling that many Gs. And in fact that's what you're *supposed* to do, is grunt. You hunch over, you're pulling against the joystick, and you're straining like you're trying to pass a watermelon, 'Unnggghhh . . . ,' and your G suit is pumped up, you know, it's trying to keep the hydrostatic level of blood up in your head, and you're hunched over trying to help it, straining yourself to do it. All you're doing is groaning. You listen to some of the tapes, you hear these guys going, 'Unnggghhh . . . unnggghhh. . . .' It's amazing the rigor it takes to do that."

The better the planes got, the worse things got for the pilots. "They used to black out sort of gradually in older jets, where you'd see the visual field sort of close down, you could hear things going on but you didn't see anything. And so it would be this gradual grayout and blackout, then you're unconscious eventually. But in the case of the F-16, crew members were going out"—he claps his hands—"like that. And they didn't know they'd passed out, and they couldn't remember that they'd passed out. And so what would happen is that, when they'd come to, it'd take them three or four minutes to really come back to it again. We lost two F-16s because of that, these guys just went out like a light."

Under these conditions, with the increasing complexity of the aircraft's electronics, and "with the philosophy of the design of these cockpits, we were at the point where we were expecting this pilot to do everything, just about—to be the janitor and the chairman of the board, make all the decisions as well as monitor a lot of these functions."

Furness was most struck by the wrong-headedness of this approach when a pilot gave him a drawing he had done of the "pilot of the future." Sitting inside the four-sided instrument panel that comprised the cockpit of that era, the ideal pilot had six arms. "He was trying to say that really what we ought to be doing is a little genetic engineering on the crew members, because they needed to have a few more appendages to operate this system."

Furness's dismay at this state of affairs led him and his fellow researchers at Armstrong to conduct a full study of people as processors of information, then redesign the cockpit to take advantage of the way people perceive and react to the outside world. They intended to make cockpits completely intuitive so that pilots could take in information without having to decode through layers of abstraction. And in order to do that, they first had to understand the nature of the human in the cockpit.

AAMRL spent years studying human perception, and the findings in those studies still guide much of the design of present-day computer interfaces. In essence, the studies concluded that humans see, hear, and feel in three dimensions. We are "spatial" creatures, and any time the provider of information deviates from a three-dimensional, multisensory means of input, it creates problems for the person taking in the information, as he or she has to "learn something extra" in order to interpret accurately and react appropriately. "We are three-dimensional beings," Furness says. "We have these two visual systems that operate in parallel, so-called 'ambient visual systems,' mediated by our peripheral retina, and a focal visual system mediated by the fovea in our eye, and these two work in conjunction with each other. The people who were designing cockpits in the past were throwing that away! We realized that we were not taking advantage of a lot of things about humans—in terms of the way we build models in our head, the cognitive process."

By stages, Furness and his team worked toward the creation of a virtual environment around the pilot—first in the cockpit, then in the pilot's helmet. As early as 1968, Furness began working on helmet-mounted displays—systems that would track the movement of the pilot's head and appropriately change the display of information superimposed over the real world that the pilot could see through his visor. By 1972, this research had evolved into a quest for development of "a virtual cockpit, a cockpit that the pilot wears," although it was not until 1977 that Furness was able to secure funding for what he then was calling a "Visually Coupled Airborne Systems Simulator" (VCASS).

Were it not for the carte blanche that military research labs were given first during the Vietnam War, then during the post-Vietnam military buildup against the perceived threat from the Soviet Union, Furness's research—which eventually totaled some $150 million in cost—never would have been undertaken. What he proposed to do with the cockpit was, given the state of computer and image-display technology at the time, outlandish, bizarre, and infinitely expensive. Only one other researcher in the world—Ivan Sutherland, at the University of Utah, who in 1968 built the world's first stereo head-mounted display—was working seriously on such a concept.

What Furness proposed was to take an ordinary flight simulator—the fuselage of an airplane, mounted on struts on a platform, outfitted with an instrument panel and a CRT display, which pitched and rolled like a flying airplane as a pilot sat in it and manipulated its controls—and turn it into a virtual cockpit in which the pilot was immersed, by means of a head-mounted display, in an artificial environment that corresponded to the outside world and that was festooned with symbols and icons furnishing, in three-dimensional sight and sound, the same information furnished in ordinary airplanes by the traditional instrument panel.

From 1977 to 1982, the AAMRL team worked on building this system, which was extremely difficult to design and construct with late 1970s computer hardware and software. Before the first PC was to hit the market, and well before these machines would have a graphical user interface, AAMRL was trying to build a full-blown VR system. The term *virtual reality* itself would not even be coined until 1989, by computer scientist Jaron Lanier—who would first be exposed to virtual world interfaces at NASA, where researchers began using AAMRL-developed technology in the mid-1980s.

The VCASS eventually took form as an eccentric and un-wieldy contraption consisting of the airplane fuselage and its platform, above which hung a huge, oddly shaped helmet that looked like an immense sci-fi insect's head. This arrangement was connected by cables and a multiport memory to eight Virtual Address eXtension (VAX) computers—huge mainframes, they took up an entire room. Inside the helmet were installed two television screens connected to Evans and Sutherland rendering engines, one drawing the left-eye view, one drawing the right-eye view. The displays were essentially computerized television sets—CRT systems that took up huge volumes of space. The computer-and-display assembly rendering the images and infor-mation the pilot needed—and updating it all as the pilot moved his head, eyes, and hands and as the simulator "flew" through space—consumed so much power that Furness likes to joke, "We had to tell Dayton Power and Light whenever we were going to turn this VCASS on."

The system was designed to render a graphical version of the outside world. The pilot with his or her head inside the VCASS helmet saw a cartoonish landscape overlaid with a grid. This envi-ronment was decorated with icons—little airplanes, for example, that were color-coded to identify them as friend or foe; icons for weaponry, fuel, runway lights, and on and on and on—that would appear and disappear as the pilot's need for information of a cer-tain type arose. The pilot could fire missiles by voice command or by touching icons. Instead of looking at a combination of the out-side world and the instrument panel displays, the pilot instead looked at a computer-generated representation of the world around the plane, augmented with information about everything from the amount of fuel left in the plane's tanks to the plane's altitude and speed, to the location, identity, and behavior of other aircraft in the sky.

The effect was a little like crawling inside the screen of a video game.

It took five years of work and some $1.5 million before the day came when Furness and his team finally were ready to turn on the complete VCASS system and stick their heads inside of it. What they saw was staggering—so much so that Furness now compares it to the day Alexander Graham Bell first called his assistant over the telephone. "If there's an occasion in the history of my career that was truly an 'aha!' thing, it was on that day, in September of 1982, when we turned on that VCASS system for the first time," he says. "It was *amazing*. I mean, we knew there was going to be a big picture, but this now was an *interactive* big picture, and it wasn't like you were looking at a picture anymore. It was like you were in a *place*. It was like somebody had reached out of the display and pulled you inside, and now you weren't looking at a picture, sitting in a cockpit looking at a picture, you were *in* the picture. You didn't even realize you were sitting in the cockpit."

The discovery led immediately to further research. "We started playing around with this, saying, 'What is going on here? This notion of *placeness*. Am I looking at something that is sort of outside in, or inside out?' " By experimenting with the display—moving, by degrees, from a 20-degree field of view to a 30-degree field of view and so on up to 120 degrees, the team discovered that at the "60- to 80-degree point, it was like a switch went off in your head. Instead of looking at a picture, all of a sudden you thought you were in a place. You had a different way of interacting with the display. You brought in a different set of innate capabilities. We did lots of experiments just to discover what you could do with this VCASS. And we realized more and more that we were onto something really big. We found that *you couldn't forget it*, because it was like this world was a *place*. And we found that people learned really quickly when they were inside of it, that there was a remarkable acceleration of the ability to learn these things, to interact with them. Naïve subjects, even my daughters"—his two daughters were in high school at the time—"and the clerical people, could come in and fly these machines—they could learn how to fly really quickly."

Furness seized upon his belief in the worth and power of this new interface with the fervor of a religious convert. Indeed, it is interesting to note that his conversion to the virtual world interface took place at nearly the same time, and under nearly the same circumstances, as a conversion he underwent, after years of tortured spiritual wandering, to the Mormon religion. During the years when he and his team were beginning development of VCASS, Furness left the Presbyterian church after a lifetime of devotion and entered what he now calls "really a down period, sort of a black period, a dark period in my life." He experimented for several years with various Christian religions, with Science of the Mind, with pyramid power, with Transcendental Meditation, and with various other faiths and occult beliefs—"looking," he says, "for something that was out there"—before spending several months in conversation and debate with Mormon friends and missionaries. Finally, just as his immersion one day in the newly developed VCASS, coming as it did after years of research, immediately and dramatically changed the course of his professional life, so did his immersion one night in prayer, coming as it did after years of searching, immediately and dramatically change the course of his personal life. "I went into my bedroom and I knelt down, and I started a prayer," he says of that night, " 'Heavenly Father,' I said, 'I've read all the things the missionaries have asked me to read, I've read in the *Book of Mormon* the things they've asked me to read, and I believe it is true. Is it?' And after I asked that question, it's like this light came into the room, this bright light, and that somebody dumped a bucket of hot Mazola oil right on the top of my head. Top of my head down to my toes. There was just never any question! It was just sort of like every particle of my being knew that it was true. And ever since that day, there has never been any doubt in my mind."

Personally and professionally settled on the course of his life, Furness was to spend five more years working on VCASS systems before things began to sour in the air force. Although his lab, now the most advanced VR lab in the world, had grown to a workforce of nearly one hundred, and was doing projects for all branches of the armed services and for NASA, military research was coming under heavier and heavier scrutiny from Congress. As the Soviet Union began collapsing in the late 1980s, military funding began to dry up, and an accompanying spate of adverse publicity had military research facilities scrambling to counter the public-relations effects of one $600 toilet seat story after another. Finally, in 1985, Furness was asked to start doing press conferences on some of AAMRL's work.

Reaction from the media was immediate and overwhelming. Furness made an initial TV appearance on the *CBS Evening News*, and was deluged from then on with requests from every American network, CNN, BBC, Australian and New Zealand television, and publications ranging from *The New York Times* to *Popular Mechanics*. Not surprisingly—given the nature of his research and the fact that he had been doing presentations on his work since he was in grade school—he turned out to be good copy. "Suddenly," he says, "my research and development stopped and was replaced by show business." He saw new VR research efforts emerging at the University of North Carolina and at MIT, and he began getting telephone calls from around the country from people wanting to know if virtual reality could be brought to bear on their own problems. Surgeons wanted to know if there was a way to superimpose X rays on the bodies of patients on whom they were doing arthroscopic surgery. Fire chiefs wanted to know if firemen wearing head-mounted displays could guide camera-equipped robot-firefighters through burning buildings. Wheelchair-bound people asked him if head-mounted displays could be made that would allow them to move through virtual environments or navigate through physical ones. "The more I thought about it," Furness recalls of these and other requests, "the more I realized, 'Well, yeah . . . you *could* do that kind of stuff.' "

Discovery of Furness by the outside world was accompanied by the retirement of his supervisor and patron, Charles Bates—a skilled bureaucratic strategist who had been Furness's boss for his entire career at Wright-Patterson—and Furness's loss of control over his program in a political football game between senators from Ohio and Texas. As part of Congress's attempt to cut the U.S. defense budget, it was proposed to close Brooks Air Force Base in San Antonio, Texas. The fight to keep Brooks open resulted in the move of Furness's research program to Texas, with the supervision of it turned over to other scientists and bureaucrats who were likely to be either uncomprehending or hostile to his life's work.

Chagrined and discouraged, Furness decided to leave the air force. He negotiated a year's sabbatical from the government, during which he toured the country, looking at schools, hospitals, offices, universities, and everywhere else he could imagine computers being put to use. Now five years old, the PC was just beginning to make heavy inroads into the worlds of business and industry, and was still a relatively rare home and school appliance. But Furness could see that it was an unstoppable juggernaut, and that the world was dramatically changed from what it had been when he entered his isolated, Edenic research lab twenty-one years before. "It was really clear to me that there was a revolution taking place in computing," he says, "and that the capacity of computers was going to continue to grow, that there was no limit. But no one was working on interfaces! We were still sitting at screens ploinking on a keyboard! And we had all this computing capacity on one end, we had this incredible human on the other side, and we had this barrier in between." The more he surveyed the computer landscape, the more opportunity he saw to spread the gospel of the virtual world interface.

Years later, Furness would write in an essay about the messianic fervor that had seized him by the end of his sabbatical wanderings:

> It became clear to me that there were thousands of applications for virtual interfaces that were ready to be invented and exploited, because even though computing technology was being developed at an intensive rate, no one was paying attention to the interface. Indeed, it was apparent that the computer interface was the primary factor limiting the utility and true impact of computing technology (just like in the fighter cockpit). We were still requiring people to be "computer-like" . . . that is, we had to interact with the computer on the computer's terms,

using the computer's arcane language, etc. Furthermore, we were constrained by an archaic keyboard and a computer screen that compressed the mind of the computer into two-dimensional symbols projected on a plate of glass. I felt that we needed the same paradigm shift that I had experienced in VCASS that first day. We needed to break the glass and enter into the mind of the machine and have the computer create a three-dimensional world with which we could interact using our natural abilities. I realized that instead of making the human computer-like, we had to do the opposite—to make the computer "human-like." This is the only way that we could get bandwidth to the brain and allow the machine to become a friendly, transparent, and seamless tool and extension of our intellect. I felt that this paradigm shift is the key to the future of computing and of the information highway. I felt that better use of information technology could ultimately help civilization in solving many of the pervasive problems that are confronting us. I felt the country needed a laboratory that would concentrate on developing human interface technology and would use, as its most powerful technology, virtual interfaces and virtual environments.

Resolved to spread the word he had writ in his lab, Furness decided to look for a university willing to let him set up a new laboratory devoted to teaching and researching virtual world interface development. What had started out as a means of bringing relief to fighter pilots had turned into a cause that burned in his heart. "I decided," he said, "that I wanted to train missionaries, I wanted to train these disciples as it were, that understood where we could go with this interface."

VR Winter

AFTER RUNNING A LAB that had worked more or less on its own for some twenty years on what was about to become popularly known as "virtual reality" or "VR," Furness emerged from Wright-Patterson like someone expelled from Paradise. He had grown up and worked in secure, patriarchal settings—first in Enka, the village owned and maintained by his father's employer, then in a securely funded federal military research lab—for nearly his entire life.

Wright-Patterson in particular had been sustained by an infinitely deep well of money. Furness found that tradition and protocol prevented Congress from looking too closely at classified projects. Asking for research money invariably was a simple ritual procedure, along these lines:

"Can I have $100 million?"

"What for?"

"You don't need to know that."

"Oh . . . okay!"

Now, for the first time, he was going out into an uncertain world—one where he would have to fend for himself in a way he had never done before.

When Furness entered his military lab in 1966, the computer was a huge mainframe that few people used and even fewer people understood. It was an exotic thing apart, kept from the general public by an elite group of High Priests in lab coats who worked in an aura of daunting mystery and magic. Now, the United States was well on its way to becoming fully computerized, as desktop computers far more powerful than the mainframes Furness had used in his VCASS project were becoming commonplace in schools, businesses, and even homes.

Furness also found that computer technology—once an arcane subject of interest to virtually no one—was fast becoming America's hottest and most celebrated commodity. Proselytizers for the computer, promising salvation through technology, roamed the country in messianic hordes of a kind not seen since legions of itinerant charismatics wandered around ancient Galilee. Called, in their modern incarnation, "technical evangelists," these preachers began emerging as gurus of a veritable new national religion.

So when he left the lab and began spreading his doctrine of salvation through virtual world interfaces, Furness was both a voice in the wilderness and a voice in a chorus.

In some respects, he was a classic techno-evangelist, spinning improbable and compelling yarns about engineering feats just around the corner that could solve every conceivable world problem. I have watched Furness work hundreds of audiences and am always struck by his ability to make outlandish visions seem plausible. With his folksy gravitas and his rather rich vocabulary, he spins yarn after yarn about technological deliverance, his enthusiasm making problems that are years away from being solved seem on the verge of solution. I have heard him promise to build "electronic prostheses" for the paralyzed, allowing them to "inhabit virtual bodies" that can travel through "virtual shopping malls," and to build headsets that "allow the blind to 'hear' a room" or even "allow the blind to see." "I want to give humans the ability," he often says, "to learn experientially, to enhance their creative abilities so that their creative juices might find easier and better expression. I want them to be able to communicate with each other, especially across vast distances. I want them to *be there*, literally reaching out and

touching someone across nine thousand miles. And I want to re-
capture lost world citizens, the ones who are lost because of physical disabilities or cognitive disabilities." He describes his mission as
an attempt to "create symbiosis between the human and the machine," and to build "a transportation system for the senses" that
will "unlock human intelligence" and "transcend human limitations."

Furness's preachy wanderings in search of a setting for his lab
eventually brought him to Seattle in 1988, where he wowed the
directors of the Washington Technology Center (WTC)—a state
government enterprise on the campus of the University of Washington—as thoroughly as he and his wife, Blackie, were wowed by
the Northwest's landscape.

The WTC had been set up in 1983 to serve as a conduit between university researchers and the state's economy. University
laboratories operating under the WTC umbrella were directed to
serve as an interface between industry and academe, helping raise
money to fund professors' research, the results of which would be
licensed to businesses or make new marketable products, thereby
creating new jobs and bringing more money into the state's economy. These labs, then, were supposed to secure funding not only
from academic departments, foundations, and government organi-
zations—the traditional underwriters of academic laboratories—
but also from businesses seeking product development.

The idea behind the WTC's complex of labs was to fill a gap
that has long existed in the United States between the market-
driven product research done in industrial laboratories and the
market-indifferent research undertaken in university laboratories.
This goal coincided neatly with another of Furness's passions—the
conviction that American industrial research had been driven into
decline by the increasingly short-term view of most corporations.
"There are two reasons industrial research is failing in this country," he said to me one day. "One is the time constant—you know,
the nine-women-can't-have-a-baby-in-one-month kind of thing.
There's a gestation period for research, and it's not one or two
years. It's more like five years, ten years. That's the Japanese approach, the time constant they use. And the other is that you have

to have an opportunity to fail, and take risks. And that's the beauty of the university, because this is an environment where you can do that, whereas in industrial laboratories, you can't."

By virtue of his reputation and the power of his personality, Furness was given a tenured faculty position by the University of Washington in that school's industrial engineering department, and a lab and seed funding by the Washington Technology Center. Late in 1989, Furness formally opened the Human Interface Technology Laboratory, and began rounding up research scientists, students, and investors to help him launch his crusade.

From the beginning, Furness found it far easier to attract people than to raise money. No sooner did he hang out his shingle than VR true believers began gravitating to the Northwest. Bob Jacobson, a noted Sacramento visionary who advised the California state legislature on technology, signed on as the HIT lab's first associate director. William Bricken, a software engineer and sage of sorts from Stanford University by way of Autodesk, a groundbreaking company that developed the world's first computer-aided design (CAD) software (programs generally used by architects), joined the HIT lab early in 1990 as a principal investigator. His arrival brought together two of the best-known figures in the VR world—Furness from the hardware side, Bricken from the software side—in the same laboratory, and by mid-1990 Furness had the beginnings of a thriving lab.

It was immediately clear, however, that Furness's new venture would resemble the lab he had left behind in Ohio no more than life for a newborn baby resembles its former life inside the womb. Accustomed to having his work funded without question, Furness now was entering the "soft money" world of university research, where lab directors and researchers alike were expected to raise their own money in order to fund their work and pay their salaries. In Furness's case, raising money was even more difficult than it was for garden-variety university laboratories because of the hybrid nature of the HIT lab. Foundations and government agencies, accustomed to funding purely academic research, looked askance at the HIT lab, with its mandate to produce technology that could be transferred to industry, because its research seemed too product-driven. Yet the very businesses the lab was supposed to benefit also looked askance at it because HIT lab researchers, being connected with a university, figured to be less dedicated to product development than the kind of researchers industrialists liked to support.

Furness soon found that the problem with trying simultaneously to be two different types of lab is that researchers have to please two masters, each with a different set of criteria. Academic researchers are expected to make intellectual progress, measured mostly by the number and quality of their publications. Industrial researchers are supposed to make material progress, measured by the degree to which their research can be parlayed into sales figures and quarterly profits. The former are driven constantly to publicize their work and its results, the latter are expected to work clandestinely, protecting the "trade secrets" in their laboratories so their sponsors can get a lead on competitors and thus increase the profit potential of their work. The ethics of university research call not only for openness, but for a high-minded disdain of directed, profit-driven work. Academics dismiss industry-directed laboratories as "warm-body operations" that do "research for hire." Industry dismisses academic laboratories as "playpens" where no substantive work—that is, work that can be turned in short order into salable products—is ever done.

The HIT lab, then, was as much a philosophical experiment as a technological one. As Dr. Emil Sarpa, Manager of External Research for Sun Microsystems, one of the earliest and most devoted supporters of Furness's operation, put it, "This is the only lab of its kind in the world in terms of its hybridization. It's a new financial-political model." He felt that his company had no choice but to invest in Furness, although whether Sun would ever earn a return on its investment was far from clear. "Nobody can figure out where the hell this is going, but it's crazy not to invest in it," Sarpa told me. "Everyone's waiting for a *commercial product* to come out of VR research."

It looked at first as if Furness's lab would not even survive, let alone come up with commercially exploitable technology. Furness turned out to have an astonishing tolerance for diversity—surprising in someone steeped for so long in the culture of the military—

that was partly a function of his temperament and partly a function of his religiosity. Once word that he was founding a laboratory spread through the U.S. VR community, people started showing up at his door unannounced, and it was not uncommon for Furness—who believes such people are "sent" to him "for a reason"—to invite them in and give them laboratory space. Given that the civilian VR world at the time consisted in large part of a motley collection of gurus, dropouts, counterculture figures, the innately mischievous, and the barely sane—virtual reality was best known in the early 1990s for having won the dubious blessing of LSD-soaked Timothy Leary—the lab in short order turned into a haven for what William Bricken gleefully called "deviantly enabled" people. Bringing potential investors through the lab on courtship tours proved to be a risky business; they were more likely to encounter someone intent on outraging them than on impressing them with the potential profitability of their research.

Perhaps because he believed in the destiny of his lab to thrive, Furness resolutely refused to try to control the behavior or appearance of his minions—except on one occasion, according to an apocryphal story attributed to the HIT lab director. A year into the life of the lab, beginning to grow desperate for money, Furness one day was wooing a group of straitlaced executives from a telecommunications company. One of his graduate students, a long-haired young man named Dav (pronounced Dave) Lion, came to work most days wearing a cotton tie-dyed dress. Lion spent a lot of time at play in the lab and had a flair for attracting attention. (He is, for the record, heterosexual.) In a break with his own principles, Furness asked him, for this one tour, either to dress in more traditional male garb or take the day off.

The story goes that the day of the pivotal tour came, and as he walked his guests through, Furness was relieved to see that Lion was nowhere in sight. After squiring his visitors around and showing them the wealth of projects under way in the HIT lab, Furness sat them down in a conference room to discuss the nuts and bolts of funding lab research. Suddenly Lion came dancing into the room, wearing a tutu and waving a small wand in the air. He pirouetted around the table, sprinkling "fairy dust" on the guests, then flitted away. The visitors from corporate America, it is said, declined to invest.

The truth of the matter is that Lion was wearing bib overalls with a Guernsey cow pattern when he burst in on the meeting, and that the visitors eventually wrote Furness his check. But the apocryphal version survives, I am convinced, because it better highlights the cultural tensions and psychological reality of the lab.

In some respects, Furness was unsurprised in the early days by the trouble he had raising money from corporations. Fervent as he was in his belief in his interface, he also knew that interest in virtual world research would inevitably wane. He had come out of Wright-Patterson just as media attention was peaking, and he knew that there would follow a period of disillusionment when investors, university administrators, and potential users of the technology would begin to realize that it would take far more work and time than they had expected to develop these new interfaces into something practical and useful. "So I anticipated that there would be a VR winter," he said. "And that the issue would be how to survive that winter. To keep things going. There were so many universities and people that had gotten into VR, then gotten disillusioned, dropped out, and in the process disappointed a lot of sponsors. And so for those who are in there for the long haul, it hurt the prospects."

The prospects were particularly hurt when the lab tried to heighten its profile at the Association for Computing Machinery's 1990 SIGGRAPH convention, held in Dallas, Texas, in August. SIGGRAPH, which stands for the Special Interest Group on Computer Graphics, is the preeminent annual computer graphics event in the world, and Furness saw the affair as an opportunity to reawaken the industry's interest in virtual reality.

Bob Jacobson, the HIT lab's associate director, was chosen to moderate a panel discussion entitled "Hip, Hype and Hope: The Three Faces of Virtual Worlds." The crowd that showed up on the day of the discussion saw Jacobson joined on stage by Esther Dyson, a computer-industry pundit and the daughter of famed physicist Freeman Dyson; Jaron Lanier, the eccentric, dreadlocked inventor who built the world's first commercially available VR headset, and who was VR's best-known (some would say "most notorious") proponent; William Bricken; Warren Robinett, head of a famed VR research lab at the University of North Carolina; Timothy Leary; and John Perry Barlow, a VR enthusiast and songwriter for the Grateful Dead.

Not surprisingly, the discussion took off into aerie realms of dream, personal philosophy, storytelling, quibbling about the appropriateness of the term *virtual reality*, the claim by Bricken that "psychology is the physics of VR"—a head scratcher, at best—and a series of incoherencies from Leary. Among the more memorable: "If you use electrons you can have any fucking reality you can imagine," and "I think that this is one of the most important meetings ever held by human beings. If we have a sense of humor we dare say that. It's only virtual anyway. And when I say it is an important meeting to human beings, I ain't saying much. Think about it."

The proceedings descended into utter bathos when Jacobson tried to open the floor for questions from the audience. Myron Krueger, a scientist who had developed immersive environments by broadcasting images on all the surfaces in a room in the early 1970s at the University of Wisconsin, in Madison, started shouting claims that his research was being suppressed and that his term *artificial reality* was preferable to *virtual reality*. Others in the audience complained vociferously that Barlow and Jacobson had forgotten to include in their pantheon of pioneers both Krueger and Morton Heilig, a cinematographer who had built the world's first VR machine—called the Sensorama—in the early 1960s. Amid rising shouts and tumult, a fight broke out, and Jacobson was shoved off the stage by Krueger.

Furness had decided he had two primary means of survival readily at hand when he set up the laboratory. One was his longstanding reputation in the military research community—a group of companies who regularly won large research contracts with the federal government and were accustomed to the arcane nature of high-tech industrial research and development with its long time lines, high-risk exploration, and uncertain outcomes. At first, it appeared that this avenue would be cut off to Furness, as his researchers adamantly refused to do military research projects. But then one of those companies—Boeing Aircraft, located in Seattle—finally managed to pass moral muster with the lab when Furness and the company reached agreement on a "virtual prototyping" project. Since Boeing made more civilian passenger jets than military aircraft and weaponry, and since the lab had no other corporate sponsors willing to pump large sums of money into it, Furness's counterculture engineers agreed to accept the company's money—a move that would bring in enough funding to keep the lab operating for nearly two years.

The prototyping project was an attempt to develop a software/hardware system that would allow airplane designers wearing helmets and data gloves to build their planes in virtual space, then have computers translate the virtual aircraft into blueprints and specs from which builders could build physical aircraft. The system relied heavily on William Bricken's software group, which was at work on a VR operating system, called Virtual Environment Operating System (VEOS), that would serve as the platform for the prototyping software.

Within a matter of months, the project ran into trouble—both because Bricken alienated his Boeing managers and because of an internal struggle at Boeing over the future direction of company-sponsored research. Bricken's vision was highly theoretical, and he chafed at the idea of doing research with a tangible product in mind. At Boeing, meanwhile, the faction favoring continued work with the HIT lab lost its battle for control of Boeing research dollars, and funding for the prototyping project was discontinued. The lab struggled along into 1992 with some more Boeing money, directed this time at an augmented reality project intended to develop goggles onto which diagrams could be projected. Engineers working on metal, Boeing hoped, could someday superimpose diagrams on the material they were working by looking at it through the goggles.

There was another, related technology on which Furness pinned nearly all his hopes for future lucrative research. While still at

Wright-Patterson, he had begun thinking about a way around the problems posed by putting displays in helmets. Pilots complained constantly that it was hard enough to see what was going on in the cockpit and the outside world under normal circumstances, and that every time Furness tried to hang a screen in their helmets, things actually got more difficult—even though the screen was giving them information they needed. In the course of trying to figure out how to give pilots necessary information without occluding their vision with a screen, Furness began thinking about beaming information directly onto the retina instead of onto a screen. "All we really wanted to do," Furness said, "was get some photons on the retina, and we were going through this whole elaborate process to get there. I kept thinking, 'Isn't there a way we could just introduce a light ray, a photon screen, directly onto the retina of the eye?' So that the retina could behave like the phosphor screen on a TV set."

By the time he arrived in Seattle, Furness had decided to put engineers to work on this method, which he had come to call the Virtual Retinal Display. The VRD is a screenless display that works by beaming a laser into the eye rather than directing an electron beam at a layer of phosphor on the back of a screen. By aiming a laser into the pupil and scanning the beam rapidly back and forth on the retina, the VRD essentially uses the retina as a screen. Because the laser scans across the entire retina—we focus with only a tiny portion of the retina, called the foveal region, when we look out at reality—the image it scans looks particularly immersive.

Displaying images in this way has a number of advantages over the use both of desktop computer screens and head-mounted displays. The VRD appears to be just as bright in daylight as it does in a dark room; images can fill the eye the way a movie screen does when seen from the front row of a theater; and the VRD headset potentially could weigh far less, and consume far less power, than a head-mounted screen display, as the vast majority of power consumed by a personal computer or television is devoted to lighting and coloring the screen.

Furness's VRD was not an entirely novel idea; researchers had known for years that it was theoretically possible to scan light across the retina. Sony, Matsushita, Hughes Aircraft, and a number of other companies had looked into retinal scanning. An ophthalmologist, Dr. Robert Webb, had built a scanner in the mid-1980s that took pictures of the retina for eye examinations, and wrote at the time that it would be possible to reverse the process—to send pictures to the retina rather than take a picture of the retina. Webb's device, though, was huge; no one who had studied the problem believed it was possible to build an efficient, lightweight retinal scanning system.

Indeed, the number of insurmountable obstacles standing in the way of building such a display device was nearly infinite, and when Furness had tried to get funding in 1990 from the National Institute of Standards and Technology to research the VRD, the institute turned him down, insisting that his design would never work. Undaunted, he put two of his first HIT lab hires—Joel Kollin, who came to the lab from the MIT Media Lab, and an engineer named Bob Burstein—to work on building a prototype. Two or three years down the road, he hoped, the two would come up with a device that worked well enough to attract some money from someone, somewhere.

With a single, faltering contract from Boeing, then, and with some seed money from the Washington Technology Center that he put to use funding his VRD research, with not much else in the way of money, and with VR's reputation still reeling in the wake of the 1990 SIGGRAPH fiasco, Furness entered 1991 in a state of quiet desperation. He did not know it yet, but the chill winds of the VR winter sweeping across the American landscape were about to burst through the doors of his laboratory.

In the Sweat of Thy Face
Shalt Thou Eat Bread

———

THE FIRST YEARS of Furness's struggle to establish the HIT lab were characterized by an odd paradox: The harder it was to raise money, the easier it was to attract talent. While Furness was out fruitlessly proselytizing to corporations and foundations, Bricken and Jacobson were fruitfully proselytizing to college students over the Internet. They posted notices to various newsgroups announcing that the HIT lab was looking for software developers, and were almost immediately deluged with replies from youngsters begging for the opportunity to come to the lab and work for little or no pay.

Bricken soon had a fairly large group of University of Washington graduate students and undergraduates from all over the country who came to the lab on summer internships working on his VEOS project. These projects seem particularly distant-future-directed when you consider that Bricken's groups were to work on them on high-end workstations from 1989 to 1992, a period when PC users in the real world were gradually upgrading to 386-based machines barely powerful enough to accommodate the move from MS-DOS to a new graphical user interface called Windows.

For Furness, this wealth of talent proved a mixed blessing at best. Although there seemed no limit to the range of his tolerance, he was a quintessential hardware engineer, and hardware engineers traditionally found software engineers to be incomprehensible, if not infuriating. Software engineers tend toward youth, irreverence, brashness, playfulness, and braggadocio. They dress sloppily and work at desks that look like an adolescent's bedroom, overflowing with discarded papers, junk-food wrappers, soft-drink cans, toys, tools, clothing. . . . Hardware engineers, by contrast, tend to be— or, at least, to seem—older, more staid. They are marked by humility and resignation. They generally sit at tidy desks, their workspaces bare, their books, papers, pens, and paper clips all neatly stored in an orderly arrangement of drawers and cubbyholes. Hardware engineers dress in shirts with button-down collars, slacks, and leather shoes. They always have hanging somewhere in their workspace a photograph of an engineering disaster—a collapsed bridge, a locomotive lying on its side, a fallen building or statue—as if to caution themselves against carelessness or hubris.

The natural incompatibility between the two types was exacerbated both by Furness, who tried to steer clear of software engineers and thus left Bricken's group alone and unsupervised, and by Bricken, who nudged his minions toward rebellion, outrage, and Bricken-worship.

Bricken was an imposing figure, a classic high-tech sage. He cultivated a mystical and eccentric air. He was given to sweeping pronouncements and long discourses on everything from boundary mathematics to the spiritual and psychological dimensions of software programming. He liked to lecture while sitting cross-legged on the floor and burning incense. His followers, being young, impressionable, and given to devotion (very much like the legions of young programmers at Microsoft, in thrall to Bill Gates), worshiped him uncritically, taking as gospel his word on the politics of industry and the HIT lab, just as they did when he pontificated on algorithms, operating systems, and the future and physics of virtual reality.

Because Furness was out of the lab most of the time, either doing "Tommy Times" before potential investors or teaching his University of Washington classes, many of Bricken's interns spent their whole tenure at the HIT lab thinking it was run by Bricken. This was an impression, people who knew him would say later, that Bricken did everything he could to heighten—possibly because he believed it himself.

Bricken cultivated in his software troops the conviction that they were isolated and mistreated in the HIT lab by its hardware engineers, who could never appreciate the ingenuity of their work. He also preached at great length on the fundamental evil of a lab ethic that called upon its researchers to publish their work gratis and let companies and other researchers benefit from their knowledge without compensating them for it. Bricken's harangues amounted to an outright subversion of Furness's mission. The guru insisted that he and his programmers were being exploited by the software companies who were underwriting HIT lab research, and he pointed to passages in certain software manuals for products developed by investors in the lab that he claimed were lifted directly from research papers written by HIT lab students. The Washington Technology Center, Bricken would tell his students, licenses your work to industry and makes lots of money off your ideas while you get nothing. Rather than slave away without reward, you should go on strike until the lab gives you a better deal.

Into this morass in the summer of 1991 came swaggering Joey King, a young undergraduate from Southwestern University, in Georgetown, Texas. King had grown up on a farm outside of Aledo, Texas, a Brazos River town of slightly more than one thousand souls in north central Texas, sixty miles west of Dallas. From early childhood, he had spent the lion's share of his time playing with and programming computers—partly out of a love of computers and partly out of a distaste for farming.

King was fourteen when he turned his back on farming for good. Slopping pigs at five o'clock one weekday morning before school, he was suddenly attacked by a massive hog that knocked him on his back and began chewing on him. King managed to reach his shovel, whack the beast over the head, and regain his feet—at which point he dispatched his adversary by crushing his skull.

Not long after, King got his first taste of the high-tech start-up world when he went to work for a small Aledo company called Electric Works Corporation. He helped write a computer program there called Digital DJ, which automated the work of a disc jockey by connecting to a radio station's traffic and billing systems, then determined what programming (taped conversations, commercials, music, etc.) to play and in what order. The program also was hooked up to a small robotic arm that extracted CDs from a radio station's library and inserted them in CD players when cued.

By 1990, Digital DJ had been adopted by 70 percent of the national radio programming market. Paid $20,000 for his two years of work, King came away feeling cheated. His employer made $50 million over the next six years, and King resolved never to get involved in a start-up again without owning equity in the company.

By the end of his freshman year at Southwestern, it looked as if that point was moot, as King gravitated toward academe rather than business. Fascinated by both computers and humans, he pursued majors in computer science and psychology and worked in his spare time at the University of North Texas Biomedical Communications Laboratory on a joint project with the GTE Telecommunications Research Laboratory, in Dallas. King interned at the GTE lab during the summer after his freshman year, doing research on teleconferencing and nonverbal communication. He was so fascinated by the work at GTE that he declared his intention to work there for the rest of his life, only to be told by his supervisor to look around at other laboratories first.

To that end, King attended the 1990 SIGGRAPH convention, watched the fight break out on stage, was intrigued rather than disgusted, and applied for and won an unpaid summer internship at the HIT lab for 1991.

Although he looks rather cherubic, amiable, and boyish, King has a tendency toward sarcasm and impatience with the rest of the world, which he deems irredeemably slow. He has dismissed years of work on the part of others, to their faces, as "crap" or "stupid." He punctuates his frequent tales of researcher imbecility or misdirection with a sarcastic "This is *beautiful*," or a resigned "This is typical," as if he is surrounded in the research community by the idiotic and the helpless. His wit, which is biting, seems all the more snappish when mediated by his voice, which is a high-pitched drawl, replete with italics, that makes King sound like Slim Pickens played at too fast a speed.

His first entry into the lab, as he remembers it, was chilling. King had turned down a lucrative summer job at the GTE Telecommunications Research Laboratory to take his unpaid internship at the HIT lab. Upon arriving in Seattle, he wondered if he had just made the biggest mistake of his life. "I go into this building," he recalls, "which isn't done. I mean, they're still running conduits, and there's no air-conditioning, I walk into this room, and it's this concrete room and there's a trampoline right in the middle of the room. A little bigger than one of those jogging trampolines. And this guy in a cotton tie-dyed dress is jumping up and down on the trampoline. And I came in [King has a tendency to switch verb tenses randomly when he tells stories] and I went, '*Oh, my God.*' I had just come two thousand miles, given up another job at GTE Research, I mean, a real research laboratory, with like *badges,* and you come in and there's like, a *receptionist,* and these big research buildings and you have *offices* and *laboratories* . . . and I come into this and I'm like, 'God, this is unbelievable.' "

King spent that summer taking in the growing chaos around Bricken and working on three-dimensional audio—part of the lab's Boeing-funded research. He went back to Texas for another year of school, then decided to come back to the HIT lab in 1992. After getting his bachelor's degree from Texas in 1993, he came north again and began combining research at the lab with his pursuit of a Ph.D. in psychology from the University of Washington.

While he was gone, the lab fell into the depths of its VR winter. Boeing pulled the plug on the last of its projects, and Furness found himself with virtually no money to keep his dream operating. He was forced to cut loose most of his researchers, cut back the salaries of those who remained, and face the real possibility of closing down his lab before he had gotten it off the ground. Bob Jacobson, the lab's associate director, left to start a new company, Worldesign. Bricken's group shrank by half, and a number of other engineers and researchers left in search of paying work. King himself came back to the lab with the understanding that he might never be paid. Furness gave King a promissory note stating that he would be paid his back salary and have a position funded for four years if a grant King was helping write, entitled "Communicating Situational Awareness," for a set of experiments to be undertaken for the Air Force Office of Strategic Research (AFOSR) was approved. As that grant was more or less the HIT lab's only hope—if it didn't come through, the lab would have to close—King signed on knowing that he might be looking elsewhere for work in a matter of months. In the meantime, he could live on savings from his GTE lab job.

Part of the reason King chose the HIT lab over paying jobs was that Furness was practically the only academic authority in the country who took King's work and vision seriously. As early as his sophomore year in college, King had resolved to work toward realizing the vision of the scientist J.C.R. Licklider, who wrote, in a famous 1960 paper, "The hope is that, in not too many years, human brains and computing machines will be coupled together very tightly and that the resulting partnership will think as no human brain has ever thought and process data in a way not approached by the information-handling machines we know today." To that end, King wanted to develop computer interfaces that were "dyadic" or "symbiotic," in that they could be designed to accept, as he put it in a 1994 paper, "facial nonverbal behavior (i.e., facial expressions, eye movement or gaze, and pupil size) . . . as a novel input channel to computer systems." King believed that a computer should have an "active or proactive" interface that could interpret human behavior and facial expressions so quickly and accurately that it could, in effect, answer questions before they were asked. Users of computers would thus be freed from the laborious process of interpreting and manipulating the interface and concentrate on the work and thought they were trying to accomplish. The computer would aid in this endeavor without the user having to exert any conscious effort via the keyboard or mouse.

King had a tendency to rant, and his comments often confused people. "I have a long-term vision that if you're going to build something like an imagination amplifier," he told me the first time I talked with him, "the first thing you should do is build a tightly coupled system that might be able to do it. So virtual environments? It's just taken for granted—*of course* you have virtual environments. It's not the pinnacle, it's just a thing—you know, that's not that spectacular or a big deal. It's really a paradigm shift. But what I'm talking about is having these interfaces which are so tightly coupled . . . not that you'll wear 'em around, that sort of spooks me out, too, this wearable computer . . . but if you want to, if you want to come in and be very creative, just to cite a simple example of how this might work: I don't know if this is possible, but I think it might be, one of the things that I do when I want to modulate my own behavior is play different music. And I'm often annoyed because I'll be doing something and the music won't be right, and I'll have to change it. And there's no reason why I should have to do that. And I don't think it would be very hard to have a machine do that for me. . . ."

King was met with skepticism and scorn wherever he turned, except when he turned to Furness. "I was trying all along to convince people that the facial expression work that I was doing, and generally all the nonverbal work that I was doing, was important, and no one in the U.S. thought it was important."

Through Furness, though, he met Fumio Hara, a professor from the Science University of Tokyo who introduced King to a huge national movement in Japan at work on the very issues King wanted to explore. Called Kansei engineering, it is a branch of engineering, founded in the early 1970s, that focuses on the human side of human/engineering connections and seeks to design "human-centered" devices and interfaces. Kansei engineers have been known to spend months studying such details as people's emotional reactions to various steering-wheel designs. King subsequently visited Hara in Japan and was exposed to a wealth of Japanese work on "facial robots" and "facial expression recognition systems" that he found "spectacular and interesting." That 1993 visit was to lead to years of collaboration between King and researchers in Japan as he continued to develop new theories of computer interface and study ways to design artificial-intelligence

(AI) systems in computers that could read and react to human facial expressions.

Even in the HIT lab King had few champions, aside from Furness and Suzanne Weghorst, a prominent research scientist with degrees in both psychology and computer science who worked with King on many of his projects. Early in 1992, however, a former HIT lab summer intern named Mike Almquist returned to the lab after graduating in computer science from the University of Delaware, working for a few months teaching classes at Silicon Graphics, and deciding he didn't want "to go to Microsoft and do the spell checker for all the words beginning with the letter *D."* Almquist joined three fellow University of Delaware alums working in Bricken's group, and he and King struck up a friendship that eventually would take on the form of a crusade.

No one really knew what to make of Almquist when he first showed up in the lab and set up shop. Short and roundish, his face is marked with a murderously mischievous look. He doesn't walk into rooms so much as burst into them, spewing wisecracks one after the other, the one-liners related to one another by tenuous puns or connections no one else can see. His speech is punctuated by piratical growls—"Arrrggghhh!" and "Avast ye, matey!" being two of his favorites—and he likes to regale listeners with his fantasies about someday finding work as a pirate. He describes himself as a formerly "dyslexic and autistic" child, and accompanies this confession with the hissing, spitting, head-shaking fit of someone trying to force a million ideas at once out of his brain through an interface that can only accommodate one statement at a time. Now, Almquist says, he has grown into a latter-day Godzilla—"I am *vast!* I romp and stomp and devour small planetoids!" To his misfortune, he often describes himself this way to objects of his romantic interest on first dates, suddenly asking them at some point during the proceedings, his voice thundering: "Do you like to eat hearty of life with bright and shiny teeth?"

Many of his first dates, not coincidentally, are also his last.

Almquist was fascinated by the HIT lab after a classmate, Dan Pezely, came back from a summer internship in 1991 and told Almquist what he had done at the lab. The two soon were commandeering empty lecture rooms at the University of Delaware, filling blackboards with designs, notes, and theories about virtual reality and Bricken's VEOS, which Almquist came to believe would be slow, clumsy and unworkable—or, in his words, "a real pig"—should it ever be completed. He came to the lab determined to trash Bricken's system and implement an alternative operating system, called Meta Operating System and Entity Shell (MOSES), that he and Pezely had dreamed up.

Almquist made an immediate impression in the lab by virtue of both his behavior and his arrival with a personal Sun workstation—an expensive rarity in those days. When he had the workstation up and running, he taped to it a large, dilapidated cardboard sign, labeled "Squish." It would be days before others in the lab learned that "Squish" was a nickname bestowed on him years before by classmates amused at an elderly and chronically confused high school teacher of Almquist's, who persisted in calling him "Mr. Almsquish."

Before long, Joey King would learn that his interests in telecommunications and human-computer symbiosis (the way people and computers interact with and complement one another) dovetailed nicely with Almquist's obsessions—virtual reality, networking, and interactive content. By mid-1993, the two were spending hours upon hours together fantasizing about future ideal interfaces and applications making use of King's tightly coupled systems and Almquist's virtual environments.

In the meantime, though, the two had to come to terms with the upheaval arising out of Furness's attempt to build a hothouse for world-changing technology.

When Almquist reentered the lab in early 1992, Bricken's revolt was in full swing. "There was a great big struggle for everyone's soul," Almquist says. "Nobody was doing any work. The morale was incredibly low." Morale was reduced in large part by the cuts Furness had been forced to enact as his funding dried up. Down to thirty-four people—seventeen of them students—working on twelve projects, the lab was struggling and uncertain of its future. "Half the people hated Tom, half the people hated William, and nobody knew what was going on." Unable to marshal anyone's attention or effort toward building his operating system, Almquist busied himself as system administrator for the lab and playing Netrek, an endless computer game played over the Internet.

Trying to sort out the lab's confusion, Almquist found himself frustrated at every turn—not only by Bricken and Furness, but by his own perverse and confused relationship with authority figures. "One aspect of the confusion was that if you write about all your great ideas, you get ripped off," he said. "But if you try to license all your great ideas to business, then you're not writing technical papers. Time and time again, I must have asked Tom thousands of times, 'Which are we? Which are we supposed to be doing?' And instead of this one or that one, it's . . . 'Yes.' "

At the same time, he found it impossible to believe in Bricken, who, Almquist felt, "educated us at the expense of Tom's dreams" by fomenting his revolt against the lab's mandate to share its research with the world. Finally Bricken's machinations grew so brazen that Furness, resolved as he was not to notice them, had no choice but to react. It turned out that Bricken had been quietly siphoning off lab hardware and software resources—some of which he had cadged out of companies with the promise that the HIT lab would write evaluations of them—and had been stockpiling them at home in the course of starting his own company. Furness learned of this when he contacted a head-mounted display company asking for a free headset, and received a scathing reply about Bricken's having gotten one months before and never delivering the lab's promised evaluation.

The day Bricken was expelled from the lab is widely remembered as the darkest day in the lab's history. People sitting outside Furness's office heard the sound of objects thrown by Bricken bouncing off the walls. Many in the software group were so devoted to their leader that they never forgave Furness for forcing him out of the lab. In the weeks following, many in Bricken's group finished up their various private projects and left angrily, spreading out to start-ups and other universities around the country.

Furness, for his part, was devastated. Whether from his inveterate optimism, his religiosity, or his lack of experience outside the hermetic and orderly world of the military research laboratory, he had badly misjudged a man he trusted as a nearly equal partner in the launch of his dream. Now, practically out of money, having exhausted the goodwill of most of the people he had lured to the lab, and out of ideas on how to start over again, he looked out over the smoldering wreckage of his domain and saw . . . Squish. Gesticulating wildly, hollering, romping, and stomping, Almquist was berating him: "Tom, this sucks. . . . We need to be going forward. . . . We're almost the laughingstock of the scientific community. . . . With all this hype and hysteria, nobody knows what to believe. I can build you a really cool VR platform, honest! Just give me people . . . equipment . . . space!"

Regarding this unaccountably arrogant kid whom he barely knew, who had come to the lab with indifferent grades from an undistinguished school, Furness found himself asking why on earth he should turn all of the HIT lab's software research over to someone who could scarcely manage to keep himself bundled in his own skin, let alone supervise other people. Then he found himself saying, "Okay, Squish . . . go ahead and do it."

While things were falling apart in the HIT lab, Furness managed somehow to find the time to subject himself to even more suffering and disappointment out in the commercial sector. In return for shares of stock and a seat on the company's board, he licensed some display technology he had developed and patented back at Wright-Patterson to a Seattle start-up named Virtual Vision, then watched in horror as the company turned itself into an object lesson in the pitfalls inventors and enthusiasts encounter when trying to forge new technology into a consumer product.

Virtual Vision was the brainchild of Seattle entrepreneur Gordon Kunster, who was introduced to Furness and his display technology by Peter Purdy, another Seattle high-tech entrepreneur. Furness had developed a way of using optics and tiny liquid-crystal-display (LCD) panels (the kind used in video camcorder viewfinders) to create, in a head-mounted display, an image that looked as big as a television screen. Purdy had been trying to design and market a head-mounted display, using Furness's technology, that could serve as a speedometer for downhill skiers. After seeing Purdy's prototype, Kunster thought he could make something more spectacular, and with more widespread use, than the simple digital readout Purdy had in mind.

Furness was drawn to both men because he was determined to find a foothold in the marketplace for head-mounted displays. Once one of these things took off in some niche market, he reasoned, the concept would be proven and the HMD would be well on its way into the mainstream.

The Virtual Vision gadget, as envisioned by Kunster, would use a prism beneath one eye to reflect into it the image displayed by an LCD panel installed in the visor. Within a matter of months, Virtual Vision developed such a headset, weighing scarcely more than a large pair of eyeglasses and attached to a battery pack worn on a belt around the user's waist. Kunster thought the device would be useful for certain industrial applications: An electrician, for example, could measure voltage and see it displayed in his or her headset without having to look away from the device being repaired, or a mechanic could refer to diagrams while working on the assembly or repair of a motor or engine.

That initial vision of building a product for a niche market, however, was almost immediately corrupted by a grandiose and seductive dream to fit the goggles with a television receiver and go after the vast consumer market. Virtual Vision started building prototypes of a mass-market headset—a far harder proposition, as consumer devices have to be infinitely easier to use, infinitely more durable, and infinitely less expensive than industrial devices used by specialists and experts—and immediately ran into production and performance problems.

These problems might have been correctable had it not been for one fatal detail: The headsets worked so spectacularly that they blinded Virtual Vision to the realities of the marketplace. The wearer could indeed see a clear picture, and it was possible to do something no one had ever been able to do before: watch television while walking around, while mowing the lawn, while sunbathing, while playing golf . . . It was impossible for Virtual Vision's executives and marketers to put a headset on, see the surprisingly crisp television picture, and not get uncontrollably excited about the device's market potential.

In their excitement, they forgot a number of important questions, such as: Why would anyone *want* to watch television while they were playing golf?

There were some in the company who wanted to proceed with relative caution. Furness and Virtual Vision's engineering staff wanted to move slowly, building a small number of headsets, testing them on the market, then optimizing and improving their design after getting feedback from their first customers. But the marketing staff—and, more important, Gordon Kunster himself—wanted to go immediately into high-volume production, as they were convinced they had a hit on their hands.

So Virtual Vision invested heavily in a manufacturing plant, enough supplies and machinery to build 50,000 headsets in short order, and a tremendous number of new hires in manufacturing, finance, inventory, and sales. The expansion, which cost millions, was to be financed by revenues from the immediate high sales through stereo and television retail outlets that the company expected. Instead, it drove Virtual Vision into Chapter 11 bankruptcy within a matter of months, as virtually no one bought the headsets.

The experience was yet another bitter blow to Furness—not only because he was so emotionally invested in the success of Virtual Vision but because, in retrospect, the reason for the company's failure was so painfully clear.

Clever as Virtual Vision's engineering was, its business strategy was laughable. Early market research, for example, showed that consumers almost unanimously would refuse to pay more than $500 for Virtual Vision's gadget. Somehow convinced in the face of that discouraging news that customers would be thoroughly seduced by the headsets once they tried them, the company put them on the market at $1,000 each, dropping the price to $799 a few sales-free weeks later.

Price aside, the contraptions suffered from two other problems, each one fatal in its own right. Virtual Vision had not taken the time to test and debug the headsets, and they proved so fragile that they sometimes broke in stores while customers were trying them on for the first time. Moreover, they were so complicated that people couldn't figure out how to use them. Since the headsets beamed their display into one eye, they required users first of all to conduct a test to determine which was their dominant eye, pick a headset with the display on the appropriate side, then go through a complicated series of adjustments before they could watch anything on them. This complexity discouraged salespeople, who didn't want to take the time to help people learn how to put the headsets on, adjust them, and turn them on when they knew their time and effort stood little chance of resulting in a sale. "One retailer told us," a Virtual Vision engineer recalled, " 'Somebody comes in here and they're looking at a VCR, a TV, I've got a thirty to fifty percent chance that they'll walk out of the store having bought one. If it's stereo equipment, maybe it's a little less, but I've still got maybe a twenty percent chance that they will walk out with a stereo, if not this time then the next time they come in. And in most cases I'm not working real hard to do that. In the case of this device, I've got maybe a two percent chance of them walking out with one, and I'm working real hard for that two percent.' "

As often happens with high-tech gadgets, Virtual Vision expected consumers by the thousands to shell out money for the goggles simply because they were a charming novelty. But in designing their goggles, Virtual Vision's engineers had created a classic solution in search of a problem. There was, in the final analysis, no compelling reason for people to wear a television set on their heads—other than to show that it could be done. The company tried selling customers on the notion that you could wear the glasses to sporting events, supplementing what you saw live with what you saw replayed and explained in detail on television. Early marketing tests showed that this might be a relatively widespread use of the goggles, except for one thing: Test subjects said that they enjoyed wearing the glasses while sitting in the stands watching a game; but when asked how long during a three-hour game they kept the glasses on, the average time turned out to be less than fifteen minutes.

The epitaph for Virtual Vision—"We fooled ourselves into

thinking it was bigger than it was," in the words of one departed engineer—could be etched on the tombstones of countless high-tech start-ups victimized by the wishful thinking that blinds so many inventors and entrepreneurs to the realities of the market-place. There were those who knew Furness in those days who wondered if that epitaph might not apply to him and his mission as well.

But then, before Furness could get around to joining those who had given up on him, nearly $8 million came walking in the door of his lab. In the spring of 1993, the Air Force Office of Strategic Research decided to fund the proposal Furness, Suzanne Weghorst, and Joey King had written, to the tune of $2.53 million. The lab was to study fighter pilots' "situational awareness"—how interfaces in virtual environments affected their understanding of and responses to things going on around them. A few months later, another $5.1 million materialized in the form of a Canadian stock-broker named Casey Harlingten, who wanted to invest in the VRD. Although the total dollar amount for the two projects, Furness liked to note with a chuckle, amounted to less than a "round-ing error" in his old Pentagon budgets, it was a tremendous amount of money for his new enterprise—enough to keep it operating for at least four more years.

With the AFOSR money, Furness paid Joey King his five months' back wages and put him and others to work planning out the four years' work the air force would be funding. The money also allowed Furness to bring in an old friend, Maxwell Wells, as as-sociate director of the HIT lab and lead researcher on the AFOSR project. Then, having put all that machinery in order, Furness turned his attention to his beloved VRD project.

By 1993, four years of HIT lab research had gone into building a crude VRD prototype that Furness had been showing off for the past year to anyone who stopped in at the lab. Although the image it scanned onto the viewer's retina was extremely poor, the device did prove that retinal scanning was possible, and Furness regaled his audiences with visions of a future in which people would be using tiny VRDs for everything from surgery to telephone calls.

His evangelism eventually led to an article in *Discover* magazine, which Casey Harlingten read on an airplane flight and was intrigued enough to visit Furness's lab. A few months after that visit, Harlingten, who had made a small fortune trading Canadian mining stocks and now was looking for high-technology investment opportunities, rounded up a group of investors, established a company in Washington called Microvision, and signed a deal to fund Furness's research for four years in return for rights to market VRD technology. At $5.1 million, the agreement was the biggest technology transfer deal the University of Washington had ever signed.

Surprisingly—or maybe not, depending upon how familiar you were with the way chaos seemed drawn to Furness—the money from both sources brought as much trouble as relief to the lab. Joey King soon found himself in a dispute with Max Wells over the direction the AFOSR project should take, and he finally hied himself in a huff off to Kyoto, Japan, where he had a standing offer to work at the Advanced Telecommunications Research (ATR) Institute—a private laboratory administered by the Japanese Ministry of Posts and Telecommunications and lavishly funded by the government, Nippon Telegraph and Telephone Corporation (NTT), and some two hundred Japanese electronics companies.

The money also brought a sudden set of new pressures, from all directions, down on Almquist's software group, which had been working more or less in secret for months, sucking up more and more lab resources without anyone really knowing what, if anything, the group was doing. Almquist, who had decided after Bricken left that the only way to succeed in the lab was to "ignore Tom, do what you have to do, and ask forgiveness later," had quietly built himself a tiny empire in the center of the lab. He had appropriated most of the lab's most powerful graphics engines and rearranged a group of cubicles into a single large, square lair, in which he stuffed desks, computers, a couch, and various other VR accoutrements. Outraged and alarmed lab researchers dubbed Almquist's creation Fort Delaware, as the only people left in the software group were Almquist and two of his fellow University of Delaware graduates.

Furness had occasionally tried to rein in Almquist and his pals by assigning someone as their supervisor, but Almquist proved ungovernable. A succession of managers—hated by Almquist either because they were hardware engineers incapable of understanding software issues or because they were Stanford graduates, all of whom he regarded as "incompetent boobs" or "idiots"—walked away from the group, tearing out their hair, after trying to deal with Almquist.

With the influx of money, though, there suddenly was a need for the software group to produce a demonstrably useful virtual environment. Furness and Wells needed one for running test subjects through, to test their "sense of presence" in a virtual environment for the air force project. Various graduate students, who were doing research for master's theses and doctoral dissertations on everything from computer science to psychology to architecture to dance, needed an environment to work with so they could gather their data, finish their writing, and graduate. Rich Johnston, an engineer Furness had hired from Virtual Vision after its bankruptcy to head up the newly funded VRD project, wanted the group to produce graphics he could use to test the VRD. Furness also was desperate for something to show the HIT lab's corporate sponsors. From the lab's inception, a group of companies, each of whom paid $50,000 annually to belong to the "Virtual Worlds Consortium" (VWC)—an organization of companies that were given a privileged look at lab research in return for their annual membership fee—met at the lab twice each year for an update on HIT lab research projects. The group included U.S. West, Boeing, Microsoft, Fujitsu Research Institute, Ford Motor Company, Telecom Italia, and other industrial and electronics giants. The last four meetings had not gone well, in large part because the software group under Bricken had not produced anything new to show. This time around, Furness wanted to knock the consortium's socks off and begin restoring the lab's reputation now that Bricken was gone. He asked Almquist to build a virtual environment in the form of a burning building—something, in Joey King's words, that "was goal-directed, had danger, and an abstract strategic task"—that users could navigate through.

Almquist, of course, was more than happy to oblige, although his teammates were not. They had been lobbying Furness for years to be given permanent lab positions, and he had persisted in putting them off. Now they were ready to quit. Almquist cajoled them into giving him three more months of work. "Let's do this stupid burning building," he said, "because when we do, it'll either be videotape fodder for our résumés, it'll let us launch a start-up, or it'll just be like, 'Ha, ha, Tom! We told you!' "

The three of them sealed off their fort so that entry could be gained only through a narrow passageway. They set to work around the clock, communicating as little as possible with people outside their cubicle. "We worked and worked and worked on the project," Almquist would recall later, "and with minor explosions here and there, continual bitch sessions, finally we came up to a couple days before the consortium meeting, and it was all coming together, but we were all very burned out, and some things weren't working quite right." With minor glitches—including the inability to get the Polhemus trackers to work—the demo was more or less done. "More or less," unfortunately, meant that it was not presentable to the consortium, and Furness's chagrin at having no new software to demonstrate was deepened when Ford subsequently dropped out of the VWC.

Once that deadline was past, Almquist and his team had time to catch up on their sleep and put the final touches on their demo—which they called "Proven" in response to Furness's constant complaints to Almquist that he and his team were "unproven," and therefore did not merit permanent lab positions. When it was done, and they could walk through it, manipulate it, populate it, and show off the capabilities of their graphics engines and input tools, they had what Almquist still defiantly calls "the best VR demo in the world at that particular time."

Even the skeptics in the lab were impressed. But because it had not been finished in time for the consortium meeting, the enemies Almquist had made in the course of siphoning off lab resources, sealing himself and his friends inside their fort, and alienating a succession of managers closed in on him to exact revenge. Max Wells, saying the demo, while impressive, was "too little, too late," began taking apart Fort Delaware. Rich Johnston, while allowing that Almquist's group had done more in three months than Bricken's group had done in three years, suggested that their accomplishment had been a fluke. When Almquist appealed to Furness for relief, Furness told him, rather coldly, that the group's resources were needed elsewhere in the lab.

In the meantime, videotapes of the burning building demo began circulating among consortium members, and Kubota Pacific—the company that manufactured the graphics engines Almquist had used to compose and show off his demo—was particularly impressed. "If you can write something like this that we can bundle with Kubotas," one of the company salespeople told Almquist, "we will buy it from you."

The praise from Kubota, combined with the hostility in the lab, drove an exhausted and righteous Almquist over the edge of incivility, and he delivered himself of a series of intemperate and vituperative remarks to anyone who came near him. The next thing he knew, his cohorts had quit and Wells, the lab's associate director, was telling him he had until the end of that day to leave the lab or be escorted out.

Burned out, demoralized, furious, vowing revenge, Almquist packed his things and slunk away. Looking back at the lab as he walked down the hall and out of the building, he was sure he saw an army of cherubim guarding the lab entrance. A flaming sword hung suspended in their midst, turning every which way.

The Soul
of a New Machinist

———

FURNESS HAD BEEN on vacation when Almquist left the HIT lab, and when he came back to find the youngster gone, he surprised many in the lab by being devastated. For all of his apparent neglect of Almquist, it turned out that he had come to regard him with affection and admiration. But being new to an environment where there were as many visionaries and visions of the future as there were people, and where the scarcity of money kept everyone on the ragged emotional edge almost all the time, Furness tended in the first years at the HIT lab to give off confusing signals to his followers. Years later, a slightly calmer Almquist would reflect, "Tom loved to burn out competent people. If you were doing something good, Tom would ride you hard and beat the crap out of you and say, 'Give me more, give me more!' But the incompetent boobs he would completely ignore. And I know it caused a lot of confusion for people. Because here they were busting their butts and not getting any recognition, except 'Do it better! Do it faster!' And that was at the time Tom's management style."

It led, Almquist said, to a number of departures of some of the lab's most talented engineers.

Yet there was never a shortage of new wetware for Furness to abuse, as eager researchers and students, lured in large part by the HIT lab's Internet newsgroup, alt.sci.virtual-worlds, kept pouring into his lab. He had little time in the wake of Almquist's departure to mourn or reflect on what had happened. Particularly and de-lightfully distracting was the sudden upturn in fortune he enjoyed in connection with his beloved VRD project.

Four months before the arrival of Canadian investor Casey Har-lingten with his $5.1 million, an eccentric and reclusive physicist-of-all-trades, who had learned of the lab from a magazine article his wife had shown him, arrived unannounced at the HIT lab and overcame his own shyness long enough to talk his way into an in-terview with Furness. The visitor, David Melville, proved to be a kindred spirit. Modest, self-effacing, and either disinterested in wealth or incapable of turning his expertise into money, he loved nothing better than solving difficult problems and fooling around in his laboratory. He was fascinated by the VRD when Furness showed the prototype to him, and he immediately had some ideas for improving it that Furness found tantalizing. By the time the in-terview was over two hours later—Melville's wife and two chil-dren, meanwhile, were waiting with epic patience out in the family car—the visitor had talked his way into an unpaid position at the lab with the understanding that he would be given a salary if Fur-ness ever managed to scrounge up funding for the VRD project.

Given the nature of this transaction, it was hard to tell whether it was between two resolute nonmaterialists or two confidence men.

For as long as he could remember, Melville had been addressing human problems with technological solutions. Growing up near Ford Ord, which was near Monterey, California, he lived in a rural area a quarter mile from the house where his grandmother, an in-valid, lived. Since his bedridden grandma could not answer tele-phone calls, Melville decided to build an intercom between his house and her bedroom, so that he could talk with her whenever he wanted; all she would have to do in order to talk back was turn her head toward the speaker box installed at her bedside. "I was al-ways building stuff," he says. "I was always a collector of things. If something broke, I would go take it apart and try and fix it. If I didn't fix it, it would go to my 'resource pile.' So I had a lot of stuff." He fashioned two intercom boxes out of various little amplifiers, switches, and speakers that he had scrounged up and saved. "The problem was coming up with a quarter mile of wire, that was the big problem. I had all this electrical cord in my box of stuff, all these varying weights, so I proceeded to solder them together and tape them up, this quarter mile of wire, six-foot pieces, two-foot pieces. . . . I strung them over the tops of trees, over hedges, to her house. And it worked! She didn't have to do anything, I could just turn it on and start talking to her, she could talk back to me."

Melville was eight years old at the time.

He remembers his youth as a series of science projects. He built sand sleds, an airplane—"although we never got it off the ground"—hot-air balloons, various other vehicles and gadgets, and spent a lot of time working on car engines. The highlight of his high school years was the gift from his chemistry professor of a kit from Bell Labs, for the construction of a solar cell—a battery that converts sunlight to electricity. He not only built the cell itself, but incorporated it into a larger, Rube Goldberg–esque device that attached a piston assembly and speaker coil to a flashlight that bounced light off a mirror onto the solar cell, which in turn was hooked up to an amplifier with a tape recorder that played the sound originating in the speaker coil. "My chemistry teacher, his mouth kind of dropped open when I showed him that. . . . I think I made his day."

Because he is, as he puts it, "interested in everything," Melville decided to major in physics rather than engineering when he entered college, as engineering was "too confining, and physics was this broad sea of knowledge." After college, he tried helping out in his father's agricultural chemical-spreading business for a while, then tried helping a friend start a business based on a new kind of air-conditioning the two had invented. From there, he gravitated to a job with a company that made equipment for microwave uplink signaling. Five years later, his company was purchased by a competitor, and Melville lost his job. He next worked for a time with a company that was building fruit-sorting equipment, on a machine that would scan a piece of fruit with light and automatically grade and sort it.

None of this was particularly fulfilling work, as Melville found directed work on single, narrow problems boring. Eventually, he moved on to California State University at Fresno, where he found a job he was to hold for the next thirteen years. Working as a laboratory technician in the engineering department, Melville worked on all manner of projects—"weird, interesting problems, trying to make things work." Tackling an array of endeavors from solar-powered vehicles to cold fusion, Melville kept building both his body of knowledge and his collection of what looked like junk to the uninitiated, but what he rather grandiosely called "resources."

In 1992, Melville's wife, Julie, tired of living in California, found a job in Seattle as a tumor registrar—someone who measures and evaluates scanned images of cancerous tumors—and the family eventually moved north.

When Furness first showed Melville the VRD, he asked if he could come up with some relatively efficient ways to scan light onto the retina. The VRD was essentially made up of three separate systems: electronics that processed the digital signals coming from a television or computer; complex optics that bent, shaped, and directed the beam of digitized light; and a scanning device that reflected and scanned the light at extremely high speeds through the pupil and back and forth across the retina. The scanner was the biggest question mark in the system; no one knew whether it was even possible to build a mechanical part that could scan light fast enough and accurately enough to make the eye see a clear image, without breaking down over time.

Melville spent four months working on the problem, eventually machining a crude metal scanner that he got working at about the same time Furness secured funding from Microvision—investor Casey Harlingten's new company—for the VRD project. Having thus proved that it was possible to make a fairly small scanner, and that it might therefore be possible to make an even smaller, commercially viable one, Melville was tasked with spending the next three or four years building as small and fast a scanner as possible, while others would be at work on the VRD's electronics and optics.

As engineers go, Melville is something of a mystic. Tall, thin, with neatly trimmed gray hair and a soft gaze that is always directed either off into space or into the miniature universe where he works (many of the parts he builds are too small to be seen with the naked eye, and thus have to be fashioned, with excruciating care, under a microscope), he spends most of his time in a reverie. At home, his wife constantly finds herself trying to bring him back to earth by asking, "Where are you now?"

Invariably, he is wandering around in a private mental museum of tiny mechanical parts. I asked him once how he pictured these things in his imagination, and he told me that they were as big as buildings and that he could walk among them, walk up to them, and examine them up close—every detail on every side.

Melville's fantasy life is more or less unimaginable to the nonengineer. I was talking with him one day when he used the phrase "fantasy magazine" in a story he was telling. Then he said, by way of definition, "You know—like *Popular Mechanics.*"

In many respects, invention is the easiest and certainly the most pleasurable part of Melville's work. Far more difficult and tedious is the explanation to someone else how to build the things he invents. This is a critically important skill, as he has to be able to explain to people running machine shops or assembly lines how to produce real versions of his visions. "An artist doesn't have to document his work," he said one day, showing me schematic drawings of the latest iteration of his scanner. "The object itself speaks for the artist. But in engineering, the product you're producing is not the object, but that drawing, the documentation." Extremely detailed, these drawings and their accompanying text explain all dimensions, materials, and shapes of every component, and how they are to be fit together into a complete machine. "Once you've made this thing, whatever it is, you have to be able to tell someone else how you made it. Because it's no good if it's only in your brain. The documentation is an argument for the object. You give these specifications to a machine shop, and they build the part, and if it comes back the way it's supposed to, then you did your job right. If it comes back wrong, there's a 99.9 percent likelihood that I didn't tell them how to do it right."

His greatest pleasure derives from invention, which he describes as a constant wrestling match, or struggle, with God. "There are all these boundaries that you just don't cross. You're always trying to get around them. We have this running joke, 'Will God let us do this?' Since we're always trying to make things as small as possible, as fast as possible, we're always at the limit, it seems like. And these are *natural* limits. So it seems like we're always having to figure out, 'What does God have in store for us on this one?' Typically, when you are"—he laughs heartily—*"working with God* on something, He doesn't give you something for nothing. You have to fight for every last little bit of ground that you're working on."

The battle is won in increments, with results appearing dramatic over time. Thus Melville loves chronicling the tendency of machines to grow smaller and more efficient. "If you took the air-conditioning systems available when the Model T was invented, they probably weighed two or three tons. And the radio stuff they had that day was probably another ton of equipment. You would have had to have a twenty-five-ton truck to haul around the equipment you can get in a little car today. Everything tends toward less and less cost, more and more function."

He sees the life's work of an inventor as a constant struggle to extend the rule of mind over matter, with the greatest invention possible being something completely immaterial. "Invention is a combination of brains and material. The more brains you use, the less material you need. So the ideal mechanism is one that doesn't exist. It's usually easy to come up with the big thing to do something. But then to get it smaller and smaller, you start coming up against these limitations. And it takes more science and more understanding of the problem to get things smaller and smaller, less and less. The idea is to have the function without the object."

Inevitably, talk of ideal inventions in his early days at the HIT lab led him to dreaming about his ideal VRD, which at the time was an apparatus the size of a midsized desk, hooked up to a computer. "We'd like to get this display to where you have this card or whatever it is"—he held up a credit card—"you can get your e-mail, web page, whatever you want on there. Phone, who knows? The ideal thing would be something I packed around with me all the time, and I'd have the sum total knowledge of life, about the entire human race, back clear to the beginning of time, available to me at my fingertips, in audio and video, be able to talk to anybody in the world when I wanted to, and be able to see things other places, in some kind of video, and it would weigh nothing, use no power, and cost nothing."

Whenever I talked with Melville, watched him work, or listened to him talking with his teammates, I was struck with how *unemployable* he was. His mind embraced too wide an expanse and too many disparate topics at once ever to focus on a single task with a deadline, or to limit its directed thinking to a problem solvable enough to deliver sales and profits to a corporate boss within a few months. Yet it also seemed to me that profit-driven research could be undertaken only when built upon the dreams, experiments, and findings of people like Melville—dreamers and undirected actors who keep tinkering with and pushing against what the rest of us take as inviolable natural laws. The deal between the HIT lab and Microvision, then, began looking to me more like a business experiment than a science experiment. In funding the VRD project, corporate America was testing the feasibility of harnessing the minds of the Dave Melvilles of the world in a way that could turn their disparate imaginings into profits.

This may have been why, when he signed the contract with Microvision, the first thing Tom Furness did was go out and recruit an engineer with real experience in the real world developing real products for real markets. The two engineers who had built the first VRD prototype—Joel Kollin and Bob Burstein—were classic university lab types who loved to solve abstract problems but had little taste for market-driven research and even less taste for deadlines. Burstein liked to experiment aimlessly, and Kollin spent his days staring into space or sitting slumped over with his forehead resting on his keyboard, either sound asleep or in some kind of trance. And while Melville clearly was a capable inventor, he could not be counted on to manage a project with both a tangible deadline and the tangible goal of making new technology marketable and transferable to the private sector.

So Furness recruited Rich Johnston, an electrical engineer with extensive industrial experience, to manage the VRD project. Johnston became available when his employer, Virtual Vision, went bankrupt, and Furness—a board member at Virtual Vision—wasted no time in inviting Johnston out to the HIT lab.

Johnston actually had seen the HIT lab four years before, in 1990, when his employer at the time—the entrepreneur Gordon Kunster, who was on the board of directors of the Washington Technology Center in those days—asked Johnston to meet with Furness and report back to Kunster on whether or not, as Johnston put it, "Tom knew what he was doing." Johnston concluded that "Tom is a sales guy. He's inspired and he's got a vision and things like that, but he doesn't really know how to get from here to there."

Johnston is one of those people who find life so hugely entertaining that their emotional range is confined to degrees and types of laughter. Thus, depending upon the situation, he laughs uproariously, lugubriously, resignedly, ruefully, childishly, mischievously, knowingly, suggestively, or in any one among hundreds of different ways in his repertoire of guffaws, chortles, laughs, chuckles, and grins. Anger rarely makes an appearance on his face, and when it does it looks like a guest who has shown up at the wrong party. Distinctly out of place and uncomfortable, it appears for a split second, then flees.

Born in upstate New York in 1954, Johnston spent his childhood and high school years in southern Florida—where the family moved when he was two—living what he now calls "a pretty typical Ward Cleaver existence, pretty much normal. Unlike most of the people at Microsoft, I wasn't a valedictorian or anything like that. I was kind of a half screw off." He entered Georgia Tech after high school because he "wanted to get out of Florida," and majored in electrical engineering "because it seemed like it would be relatively easy to do." He stayed at Georgia Tech for his master's degree "not so much because I wanted to continue my education, but at that point in my life I was very into paddling whitewater and things like that. I was having too much fun to not take the summer after graduation off, and since nobody that I interviewed with seemed to be inclined to be happy with me not coming to work directly after school, I just decided to stay in school. School was easy."

After getting his master's degree in 1978, Johnston interviewed with most of the country's major electrical-engineering employers, who came dutifully trooping to Georgia Tech every year in search of new talent. Having seen most of the country during his whitewater summers, Johnston decided in advance that he would "take the job that came up highest on the 'where I want to live' list. And so I ended up with Boeing. It was actually my lowest-paying job offer. But I figured it was more important to like where I lived than how much money I made." He turned down offers from Westinghouse, Texas Instruments, General Dynamics, and Hughes Aircraft solely because of where they were located. "It was strictly a lifestyle decision. It wasn't money, it wasn't a good job . . . it actually was one of the crummier-sounding jobs. It just seemed like a decent place to live—there were actually rivers and mountains."

The digital-age Northwest owes its prosperity to the Johnstons of the world—people, educated in science and engineering, blessed with far more talent than ambition, who gravitated to Washington because of its natural splendor and its storied ethic of under-achievement. Boeing and other employers in those days often boasted of the "Mt. Rainier factor"—an environment and lifestyle so attractive that people would accept far lower salaries than they would almost anywhere else in the country. This regional allure, combined with a Boeing resurgence in the late 1970s that had the company hiring and growing at an astronomical rate, brought into Seattle an influx of software and hardware engineers that was to lay the foundation for the coming Microsoft era.

During his Boeing years, Johnston worked on a variety of projects, most of which had to do with computer technology. Much of his time was spent in research labs or on government contracts, working on computer hardware, digital signal processes, and software for flight-simulator graphics display systems. After four years there, he settled down in 1982 to work on a project investigating a new hardware architecture for computer graphics, which at the time were extremely crude and expensive. The project was underwritten by the U.S. Defense Department's Advance Research Projects Agency, or DARPA—the agency that funds experimental research projects. (The present-day Internet, to cite a famous example, began as a DARPA project, called the ARPAnet, in the 1960s.) Johnston designed a system, called a "Z-buffer" system, that could make the display of three-dimensional worlds immeasurably cheaper and faster, thus making flight and battle simulators far more realistic both in terms of the quality of their graphical displays and their rendering speed. The Z-buffer eventually was to be a critical component in simulator technology—one of the first real implementations of virtual reality—and it helped facilitate the development of SIMNET, a worldwide Internet-linked set of simulators on which soldiers in all the U.S. armed forces can fight simulated battles as if they are operating real tanks, ships, submarines, or planes in actual battles.

Johnston and his cohorts became fervent evangelists for the Z-buffer, and soon they found themselves bidding on contracts with DARPA to work toward implementation of full Z-buffered battlefield simulation systems. The Z-buffer made storage and retrieval of what now are called "real-time databases"—essentially, the information files the computer retrieves when it is asked to display and render particular airports or other environments accurately—and thus promised to be something of a hot commodity in the lucrative defense-contract market.

Indeed, Boeing soon was pursuing a number of Z-buffer-based initiatives with DARPA, and landed a highly prized contract to build a flight simulator for the B-1 bomber—a massive, complicated computing project that would effectively redefine the capabilities and performance of flight simulators.

By this time, though, Johnston's teammates had had their fill of a common rite of passage at Boeing. The company layered their group with so much bureaucracy that everyone but Johnston left in frustration to form their own computer graphics company, which they called Delta Graphics, in 1983. Johnston, who wanted to stay and work on the B-1 project, ended up no less frustrated than his former teammates, and left less than a year later to sign on with Delta as its chief engineer. By January 1986, the company had refined Z-buffer performance to the point where it was under contract to build hundreds of battle simulators. Delta was then bought by a larger company, Bolt, Beranek and Newman (BBN), that December, and Johnston learned the same lesson that Joey King had learned in high school: If you're going to get involved in a start-up, be an equity partner. The deal made Delta's owners millionaires and left Johnston with $150,000. "You win some, you lose some," he would say often. "The biggest mistake I made was saying I'd stay at Boeing and do the B-1 project."

BBN asked Johnston to move to company headquarters in Boston a year later. After spending the summer of 1988 there, Johnston decided against moving, quit his job, and went off to work for a new start-up, Neopath, in March 1989. Neopath was trying to build an apparatus for the automated reading of Pap smears. "It turned out to be a horribly difficult problem to develop that machine," Johnston said later. The company struggled through a series of cash infusions from venture capitalists toward a finished product and federal approval until, four years and four company presidents later, with its product still under development, Johnston left again, this time to head up the engineering department at Virtual Vision.

When Johnston joined the HIT lab, he was pleased to see that Furness had signed a brilliant young graduate student at the University of Washington, Mike Tidwell, as the project's optical engineer. Tidwell had graduated from Georgia Tech University in 1993 and come to the University of Washington to get a master's degree in electrical engineering. At twenty-five years old, he was unrelentingly sarcastic and impatient—traits that Johnston, who prided himself on his own forthrightness, admired. Tall, thin, and gangly, he wore his hair short and combed straight forward, and his face was decorated with a pair of wire-rimmed spectacles and a mouth set in a pronounced, waggish sneer. His favorite word, as far as I could tell, was "asshole." Whenever anyone other than Melville or Johnston said something to him that he took to be true, he most likely would answer, "Well . . . *duh!*" If he heard anything he took to be false or misinformed, he would complain about it for years.

Tidwell prided himself on his cynicism and outspokenness. "Dave's probably not as much fun for you as someone like me or Rich, who has no control over their behavior, basically," he said the first time we spoke at length. He frequently professed to care little either for lab director Furness's philanthropic dreams, which made no sense to him, or for the greedy dreams of his paymasters at Microvision. He signed on to the VRD project, he said repeatedly, because he needed a subject for his master's thesis, and he intended to publish the thesis when his work was done no matter how hard Microvision tried to stop him from doing so. He refused to consider the notion that the work Microvision paid him to do should be regarded as proprietary, and he viewed the company as an evil adversary from the first day he signed on to work at the HIT lab.

Tidwell seemed to work at similar cross-purposes in his personal life. Being an engineer, he was exceedingly rational, orderly, and tidy, both at work and at home. But he suffered from an odd kind of romanticism that made him fatally attracted to English majors. He found the artistic, irrational, emotional world literary women inhabited to be fascinating and exciting, and he was to date a succession of literature students during his years at the HIT lab. These relationships always foundered, and Tidwell lived largely in a state of outraged agony. It seemed that he was constantly breaking up with someone because she was a slob. When not railing at Microvision, he would sit in the lab and rail at the latest woman in his life. Her apartment, he would complain, was always a mess, and Tidwell's relationships were always punctuated with the same epitaph: "How can she live like that?"

With this core team in place, and with others hired to handle the VRD system's electronics, Johnston turned his attention late in 1994 to redirecting VRD research. He wanted to develop a series of prototypes that would be increasingly small and portable, with the idea of being able to begin gradually turning components and systems over to Microvision by some time in 1996. The company could then begin developing and marketing VRD technology in the private sector. Johnston saw himself as the rational agent who could help Furness, the visionary and dreamer, get "from here to there" before the Microvision contract would run out in November 1997.

While Johnston and his new team were building up the HIT lab's hardware effort, its wetware wing was suffering through the absence of Joey King. King had been driven to Japan's Advanced Telecommunications Research (ATR) Institute not only by his frustration with Furness and the lab, but by an inability to get along with his intellectual masters in the University of Washington psychology department, where he was trying to embark on an unconventional course of graduate study. King wanted to get his Ph.D. by studying human emotion in the context of human-computer interaction, and the necessarily interdisciplinary approach he wanted to take wasn't flying in the psychology department, which was resolutely traditional and leery of cooperating with other disciplines. It didn't help that King would rant at his mentors, delivering such pronouncements as, "I *hate* disciplinary studies. I'm very much opposed to the university as it now stands. If the current research university dies—I mean, it's only been around for fifty years or so—I don't think that is a big loss. This place is just ridiculous! Everyone locked in these little offices, it's a *big deal* when someone's an affiliate faculty member in another department. . . ."

His constant fulminations finally led members of the department to mount a campaign to get him out of their bailiwick. Among the many angry letters in his file at the university is King's personal favorite, addressed to him, declaring, "You concentrate too much on big-picture thinking."

"So I decided to leave this university," King said later, "which is writing me nasty letters and threatening to get rid of me and not funding me, and I'm in this little hovel of a lab, a little dusty room, and I go over to Japan and suddenly I'm in this office of a Japanese research institute, with a team of assistants, a laboratory, and pretty much an unlimited budget." Indeed, he was in a kind of research Nirvana, ATR being the crown jewel of research labs in Japan. "I mean, if you need any equipment—this is beautiful—ATR has like two hundred member companies. They're sort of coerced by the government to be members. We had like these catalogs of *stuff.* So let's say I needed a laser disc writer? That's a two-hundred-thousand-dollar piece of equipment? I'd call Sony up, and they'd ship it to me on 'indefinite loan.' "

King was particularly interested in a project at ATR called "Virtual Space Teleconferencing," by means of which as many as six to eight people at a time, from different places around the world, could "meet" via the Internet in a shared virtual space. ATR had a system in which all of the virtual environment graphics were stored on every participant's computer, and the only information that had to be passed through the Internet among all the distributed workstations were changes in the environment. This approach solved a great deal of the bandwidth problem in distributed virtual worlds technology, as the amount of information flowing between workstations was infinitely less than under the conventional approach, in which all the graphical data about the virtual environment is stored in a central server that constantly updates all the graphics on all the participants' workstations.

In order for such a system to work properly, it needed to be equipped with eye tracking, face tracking, gesture recognition, and other input modes dear to King's heart. King was interested in how emotion and other nonverbal cues would be transmitted and understood in virtual space. ATR scientists had developed sophisticated recognition systems for their teleconferencing computer networks, so that artificial intelligence could recognize and react to such things as human facial expression and eye movement. Should a computer user frown, for example, the system would have the icon or avatar representing that person squint an eye or turn down the corners of its mouth. "They had a huge signal processing group that was doing all this work," King recalled later, "and I basically had that environment to do research with." After mulling over possibilities of research avenues, King decided to concentrate on how humans react to and evaluate different kinds of software agents—graphical representations of software programs that perform tasks for users.

King devised an experiment where he and fellow ATR researcher Jun Ohya showed test subjects forty different "agents," ranging from detailed human figures to crude caricatures to little happy faces, saki urns, boxes, spheres. . . . The test subjects—half from Eastern cultures, half from the West—were asked to assess the intelligence and capabilities of the agents based on their appearance, and their facial expressions were recorded while they reacted to the different agents. King was surprised at first to see that "the Japanese thought that the caricatures and these three-dimensional human forms were the same, had the same amount of agency, and Westerners thought there was a progression, that the agency capability was very much related to complexity and realism." Upon reflection, however, this didn't strike him as all that odd: "It doesn't take a genius to look around Japan and see comic book stores that are the size of tall buildings. I mean, these people really put a lot of faith in caricatures."

King was doing this research well before Microsoft and other American computer companies started throwing prodigious resources and faith into the development of such software agents as Microsoft Bob, the bespectacled happy face that was supposed to make computers as easy to use as toasters. King decided that agents were a bad idea at that point in the development of artificial intelligence. It was clear that they would lead to more confusion than enlightenment on the part of computer users, who would impute far more intelligence and capability to the agent than it actually had. "There's a lot of reasons agents are going to go wrong," he said, "and only a limited number of reasons that agents are going to go right."

King took part in another project, though, that was to give the world an outsized and misbegotten notion about the power and capabilities of these creatures. Fujitsu Semiconductor, a huge Japanese electronics conglomerate, had deployed eleven thousand automatic teller machines (ATMs) in Japan, then looked on in horror as Japanese bank customers refused to use them at all, even after an expensive education campaign mounted by Fujitsu. The company finally came to ATR to ask researchers there to find out why, and to devise a way to get people to start using the machines.

The engineers decided to start out by going to banks and watching what happened.

King had always found Japanese banks odd. "You go into these places," he says, "and there's forty people working in a little bank branch! In this country, there might be three. The places are *packed*. And the reason is, banks in Japan don't use computers, so you have to have twelve people on abacuses checking everything." The customer is met by a uniformed man—a greeter—who asks what sort of transaction you intend to do, then guides you to the appropriate part of the bank. Once there, you might spend several minutes in conversation with two or more bank employees in the course of completing a simple transaction.

King suggested that Fujitsu add an agent to the automatic teller machines, in the form of a little screen with a cartoon figure that greets the customer as he or she approaches the machine. Given the highly interactive form of normal Japanese bank transactions, and given the faith his test subjects had shown in crude caricatures, he suspected that a cartoon figure might make ATMs acceptable to Japanese customers. "It worked like a charm!" he said years later, still surprised. "Basically, it didn't do anything, except that when you stepped up to the machine it bowed profusely and said something. I've still got pictures of old ladies bowing to these things."

From Fujitsu's and King's point of view, the agent worked *too* well. Customers began demanding that the ATMs, which only operated from nine A.M. to five P.M., be kept running all the time— something the tradition-bound Japanese banking industry was loath to allow. And the software industry—in particular, Microsoft, which would eventually spend $30 million developing and marketing Microsoft Bob (a market bomb)—became enamored of the notion that software agents could turn everyone on the planet into an enthusiastic computer buyer and user.

Typically, King found himself at odds with the very people who took tremendous interest in his work. "Microsoft's really interested in something I'm not," he said years later. "Something I did as an accident. I wasn't interested in agents. I'm *still* not interested in agents. I don't think I'm *ever* going to be interested in agents! I'm interested in emotion, particularly toward machines. I got interested in agents from the standpoint of wanting to know about emotion. One of my contentions was that emotions may be different in virtual environments. That's why I decided to do those experiments at ATR."

Back at the HIT lab, meanwhile, Rich Johnston, once he started studying the VRD project in earnest, was so dismayed at the poor quality of the prototype and at the technical barriers he saw looming before him that he concluded something odd was going on: Either Microvision's owner/investors didn't know what they were investing in, or they were investing in it for reasons other than carrying the project through to completion. "I think they thought they could get in here," he said, "put a little money in, sign this technology transfer agreement, create a whole bunch of hype, take their company public, get a bunch of money, get out, and not worry about what happened afterward."

This deduction was based on the dim prospects he saw for ever turning Furness's idea into a marketable product.

Johnston approaches all projects in the same way, first breaking them down into separate problems to be solved. He then divides these problems into two categories, which he calls "technical breakthroughs that are needed" and "engineering issues." The first are "things that there may or may not be a physical way to do." The second are issues "you know are solvable. They're issues of schedule, time; they cost a little more money than you'd like, but you know you'll eventually get it done." There is no point, of course, in working on the second set of problems without knowing whether the first set can be solved.

Johnston identified three potentially insoluble problems. Least vexing of the three was the problem of finding color image sources for a lightweight, wearable display unit. The VRD used a laser to beam light into the retina, and to date only red laser diodes had been invented. Color images are formed by mixing three beams— red, green, and blue—together. In order to generate blue and green laser beams, Johnston and his team had to use gas lasers—large, cumbersome, complicated pieces of machinery that could never be part of a wearable display system.

Difficult as this problem was, Johnston knew that there was so much money to be made from blue and green laser diodes that he wouldn't have to worry about them being available when he needed them for the VRD. "The original VRD proposal said that we would work on that problem," he said, "but I didn't think it made any sense at all. It would cost way too much money, it was a totally different area, very complex, and I knew lots of people were working on it anyway, people with a lot more money than we had. There's a hell of an economic incentive to get blue laser diodes." Since invention of a blue laser diode could make billions for the Sonys and 3Ms of the world, their laboratories—directed toward more immediately profitable research than that undertaken in academic laboratories—were already hard at work on the problem. Blue laser technology would allow manufacturers of laser printers to double the dots per inch on their machines, and manufacturers of CDs to store probably four times as much information on them. "If you use a blue device," Johnston explained, "you can get full-length motion pictures on a five-inch disc. So there's obviously a huge reason for people to work toward doing that."

The other two problems were specific to the VRD and to the anatomy of the eye, however, and Johnston had severe doubts about finding solutions to them. Screens—and, for that matter, reality—work by broadcasting light profligately, knowing that only a tiny portion of it has to reach the pupil in order to be directed through the lens and cornea onto the retina. Moreover, because the pupil is tiny—two to seven millimeters in diameter, depending on light conditions—the light forms a faithful picture on the retina by entering the eye at a wide angle—the light, in effect, pivots at the pupil, spreading out over the retina at about the same angle as it enters the pupil. You see clear, crisp details in the center of your visual field because the eye's detail receptors are located in the center of the retina, or foveal region—an area estimated at plus or minus two degrees around the eye's optical axis. (This is why you have to move your eyeballs when reading text.) The eye's field of view is approximately 140 degrees, with the bulk being devoted to peripheral vision—the portion of the retina that sees motion better than color or detail. "My guess," Johnston said, "is that this evolved so that if motion occurred, your attention was drawn to it, in which case you turned that way and saw in detail what was about to eat you."

In order to understand how the VRD was supposed to work, and why it offered a potentially far higher resolution display than screens did, you have to think of the retina as a screen, and the VRD's laser as analogous to the electron beam scanning the back of a computer or television screen.

Monitors and screens are illuminated and colored by this thin beam of electrons that sweeps at high speed back and forth, up and down, on the back of the screen, with the line zigzagging its way to the bottom right corner and beginning again at the top left corner before the light in that top corner has had time to fade away. The electrons hit a layer of phosphor on the back of the screen, making the phosphor glow. The beam draws each line in an image one dot—or "pixel"—at a time, at extremely high speed. By constantly "refreshing" the image, pixel by pixel (there are 786,432 pixels on an industry-standard 1024-by-768-pixel computer monitor), the display system makes the array of individual pixels appear—to the human brain, at least—to be a single, stable image.

The VRD was designed to paint the retina in the same way. The VRD's laser would be directed through the center of the pupil and would paint back and forth and up and down the retina fast enough—painting the entire image sixty times per second, at a minimum—to begin again at the top before the brain's memory of the light faded from that first painted spot on the retina. This feat was made more complicated by the desire of Furness to make the VRD's display seem more immersive by using more of the retina. In order to direct the laser through the two-millimeter pupil and paint with it across the whole retina, the beam had to be scanned at an extremely wide angle. It was like trying to paint a billboard at superhuman speed by reaching with a long brush through a tiny hole—which, to make matters worse, was moving.

This matter of the pupil's mobility threatened to make any

future VRD device impossible to use. In order to see a VRD-broadcast image on Furness and Kollin's prototype, a user had to very carefully align his or her pupil with a tiny dot, called the "exit pupil," that could be seen floating in the center of a large lens on the VRD. It was not unlike trying to look through a high-powered microscope. It took considerable concentration and effort to find the dot, focus on it, then keep your pupil from straying off of the exit pupil and losing sight of the image. Furness and Kollin originally hoped to add eye tracking to the VRD so that it could monitor movements of the user's eye and move the exit pupil around to keep it aligned with the user's pupil. But Johnston soon discovered that eye tracking would add hundreds of dollars to the construction cost of each VRD unit. "In my mind," he said, "to make this thing commercially viable, we need to be able to build displays for on the order of twenty dollars each. If you can't do that, you're not going to sell them. You may make a theoretical nice thing, but you're not going to sell much." Further, an eye-tracker-guided VRD would have to move all of its machinery around as fast as a human could move his or her eye—a virtual impossibility.

Only slightly less vexing was the invention and construction of a device that could scan the laser beam back and forth across the retina. "How do you take and move an optical beam of light back and forth that fast?" Johnston kept asking himself. "It's a very difficult problem."

In the first VRD prototype, Joel Kollin had built a scanner out of crystal. Called an acoustical-optical scanner, it moved light back and forth by means of electrical pulses that applied and removed pressure on the crystal, causing it to compress and decompress as waves of light passed through it. The compressed and decompressed parts thus formed a "diffraction grating" that bent the light passing through. By changing the spacing of the compressed and decompressed sections of the crystal, the grating's frequency was changed, thus scanning the light by changing the way it was bent. "You can scan light real fast with an acoustical-optical crystal," Johnston said. "They have a number of problems, though: They do it over a very small angle, and they require a large amount of optics to get the beam going into them just right and to form a good circular beam coming out. So it makes for a big system." Since they also cost $5,000 each, Johnston added, "There's no way you can make any kind of commercially viable display out of this."

While Johnston regarded these three problems as the only ones with no apparent solution, he did not regard them as the most complicated parts of the VRD project. "There were a hundred other things that had to be done," he said. "Probably the most complex part of the system isn't any of those three things. It's probably the electronics and the timing, how everything has to play together when we build it. Although while it may be complex, may take a long time, you know it can be done—it's just a matter of doing it, figuring it out."

Mike Almquist had exited the HIT lab with as much determination as disappointment. While on the one hand he was devastated—"I had thought the lab would be the one place in the world where I could get all these ideas out of my head that were trying to get out," he said—on the other he was energized and enraged. "I will succeed," he said over and over again to himself. "I will show them!"

Unlikely as it seemed that Almquist had much chance of realizing any of his outsized dreams, he did have an ace or two in the hole. Kubota Pacific, maker and marketer of the graphics engines Almquist and his friends had used to make their burning building demo, had been trying for years, without success, to make inroads into the high-end graphics market owned entirely by Silicon Graphics. Now Kubota salesmen were finding that videotapes of the demo served as a compelling lure to potential customers at trade shows. Near the end of his time at the HIT lab, a Kubota salesman had said to Almquist that if he could write VR software that "will make Kubotas sell," the company would bundle it with every graphics engine it sold. Legal restrictions on entrepreneurial ventures by HIT lab employees had prevented Almquist from cutting a deal with Kubota then; now, though, the restrictions were null and void as far as he was concerned.

Once safely out of the lab, Almquist incorporated a company named Ambiente, cajoled two of his former HIT lab cohorts into joining forces with him, and borrowed $10,000 from his parents to get started. Then the three of them started building a VR system for Kubota.

For a month, the three worked out of a side office at Kubota's suite of offices in Bellevue, across Lake Washington from the HIT lab. Almquist and his partners started over more or less from scratch, both to improve their demo software and to avoid using code they feared might be the property of the HIT lab.

Almquist's exuberance was short-lived. At that year's SIG-GRAPH conference, he heard that Kubota was shutting down its American operation, Kubota Pacific. His Kubota cohorts at the conference denied the news at first when he asked them about it, but no sooner did he get back to Seattle than they finally admitted that Kubota Japan was cutting off their funding and allowing them to stay in business only if they could raise their own money. The Ambiente partners worked another month, considerably distracted, then suddenly got word that Kubota was shutting down its Seattle office immediately. "Get out here quick," a sympathetic Kubota salesman told them. "Take as much of our equipment as you can haul away."

Almquist and his friends loaded up their car with three computer systems' worth of hardware and software, drove back across the lake, distributed it among the three of them, and tried to figure out what to do next.

An answer of sorts came from a professor in the University of Washington oceanography department who had worked some months in the past with a group of students in the HIT lab on software that could "visualize" sea-floor topography. The professor wanted Ambiente to develop software that could take in sonar signals that were swept across the ocean floor and turn the sound into graphics rendered on computer screens. After Almquist said that such a project could cost in the neighborhood of $50,000, he agreed to do it for somewhere between $7,000 and $10,000, depending on various funding contingencies facing the college prof.

With their savings draining away and with no certainty that their one client would ever get around to paying them, the Ambiente partners next did something that seems self-destructive and insane in retrospect: They rented office space—"incredibly cheap office space," Almquist says, but a drain on their budget nonetheless. The space was a large room in the basement entryway to a state-subsidized housing complex in a fading neighborhood on Seattle's Capitol Hill. "It was surreal," Almquist later said. "It was filled with a bunch of low-income people and a lot of old people. There was no entrance—the entrance to our office was the entryway to the whole thing. So whenever we brought customers, clients, people in, there would be like old people walking through asking for quarters."

It came to be a symbol of Ambiente's dismal prospects. Almquist and his friends, rather than feeling daunted or downtrodden, succumbed to "visions of grandeur. We had, like, some savings, ten thousand from my parents, five thousand from one of my friend's parents, and this nebulous seven to ten thousand from the University of Washington. And we ran out and bought seventy-five sheets of drywall, and had this grand vision for erecting like fifteen walls. We had all been reading books about start-up companies, and one of them was *Sunburst: The Ascent of Sun Microsystems.* And they talked in there about how they went out to start this company, they were going to suck down as many people and as much money as possible, and they would either make it incredibly big or make the biggest crater in the world. So we were like, 'Okay, all or nothing, guys, let's do the same thing!' "

It had taken Almquist more than two years to understand what Rich Johnston understood almost from the day he first set foot in the HIT lab: Furness was visionary in the most dangerous sense of the word. He had a way not only of seeing the preferred as the actual, but of making other people see it that way as well; and those who did not bring superhuman skepticism to their dealings with Furness were headed, like Almquist, for a crushing disappointment.

Nearly everyone in the high-tech engineering world falls into one of two categories: evangelists (like Apple cofounder Steve Jobs) or pragmatists (like Apple cofounder Steve Wozniak). The first, like Furness, have a passion for dreaming and a gift for spellbinding speech. The second, like Johnston, tend toward disbelief and passionless analysis. They define, attack, and solve complex problems in tiny increments while their opposite numbers are off rhapsodizing about the big picture. The two also are inextricably linked, since the first cannot progress toward realization of their visions without the backbreaking work and hardheaded thinking of the second—who in turn rely on their visionary counterparts for inspiration and a sense of direction.

Yet any practical engineer will tell you that the evangelist is more bane than benefactor—as Johnston was more than happy to point out to anyone who would listen. "Tom, as you probably noticed, is not as technically detailed as I am," he said to me one day. "He's an evangelist, a dreamer. A very good salesman, exciting. And he gets very enthusiastic very quickly about things—always believes that everything's going to go right, and that people are waiting to drop money on all these things. But sometimes there's a lot more to getting from here to there than he expects."

Johnston spent a great deal of time serving as a human reality check on Furness's enthusiasms, which were made all the more infectious by the director's considerable charm. His homespun, self-effacing manner set him dramatically apart from other computer-world visionaries, who tend to congregate more toward the blowhard end of the behavior-and-vocabulary spectrum. Furness also believed in the potential of technology to ease human suffering the way St. Augustine believed in Catholicism—hence his enthusiasm for projects like the one easing Parkinson's disease symptoms or treating arachnophobia. For Furness, the promotion of technology was more a matter of saving the world than of winning a competition or accruing personal wealth, and he exuded sincerity and compassion so palpably that people found themselves involuntarily rooting for him.

His eloquence always ramped up several notches whenever he looked into the future: "And those worlds that we'll visit will not only be the ones that we synthesize, but will actually be worlds we visit in a 'telepresent' sense. Where we go to another physical place, but we don't have to be there physically. We can walk along an insect's eye, or on the surface of a molecule. . . . What's it going to mean? What are we going to learn? What'll we be able to do in the future, in terms of modern alchemy?"

Talk like this, which always had Furness's audiences looking excitedly around the lab for the headset that would take them to these places *right now*, was nearly always part of Furness's demonstrations of the VRD prototype. You could usually find Johnston standing off to one side at these events, trying to figure out how to lower the unreasonable expectations brought on by his boss's feverish pronouncements.

One Furnessian hallucination in particular came to serve as a kind of leitmotif in Johnston's professional life: the idea that the VRD might be able to "cure" blindness. Furness had stumbled onto the possibility that the blind could see VRD-displayed images two years before, by happenstance, when a visitor to the lab had put an injured eye—it had been blinded in an industrial accident—up to the VRD and seen the image it was displaying. "Why can I see this with my blind eye?" he asked Furness. "I don't know," answered the perplexed—and thrilled—director.

It turned out that certain forms of blindness—advanced glaucoma, for example, or blindness caused by an accident that damaged part of the eye while leaving the retina intact—could be overcome by the VRD, apparently because the laser beam was narrow enough to direct light and its image through obstacles that kept ordinary light out. "What this is going to come down to," Johnston said, "is you're going to need a retina for this to make any difference. And most visual impairments involve retinal damage. I know Tom is very enthusiastic about this; I tend to be a little less so. Although there *are* some people it can potentially help. Whether the number of them is enough that you actually can justify the cost of designing and developing a system remains to be seen."

Unfortunately, the tendency of Furness to see the best of all possible worlds opening up before him and the tendency of the media to exaggerate any potential technological advance doubly exaggerated the potential of the VRD to relieve blindness, and word that the HIT lab had a device that might someday cure blindness circulated with shocking speed around the world. Or so it seemed to Johnston, who got an amazing number of telephone calls from blind people who had heard about the VRD somewhere—the most distressing, to him, being one from a man in the Deep South who had blinded himself accidentally with a shotgun while hunting wild turkeys—and he was driven to near-apoplexy by Furness's promotion of the possibility. Time and again, whenever I saw Johnston give a demonstration of the VRD prototype, someone would ask him if it could cure blindness. Johnston would open his mouth as if to snap. "No, goddammit, no!" Then he'd stop, his hands in midair, emit a tiny sigh of exasperation, smile, and launch into a long-memorized explanation about the slim possibility that *some* visual impairments possibly *could* be alleviated by the VRD, but that no one in the lab knew for sure yet what its potential really was. Then he would resume his demo.

Although Johnston regarded a lot of Furness's publicizing as a distraction from the lab's real work—he often would ask Furness if he hadn't gone "over the line" in scheduling so many demos and press conferences—he nevertheless admired the director. "I could not do what Tom does," he said. "I can't go out and sell stuff like that. I usually don't dream up brilliant new ideas. Tell me what the idea is and I can take it from there, put a team together, make it into something real. But I'm not the guy who's going to come up with a brand-new idea, who's going to go out and talk to investors and explain how it works and why it's better and everything else; I'm not going to get the guys excited to begin with, I'm not the guy who's going to run around stirring up the audience."

Even so, Furness's incessant stirring always elicited showy exasperation from Johnston whenever he found himself in attendance at one of the director's rhapsodies. Johnston spent so much time compensating for Furness's enthusiasm that he often felt it was his job not so much to move the VRD technology forward as it was to deflate the extravagant expectations of people who had first heard of it from Furness.

Unfortunately for Johnston, the VRD itself had a way of subverting his reality checks and pouring fuel on the fires stoked by Furness's fantasy. One evening, Furness ushered into the lab a group of visitors from Seattle's Community Services for the Blind and Partially Sighted. While delivering a few introductory remarks and passing copies of a document around to the group, Furness noticed one woman who had arrived with a seeing-eye dog and who kept trying without apparent success to read her copy of the document by placing one corner of it flush against her eyeglasses. Then, when the group was brought down to the lab where the VRD itself was stored, she was the first to volunteer to look into its lens.

She made her way, with help, up to the lab bench on which was mounted a large contraption with a lens pointing straight upward. Unseen by her, on a computer monitor off in a corner of the room, was a vivid, colorful photograph of a toucan surrounded by lush jungle foliage—the picture being transmitted to the VRD. With Furness at her elbow, the woman leaned over the lens, moving her head every which way as the lab director explained that she needed to line her eye up with a tiny red dot that appeared to be floating on the lens.

"Can you see the bright spot?" he asked after a few moments.

"I . . . don't know," she answered.

A few more seconds passed, during which she kept maneuvering her eye over the lens. She seemed confused, hesitant, and uncertain.

What happened next, though, sent chills up the spines of everyone else in the room. The woman's mouth suddenly dropped open and she gasped, putting her hand to her chest and beginning to tremble from excitement.

"I can see it!" she shouted. "I can see it!"

The picture of the toucan had suddenly filled her eye.

PARTURITION

———

Buddy, Can You Paradigm?

WHILE FURNESS HIMSELF FELT at the beginning of 1994 that he was barely managing to keep his quest and his lab alive, it seemed to me that his cause was spreading out and taking root in innumerable subtle ways around the country. His incessant publicity campaign had brought in the Microvision investment; his students and researchers had won the AFOSR contract, which in research circles was highly prized and prestigious; his brightest protégé, Joey King, was working on virtual reality in one of Japan's most important research labs; there were now twenty-five paying members of the Virtual Worlds Consortium; and research papers from the HIT lab were circulating in growing numbers among client companies, in technology industry publications, and in scholarly journals around the world.

Furness's cause was also being furthered in other, less expected ways. The software group that had fled or been exiled from the lab moved out across the country, spreading the gospel of virtual reality wherever its members went. A former HIT lab student, Aaron Pulkka, found work as a software engineer at Disney; two other students moved to Chicago to work for VictorMaxx, a head-mounted display company; Mike Almquist and his two Fort

Delaware HIT lab cohorts, Marc Cygnus and Dan Pirone, had founded Ambiente, their VR software company; Bob Jacobson, the former associate director of the lab, had a VR company called Worldesign up and running across town in the Ballard district of Seattle; and countless other engineering, computer science, psychology, and architecture students had graduated from the HIT lab with advanced degrees from the University of Washington and taken their expertise and fervor out into the world.

All of this was rather haphazard and chaotic, little of it contributed directly to the care and feeding of the HIT lab, and many of these disciples were furious with Furness; but there was no question that the dreamer/director's effort was very much alive and kicking.

The lab's profile, in fact, had grown to the point where it helped build up in Seattle a critical mass of VR programming and designing talent. In this respect, the years 1993 and 1994 proved a historic turning point for Furness, as two promising new VR companies—one making software, the other hardware—set up shop in Seattle, their respective launches testifying eloquently to the rising credibility of both the lab and the industry it was trying to promote.

The first of these companies—Virtual i/O, a manufacturer of head-mounted displays—began developing its first product in May 1993. Virtual i/O was followed nine months later by Zombie Virtual Reality Entertainment, a VR gaming company founded by two research scientists who moved out to Seattle after leaving the famed David Sarnoff Research Center, in Princeton, New Jersey. Their establishment in Seattle marked the beginning of a sea change in the VR industry: Driven and supported from its beginnings by the military-industrial complex, it had advanced to the point where it was being driven and supported more and more by the entertainment-industrial complex.

Virtual i/O was founded by Greg Amadon, a television cameraman-turned-entrepreneur; Linden Rhoads, a geologist by training who had met Amadon when he hired her at his previous start-up, Cellular Technical Services (CTS); and Wolfgang Mack, a chemical engineer who left IBM and moved to Seattle from Texas to help launch Virtual i/O.

All three founders shared a vision based on Amadon's interpretation of the history of the cellular telephone. First had come the "car phone," which required nearly a full trunk's worth of batteries and other equipment to operate; next had come a smaller version that could run off the car battery; then had come a portable phone that could be carried in a bag and that required a briefcase-sized battery pack; finally, the technology advanced to the point where people could carry pocket-sized telephones around, sending and receiving calls from nearly anywhere in the world.

Virtual i/O's founders believed that display technology for computers and televisions was already moving along an identical path, albeit somewhat more slowly. Computers, Amadon liked to tell investors and reporters, started out as massive mainframes, shrunk down into refrigerator-sized minicomputers, then desktop-sized microcomputers, then laptops. Next would come computers with wearable, eyeglasses-sized displays, foldable keyboards, and processor hardware small enough to fit into a box the size of a small cell phone. Users would be able to carry the whole works in their pockets, putting the screen/eyeglasses on and unfolding the keyboard whenever and wherever they wanted to work. Eventually, the three components would be wirelessly connected with one another—and, for that matter, with other computers.

Amadon had done rather well—financially, at least—with his first start-up, and he took to his second venture with the enthusiasm of an adrenaline addict. Cellular Technical Services, a company that developed real-time billing software for cellular telephone companies, had gone public in 1991 during a tremendous boom in the cell phone industry. Immediately after its initial public offering (IPO), amid rumors that CTS was about to win some large contracts with major cellular phone companies, its stock shot up from $3 to $30 per share. While the deals never materialized, the stock plummeted, and Amadon was forced out as the company's CEO in late 1992, he nonetheless made a substantial amount of money in the process of riding the CTS roller coaster. He and his cofounders charted a similar course toward an

IPO for Virtual i/O, planning to ship its first product in early 1995 and go public amid tremendous hype and publicity at the end of that year, making another killing in the stock market.

It is impossible to overstate the allure of stock options in the minds of high-tech start-up founders and employees. Ever since Microsoft began making millionaires out of twenty-five-year-olds who had put in as little as four years with the company, the hard-work-to-quick-riches paradigm had rewritten the rules of employment in the Pacific Northwest. The remote possibility that a burst of round-the-clock work for very little pay would be rewarded with overnight wealth had a way of turning into a high likelihood in the minds of youngsters seduced by the technological cutting edge. By making stock options the paramount feature in compensation packages for employees, and by making more or less the same pitch to prospective workers that they made to prospective investors, the executives running start-ups were creating in their workforce the same demands and expectations they were creating in their backers. New employees were less interested in working conditions, medical benefits, and long-term prospects than they were in a spectacular short-term return.

Virtual i/O's founders were undaunted by the pressures they put on themselves from investors and investor/employees alike. They had high hopes for their company's product line, which they planned to have developed and on the market, virtually without competition, when a host of other computer- and entertainment-industry developments converged to make the wearable display market take off. Amadon, Rhoads, and Mack expected one day to be selling head-mounted displays by the hundreds of thousands for viewing television and movies, for high-end industrial uses, and for computer gaming—a form of entertainment they expected to transform when they brought out a head-tracking-equipped display that would allow commercial video and computer games to become as immersive as the HIT lab's Polhemus-equipped displays were. By the end of 1995, Rhoads predicted, Virtual i/O would be selling twenty thousand units per month, on its way to what she called a "modest goal": first-year sales of $20 million.

Virtual i/O charted a product-development course that called for the release first of all of a video-viewing headset that would hook up to televisions and VCRs; next would come a similar unit, with head-tracking, that would hook up to all PCs and game machines; next, a high-priced, custom-made, high-definition TV unit for use in medicine and engineering; after that would come an eyeglasses-sized display that would hook up to a computer microprocessor unit, making possible a screenless laptop computer—a machine that would weigh less than a pound and run indefinitely on two AA batteries. Any one of these product lines, the three reasoned, would generate millions upon millions in profits. If Virtual i/O managed to develop and market all of them, they could end up with a company bigger and more valuable than Microsoft.

While the market for head-mounted displays was as yet non-existent and undefined, Amadon felt that it was potentially a huge market, if someone could only manage to develop a reliable and well-designed headset. He also believed that he had a tremendous technological advantage over potential competitors: He had tracked down and struck a deal with one of the world's leading optics engineers, Richard Rallison, who had several optical-system patents on head-mounted display technology he had developed for the U.S. military. Rallison, something of an eccentric, was a self-styled "optical plumber" who would commute by ultralight airplane for the next several years from his remote ranch outside of Paradise, Utah, to Seattle to work with Virtual i/O.

While Wolfgang Mack worked closely with Rallison and concentrated on industrial design of the first Virtual i/O headsets, Amadon and Rhoads commenced a frenzied round of evangelizing to computer-game companies, software companies, and investors. Rhoads was able to parlay a family connection with Tele-Communications, Inc. (TCI), magnate John Malone into a purchase by TCI of 35 percent of Virtual i/O. With TCI on board, the start-up was able to talk Logitech, manufacturer of computer mice and other peripherals, into buying 5 percent of the company. Although Virtual i/O's founders never revealed the size of that initial round of fund-raising, it was believed to have been in the neighborhood of $20 million.

This relatively phenomenal amount of money invested in a

product line that struck most people as weird and futuristic, at best, gave the start-up extensive credibility in Seattle, and engendered the expectation in the community around the HIT lab that the head-mounted-display market was finally going to take off.

Amadon and Rhoads counted on the TCI/Logitech investments to give them entrée into the software and entertainment companies they desperately needed to provide applications and uses for their coming headsets. They spent the company's first year circling the globe in search of industrial partners on both the hardware and software sides, on the theory that the head-mounted-display market would develop exactly as the PC market had, with hardware and software advances egging and helping each other along toward worldwide acceptance.

The two had a combined power of persuasion that bordered on the hypnotic. Amadon, who was tall and stout, generally wore custom-tailored suits that gave him an air of high seriousness, which was considerably enhanced by a sober mien and soft-spokenness that brought Gary Cooper to mind. His taciturnity gave listeners the impression that he was understating the potential of his company's product even when he was projecting extravagant sales and profits. Rhoads, by contrast, seemed a barely harnessable bundle of kinetic energy. Her grooming was uncertain, her clothes—generally a jacket and skirt—never seemed to fit quite right or sit quite comfortably on her body, and she spoke and moved with such high speed and abrupt change of direction that it was impossible to follow or keep up with her. Earrings, or other objects anywhere within reach, often flew off in one direction or another without warning. Her hair, which she wore long, had a habit of flinging hanks of itself around, and sometimes a stray strand of it would stick, incongruously, to some part of her face, where it would sit unnoticed by her for minutes at a time. Finally—suddenly irritated—she would start swatting at it, eventually making contact by accident.

Rhoads believed that Virtual i/O was insured against failure because she and Amadon had carefully studied the short, lamentable history of the head-mounted-display market and learned from the mistakes of its predecessors. Previous HMD companies, she said, had adopted a "helmet paradigm," calling for users to cut themselves off from the outside world by encasing their heads in a helmet with a screen in front of their eyes. The headsets were uncomfortably heavy, and the isolation from the surrounding environment was often disorienting and sometimes nauseating. Virtual i/O was introducing an "eyeglasses paradigm," offering lightweight headsets that were nearly as comfortable as tennis visors or eyeglasses. Because users would be able to see around the eyepieces, because they would still be in contact with their surroundings, and because the headsets would be so comfortable, Virtual i/O was effectively eliminating nearly all obstacles that formerly stood in the way of HMD purchases.

Rhoads became quite practiced at ticking off the lessons Virtual i/O learned from Virtual Vision—another "eyeglasses paradigm" company—as she often was asked why she thought her company would succeed where that other Seattle company had failed just months before. She pointed out heatedly that she and Amadon had put far more thought into "usability" than had Virtual Vision's engineers. Where Virtual Vision required users to go through a relatively complex exercise to determine which was their dominant eye before selecting a headset, and had put the volume and picture controls in a place awkward both to reach and to see (on a pack that was worn on a belt), Virtual i/O was designing a headset that required no preparation or instruction to use, with its controls on the visor, where they could be easily reached and manipulated without requiring the user to take his or her eyes off the screen. Virtual i/O's design, she said, was not only more intuitive, but also more useful, as it could be plugged into a television, VCR, PC, video camera, or game machine, while Virtual Vision's could be used only to watch television or operate a camcorder.

Amadon and Rhoads foresaw an extensive early adopter market, including airlines that would install headsets in passenger seats, allowing travelers to pick from a menu of movies—including R- and X-rated ones, since they could be watched in private— rather than having to settle for the single offering on a single screen that airlines traditionally made available. They also planned to target dentists' offices, where headsets could be used by patients who wanted to be distracted by movies while dentists were working them over, and exercise-machine users, who could alleviate the boredom of exercise either by watching movies or running, cycling, or rowing through "virtual landscapes." Eventually, Virtual i/O would help give birth to a whole new software industry: three-dimensional TV. An art form that must be shot with expensive, double-lensed "stereo" cameras, it had been held back, the two were convinced, by the lack of a compelling stereo display device.

Amadon and Rhoads also expected hard-core video game players to take to their second product—the goggles equipped with the head-tracking unit—in such numbers that nearly every video game company in the world would be producing immersive three-dimensional games, the hardware and software mutually pushing and pulling each other toward mass-market acceptance.

The company entered 1994 frantically trying to develop its first headset and the market for it. All three founders, filled with revolutionary fervor, told whoever would listen that they were out to change the world. "Every CRT screen out there," Rhoads said with characteristic bravado, "is a potential target."

The move to Seattle from Sarnoff labs by Mark Long and Joanna Alexander was occasioned in part by the HIT lab, in part by the rather favorable comparisons Seattle made with New Jersey, and in part by Virtual i/O, which was attacking from the hardware side the same VR front that Long and Alexander wanted to work from the software side.

But mostly the move was occasioned by the conviction on the part of Zombie's cofounders that the world at long last was ready to line up and pay millions for VR entertainment software.

From the software realm, the leap to virtual reality looked substantially less daring than it did from the hardware world. Consumers were beginning to buy PCs with CD-ROM drives by the millions, and multimedia was hot investment territory. Nearly everyone in the software, entertainment, and publishing industry was intent on developing CD-ROM multimedia titles, and each new title represented a significant advance in computer graphics and verisimilitude over its predecessors. Since virtual reality looked like a simple extension of multimedia computing, and multimedia was on everyone's mind, it proved easy for Long and Alexander to find backers for a company formed to create VR titles for CD-ROM. So with money obtained from N. J. Nicholas, former president of Time, Inc., and former co-CEO of Time Warner, and Michael Tannen, a prominent entertainment-industry lawyer, the two quit their jobs at Sarnoff and headed west to catch the VR wave that was swelling in Seattle.

Long and Alexander both have long histories in virtual reality, and both sport the classic VR look made popular—or infamous—by the Timothy Learyoid enthusiasts who first brought the interface to widespread public attention. Long cultivates a look halfway between that of a cyborg and a motorcycle hoodlum. His head is shaved, his eyes close set. He has a wreath of thorns tattooed around the biceps on his left arm, just below the sleeve of his T-shirt. Alexander is a statuesque redhead who favors miniskirts or tight jeans worn with oversized boots and undersized crop tops. She has a pierced navel that peers out at the interested onlooker from under her top, and a pierced nipple—which she declines, with uncharacteristic demureness, to exhibit when asked.

After growing up in what he likes to call "the great state of Texas," spending portions of his life in El Paso, San Antonio, and Houston, Long entered the University of Texas at Austin in 1975, eventually earning "a bullshit degree" in communication studies. From there, he went into the U.S. Army, where he was to spend the next eight and a half years, a good part of it in the Special Forces as an army Ranger.

At the end of his career, Long found himself working on a new, "really disastrous weapons system called the Sergeant York. It was this tank with a Swedish 40-millimeter naval gun sitting on it. It was *insane*. . . . It weighed seventy-three tons, it was nine feet tall, and the army wouldn't let it go. It finally got on *60 Minutes*—that's what a disaster it was."

Rather than kill the monster after it became a national scandal, Congress mandated a series of expensive tests to find a use for it. Long was assigned to the testing program, and soon found himself learning the ins and outs of the army's new SIMNET system—the same system for which HIT lab engineer Richard Johnston had developed computer graphics back at Boeing. "They were able to mock up the system, put guys in it and try to make them shoot down simple aircraft, come up with tactics," Long recalls. The system put soldiers in various locations in the same virtual environment, where they could do battle with one another. "That's where I first heard about networked shared virtual environments."

Long retired from the army and took his newfound knowledge off to General Dynamics, where he worked from 1988 to 1991 on integrating SIMNET with the government's Battlefield Integration Center, as part of what eventually became an Internet-mediated virtual-war gaming system in which soldiers in various kinds of simulators could fight full-scale battles to the virtual death.

Before SIMNET, computerized battlefield studies were primitive and of dubious worth. Soldiers would enter data into computers—number of tanks, number of bombers, number of troops, types of weaponry, and so on, along with information about how these systems would be deployed and against what sort of enemy—then let the computer analyze the data and calculate likely outcomes. "At General Dynamics," Long said, "we were trying to integrate what's called 'Man in the Loop Simulation.' You could put guys in simulators and have them shoot, come up with tactics. We could play theater-level war games where guys making decisions could impact the game."

It was a classic lesson in the value of real-time simulation systems, as soldiers could learn tactics, capabilities of enemy weapons systems and other aspects of battle, and train their minds and reflexes in a way that was either impossible on older computer systems or impossibly dangerous and infinitely more expensive in live-fire exercises. As Furness had discovered at Wright-Patterson years before, the elimination of the abstract layer of data between a human and his or her environment, and its replacement by images, or "visualizations" of the data, enabled people to learn at astronomically faster rates.

Near the end of his time at General Dynamics, Long made a presentation to the Sarnoff Research Center on a military project he thought General Dynamics and Sarnoff should do together. The presentation, made to a group led by research scientist Joanna Alexander, led to Alexander's hiring of Long in June 1992 to work with her on the development of synthetic environments.

It can be hard for even the most resolute resister of stereotypes to reconcile Alexander's appearance with her career. She looks like a libertine and has the résumé of a nerd. She earned a degree in mathematics from Yale University in 1982, then spent two years teaching at Florida State University before moving on to the Max Planck Institute, where she worked on fending off clumsy male advances and studying nuclear target development and postaccelerator analysis. In 1985, she went to Princeton University, where she earned her master's degree in chemical engineering in 1988. She began working at Sarnoff when she was finishing up her degree, and was head of the Synthetic Environment Research Group, which she had formed, when Long showed up for his presentation.

As had Long when he first encountered SIMNET, Alexander experienced a VR epiphany during her first days at Sarnoff, when she was working on electron-beam performance analysis. Sarnoff scientists had been trying for months to figure out why these beams would shift in focus as the voltage powering them was increased. For six months, researchers pored over thousands of pages of data trying to analyze and correct the problem. Alexander, meanwhile, was put to work on a set of software tools that would enable them to visualize the data in three dimensions. The graphic computer simulation allowed them to see the performance of the beam and its generator rather than forcing them, as the alphanumeric interface did, to extrapolate a mental image from pages upon pages of figures. "Within three minutes of having the data up," she said to me, still greatly excited eight years after the event, "we realized that what happened was as you increased the applied voltage, the core rotates. That's all it was—and if you just had a way of looking at it like that, it's completely clear. I *love* epiphanies like that. To me, that was particularly fascinating, and kind of got me into the whole business of data visualization and virtual reality."

Among the Sarnoff Research Center's many groundbreaking discoveries were the invention of television and the LCD; and in

1992 the Hasbro Corporation, which believed that VR game systems were ready for mass-market development, came to Sarnoff in the hopes that the center could help develop a display system for a VR game machine Hasbro wanted to develop. Long and Alexander convinced them to let Sarnoff develop the whole system. Hasbro went along. As a result, Long said with a hearty laugh, "they eventually spent $51 million and never came to market."

Still, the Hasbro fiasco was more encouraging than discouraging to the two about the future of virtual reality. They felt it was a glimpse into the near future, when, Alexander says, "there were going to be game devices like in the two-hundred-dollar range that are going to be the equivalent of what quarter-million-dollar computers are right now." They also had come in contact through Hasbro with the computer game industry, which Long thought was "amazing, very much like research and development. High-payoff, high-risk engineering. Game guys are always on the cutting edge. These little game companies have some of the best engineers in virtual reality that there are."

By June 1994, Long and Alexander were set up in the refurbished old State Hotel in Seattle's historic, arty Pioneer Square district. Their fledgling company immediately took on the look of an art-industry rather than engineering-industry enterprise. Half of Zombie's employees—and, for that matter, half of its founding management—was female, and more than half came from art rather than engineering backgrounds. To walk through Zombie's offices was to walk through a sea of asymmetrical haircuts, nose rings, wildly and oddly colored hair, and attire that looked more like costume than clothing.

There also was a certain elusive pungent quality to the air at Zombie, reminiscent of rock festivals, that eventually was explained by a piece of e-mail a company employee thoughtfully copied to me. A scolding missive from a manager to her product team, the relevant part read, "I'd prefer it if you didn't smoke illegal substances during working hours."

Among the reasons Long and Alexander were drawn to games was a belief they shared with HIT lab director Furness that the effort on the software side must shift from engineering to art if the

VR market is ever to grow. "Applications," Alexander said, "is the one area that's constantly neglected, the stumbling point in any new technological area. In Sarnoff, when they were in the early days of doing records, stereo sound, the engineers who created the record players wouldn't write the music to play on it. Yet in this software area where you're creating content that is just as creative as music, you have engineers creating the content for it."

Part of their focus on content led Alexander and Long to mull over the possibilities in gaming that lay in the emergence of head-tracking on HMDs. If someone playing a computer game could effectively be inside a game, immersed in a fictional world, surrounded by friends and enemies alike, what sort of game could, or should, that be? After thinking and talking for months about what exactly they could compose, given the shortcomings of computer hardware, that would compel a hard-core game player to go out and spend $300 on headgear, Long and Alexander came up with a game they called "Locus."

Locus, which was to be Zombie's first product, would begin with an outside view of several arenas, floating in outer space, variously shaped as doughnuts, spheres, figure eights, and so on. Inside each space station would be an arena with a goal in its center. The player and his or her teammates were to try to steal balls from other players and get them into the goal, all the while trying to prevent opponents from stealing the ball, trying to prevent opponents from scoring, fending off opponents intent on putting the player out of commission, and assaulting other opponents in the hope of eliminating them from the game. The player would travel through the game in a high-speed vehicle—a brief sequence at the game's beginning showed a helmeted player climbing into it—that skims along the arena's surface, the walls, floors, and ceilings all being part of the same curved, enclosing plane.

Long's vision for the game was captured in a short document he wrote entitled "Setting and Story Line":

> LOCUS is set in an alternative future, about 100 years from now (2095). The Earth is crowded, polluted, and economically stratified. Super powers and non-super powers alike invested

their resources in space exploration and settlement. This required smaller nations to pool their resources and collaborate, thus fostering cultural cross-pollination. At the same time large corporations involved with software, telecommunications, fossil fuels, garbage reclamation, and other macro-interests gained enormous power. Financial interests and the quest for space weakened political boundaries. Nations diffused, fragmenting into consortiums of diverse interest groups: confederations of city-states, large telecommunication corporations, and Mafia-like gangs to name a few. These confederations are called "metropols."

Meanwhile, the destitute, passive citizens of these metropols turned to spectator sports to escape. These masses, though powerless individually, had enough power together to shape the state of future sports. They ultimately rejected former giant games of sport, and began to notice a new game phenomenon, LOCUS.

A game created to test and take advantage of new space technologies, LOCUS is held in off-world arenas near Earth. Game events are massively covered by all media, and live action is viewed via satellite uplinks over the globe. Though citizens do not watch the game in person, the viewing audience is felt on the field via audio feedback links.

Grandiloquent as this sounds, and rich as the story element is, the remarkable thing about the document is that it was inspired almost entirely by the need of the writer to explain the featureless curved surface that would surround the player in Locus. It is as if a filmmaker in the early days of moving pictures, driven to explain the fact that his movie was in black and white, wrote an elaborate screenplay about a man inhabiting a colorless world.

With this paradigm in mind, Zombie set out in mid-1994 to enter the VR marketplace within months of the time when Virtual i/O launched its head-tracker-equipped HMD. Their target market, Long admitted freely, was small—"about two million hardcore game players"—but they were convinced that when the two companies hit that market with their combined hardware-software assault, the computer game world would never be the same again. And once that beachhead was established, world domination was imminent!

With his VRD effort securely funded for the next few years, and with his research-and-development team in place, Tom Furness should have felt vindicated and triumphant. After years of being told his idea—scanning images directly onto the retina and eliminating the need for expensive, heavy, power-hungry screens—would not work, he had secured a multimillion-dollar funding package and was well on his way to turning a working lab prototype—something he had been told repeatedly could never be built—into a marketable product. He had come to regard the VRD as the culmination of his "life's work," and he could see the day when it was deployed everywhere, in all manner of devices.

No sooner had he inked the deal with Microvision, however, than Furness began seeing signs of trouble. His new industrial partners were having abysmal luck in getting other investors to pour money into their company, and Furness was convinced that their misfortune had less to do with the unreliability of his technology than with their unreliability as businessmen.

Furness's partnership with Microvision was borne of a combination of his eagerness to believe in people, the uninformed greed of the company's founders, and the fact that by the time Microvision's eventual founder, the Canadian stockbroker Casey Harlingten, showed up at the HIT lab, Furness had nowhere else to turn for money. His lab was in financial trouble, and no one on earth, it seemed, was interested in investing in the high-risk, unproven technology he was peddling.

It soon became apparent that the Furness/Microvision marriage was based on mutual ignorance. Harlingten was by all accounts as ignorant of technology and the electronics hardware business as Furness was about human nature. Furness utterly lacked suspicion or skepticism about people, his religion and instinct compelling him to believe that all people were either inherently good and honorable or redeemable. His innocence, it was often said by people in the HIT lab, was compounded by inexperience, as he had spent his entire career in government labs and knew nothing about the deviousness and ruthlessness of the business world.

At first, Furness had been thrilled and surprised by the emergence of Harlingten—particularly when he handed Furness a $250,000 "earnest money" check to forestall the director from signing with another company while Harlingten was off raising the $5.1 million Furness said he needed to complete a serious technology-development effort. Harlingten then brought in two more Canadian brokers—George Hatch and David Hunter—and formed a partnership they called the "H Group" to go out and raise money to launch a VRD start-up.

Almost immediately, the H Group raised $3.5 million from several individual investors, and began negotiating a technology-transfer agreement with the University of Washington. Among the principal elements of the agreement were these: The University of Washington would have a 9 percent equity interest in the new company; Microvision would pay $5.1 million to the HIT lab, in quarterly installments over four years, in return for getting an exclusive license to the VRD technology; and eventually the University of Washington would be paid royalties on sales of all Microvision products that included VRD technology.

In return, the HIT lab was obligated to do nothing but pure research. "We didn't even have to really deliver anything to Microvision," Furness said, "because this was basically a research contract. At the end of four years, the only thing we had to deliver were papers."

To Furness, the agreement—which he desperately needed, as his lab was mired in poverty and on the verge of closing down when Harlingten showed up—opened the door to an intellectually and fiscally rich future. "This was really a sweet deal for the university and a sweet deal for the lab," he said, "because not only would we be able to do R&D on this money, we'd also, with the royalty stream, be able to basically have another seed pot and continue on, and the company would be able to start off with some really world-changing technology. This was really a paradigm shift—a whole new way of doing images. All the screens that exist on the earth—movie screens, computer screens, TV screens—all of them ultimately could be affected by this."

It also was potentially a sweet deal for Furness. He and Joel Kollin, as coinventors of the VRD, were each given one hundred thousand shares of Microvision stock, according to a University of Washington policy that awarded inventors one-third of the school's take from technology-transfer deals. (The two eventually gave portions of their packages to Bob Burstein, who helped Kollin build the first prototype.) In addition, Furness was promised an additional 1 million shares of company stock—an allotment equal to those given Microvision's founders. In return for the extra shares, Furness signed on as chairman of the company's scientific advisory board and traveled around the world with the company principals during their second round of fund-raising. His presence on these trips was vital to Microvision, as none of the stockbrokers had backgrounds in technology or even in running a business.

Almost from the day they founded Microvision, the H Group ran into trouble of one kind or another. For a number of reasons—not the least of which was the company's lack of material assets—they seemed profoundly unattractive to investors. This was not particularly surprising to Furness, as Microvision had nothing to show venture capitalists aside from the HIT lab's crude prototype, the VRD's inventor, and a downtown office with a telephone in it. There were no Microvision engineers or lab facilities, and the company's three principals had no experience in running a technology start-up.

Matters were not helped when the stock market crashed in early 1994, all but eliminating Microvision's already slim chances of rounding up more investors.

Furness watched with increasing dismay as the H Group staggered through the first half of 1994. Finally, deciding that they needed business experience in the company, the group brought in Ron Erickson, former president of Egghead Software, as a board member; a Vancouver, B.C., engineer named Stephen Willey (pronounced "wily") to serve as technical liaison with the lab and give the company some engineering cachet; and a manager named Rick

Rutkowski, who previously had run a software company called Lone Wolf—which eventually was bought by Microsoft cofounder Paul Allen's investment company, Vulcan Ventures. There it disappeared, as many of Vulcan's companies did, into what one former Lone Wolf employee called "the black hole of being a Paul Allen company."

Rather than bring stability and credibility, though, the new arrivals brought tension and chaos. In short order, Erickson and Rutkowski had a falling out, with the result that Erickson and his faction were ousted from the company, and Rutkowski went on to cajole the founding H Group members into giving up large portions of their stock so that he could make the company more attractive to other investors. "It was just a mess," Furness later said, "watching this whole company self-destruct before our eyes, with all these fights that were going on."

When the dust cleared, Microvision had been taken over by two mysterious figures, in Rutkowski and Willey, with rather vaguely described backgrounds and plans for the future that they didn't want anyone else to know. Rutkowski habitually talked in long, nebulous, overblown paragraphs that befogged the minds of his listeners; and Willey—a small, ferretlike man with rapid speech and high-speed physical mannerisms, including eyes that darted incessantly around the room looking at everything except his interlocutor—constantly complained about the openness of the HIT lab and the onerous terms of Microvision's contract with the university. Both men inspired deep distrust and profound misgivings on the part of everyone in the lab. The only HIT lab researcher who held out any hope for them at all was the philosopher-physicist David Melville, and even his defense of the two was lukewarm, at best: "I believe in giving them some benefit of the doubt."

For all their failings, though, the two did manage to raise another $4 million for Microvision, largely because of the reputation of Furness and the rearranging of the company portfolio forced on his partners by Rutkowski. The original investors had kept too much of the company's stock for themselves, and only by releasing significant portions of their holdings—in effect, dropping the price per share they were charging new investors—could they bring new money in.

Even with the new money, though, it was soon clear, not only to the lab but to Microvision's managers, that the company was burning through its money too fast to have anything left over by the time the HIT lab could hand over any salable technology to Microvision. Growing increasingly desperate month by month, Willey and Rutkowski set off on a renewed worldwide search both for new investors and for deep-pocketed corporations to help fund product development.

The two also began questioning the HIT lab's management of their money, even though their contract with the university contained virtually no performance criteria for the lab to meet. Rutkowski and Willey began trying to micromanage the project. During Microvision's quarterly reviews of the HIT lab's progress, Willey grew increasingly impatient, demanding ever more vociferously that Furness change the direction of the project into what the director contemptuously called a "warm-body operation": one in which the lab unquestioningly served the interests of its corporate sponsor rather than conduct pure research for the sake of adding to the world's store of technical knowledge. "We're doing core technical research over here," Furness would say to Willey. "It's not our job to develop the technology on our own to the point where it's a product!"

In Furness's view, Microvision should have been building its own engineering facilities, taking the research results learned in the HIT lab and doing product development on top of it. But Microvision instead took what little money it had to spend outside the lab and hired marketing people rather than engineers. The company refused to begin building a lab, buying equipment, or doing any product development of its own. Rutkowski and Willey decided that Microvision would essentially be a broker rather than a manufacturer. Instead of making retinal scanner products or parts, it would sell the technology it had licensed from the University of Washington to established manufacturers like Sony and Motorola. In essence, Microvision would simply pass along the fruits of the HIT lab's research, skimming off money in its role as gatekeeper.

To Furness, this was a disaster. Not only would Rutkowski and Willey never find investors willing to buy into a company with no material assets; they also would never find manufacturers willing to front them money for the sake of gaining rights to technology that the sellers were not even developing themselves. "Our whole point in our arguments with them," Furness said, "was that they didn't have anything to market. They had no company, basically." His inexperience in the business world notwithstanding, Furness was convinced that he had hooked up with fools. Whenever anyone asked him about Microvision, he would lament, "They don't know what they're doing!"

Furness did have one major consolation in his travails with Microvision. On the engineering side, in the safe confines of his laboratory, his VRD team was doing the kind of work he loved watching: pure engineering, where problems were tangible, identifiable, and predictable, and where solutions were trustworthy. Maddening and difficult as breakthrough engineering could be, it was at least governed by consistent rules.

Furness and Rich Johnston, the engineer in charge of the VRD project, both knew that the key question to be answered before the viability of retinal scanning could be asserted was whether or not it was possible to build a reliable scanner. A tiny mechanical part had to be made that could scan light back and forth across the retina at high speed for years without breaking down or faltering. The first order of business for Johnston's team, then, was to find a device that could replace the cumbersome crystal—the acoustical-optical scanner—that was in the lab's first prototype.

Johnston held out some hope because David Melville, during the pre-Microvision months when he had been volunteering in the HIT lab, had been able to build a primitive scanning device. Crude as it was, that first machined scanner—referred to in Melville's subsequent patent filing as "The First Embodiment"—proved that it was possible, in Melville's words, to "bounce light off a vibrating surface and get an image you could see."

One of Johnston's first moves when he took over the VRD project was to hire a graduate student to search the universe for literature on scanning procedures. After the student found hundreds of theoretically potential techniques, the VRD team settled on the "mechanical-resonant" scanning method because, Johnston said, "with limited funding, there's only so much you can pursue at one time. We figured that if it failed, that if we came to an insurmountable roadblock for some reason, we could go back and pick up some of the other methods. Dave also had already developed one, and the results he'd gotten with his initial experiments were pretty positive. It might not necessarily give us the optimal solution, but it looked like it had the least risk of not working and would take a lot less time to develop."

Melville, who is an astonishingly patient man, spent nine months or so reading, drawing, and tinkering, eventually putting parts together until he came up with something he thought could be made to work.

The hardest thing to visualize about this invention of Melville's—particularly when you think about the confluence in his design of simplicity with complexity—is the diminutiveness of the thing. Containing twenty-five parts so tiny that many of them had to be made and assembled under a microscope, the scanner is a tiny turbine, 1-by-½-by-¼-inch in size. Seen with the naked eye, it looks like part of a toy: a thin band stretching between two steel cubes, with some minute struts under the protrusions in the center of the band. But seen under Melville's microscope, it looks like a massive, complex piece of machinery, all bolts and blocks and coils and wires.

The parts in this dynamo were so small that Melville spent almost as much time making tools to build it as he did designing and building the device itself. One day, afraid to exhale lest I unleash a gale of destruction on the Lilliputian watch works under his microscope, I watched as Melville used a homemade device—a hollow rubber tube with a tiny, hollow needle in one end—to pick up square flecks of steel so small that they looked, without the aid of the microscope, like dust motes. Sucking carefully through one end of the tube, Melville would use the opposite, needle-fitted end to pick up these flecks and put them in place on the scanner.

In essence, Melville's scanner is a thin steel band stretched over two magnetic coils. The coils are positioned under opposite ends of the squarish wings in the center of the band. Electric currents are sent through the coils at extremely high speeds, positive charge on one side, negative on the other, then negative on the first side, positive on the other, so that as one coil pushes its end of the wing, the other simultaneously pulls its end down. Light from the image source hits the scanner, bounces up to a flat mirror-and-galvanometer arrangement (this mirror is the vertical scanner, shifting slightly at carefully timed intervals in order to direct the beam up or down when the horizontal scanner reaches the end of a scanned line), then bounces back down to the scanner before bouncing off to the retina.

This apparently redundant up-and-back bouncing of the light from the scanner to the mirror and back to the scanner instead of directly into the eye doubles the "scan angle" of light into the eye, which doubles the portion of retina hit by the light, and which thereby makes the image appear twice as large.

The key to the scanner's operability is a property in matter called "resonance"—a particular frequency at which mechanical parts "want" to vibrate. Hit a tuning fork once, and it vibrates at its resonant frequency; it will continue vibrating for an astonishingly long time without further encouragement, as it takes very little energy to keep something quivering happily along at its resonant frequency. And because materials naturally tend to vibrate at their resonance, it is very difficult to move them off of it—a significant advantage in the case of the VRD, for the scanner would eventually have to operate on head-mounted displays that would be subject to unexpected movement and buffeting. So by opting for a mechanical resonant scanner, the VRD team was getting stability and efficiency thrown in for free.

The specific resonance of any mechanical part is determined by a number of things, including its density, weight, and length. Thus engineers can get the rate of vibration they want in a given part by manipulating its size and shape—building it, in other words, to resonate at a particular frequency. By designing a mechanical part to vibrate at a certain resonance, the engineer gets a part that can run reliably and steadily on very little energy. In the case of the scanner, Melville also was able to subject it to severe contortion because of a peculiarity of iron: Iron compounds have a specific stress limit, and as long as you subject them to stress below that limit, they can run forever without wearing out or breaking down. This was critical to the success of the spring steel component in the scanner, for it was violently and repeatedly twisted, and would have to withstand that punishment almost constantly for years at a time.

Melville's first scanner—the cylindrical one he had built at home—was a simple exercise in exploring whether he could exploit and control resonance to display images. With that proven, he went on to develop a second version with an eye toward potential mass production.

Melville and Johnston began by laying out some preliminary specifications—maximum angle of scan, resolution, and so on—and Melville set to work building a device he could test. The first new prototype, being much smaller and theoretically faster than the primitive scanner Melville had previously mocked up, nevertheless resembled its predecessor in one important respect: It had a piece of mirror glass mounted on top of the spring steel. The VRD team felt that the mirror was indispensable, as mirror glass reflects more than 99 percent of the light beamed onto it. While other surfaces can be made to reflect that much light, mirrors offered a readily available reflective source.

Melville immediately ran into a problem, however: When the scanner ran at rates fast enough to render VGA-quality images, the mirror would fly off. He could not get the mirror and spring steel combination to withstand its own resonance. "It was moving back and forth at almost sixteen thousand times a second," he said to me one day, "which is a lot of G-forces; you're accelerating and decelerating. The tips of that thing move almost at the speed of sound." Day after day, he would leave the lab with his scanner running, only to come back in the morning to find the mirror pieces lying on the ground.

After weeks spent trying to find an adhesive that could keep the glass in place, Melville finally scrounged one up: a mirror glue sold at a local Schuck's Auto Supply outlet near the lab.

Once the mirror was properly held in place, though, Melville ran into a second problem: His scanner could not deliver the scan angles his equations had predicted. It took exhaustive and lengthy testing to determine that the steel-and-glass assembly had two different resonances—one around the center of rotation, the other about the center of the assembly's mass. The first was a line through the center of the steel spring, the other just above the spring, as the addition of the mirror on top of the spring raised the center of mass. The two resonances beat against one another, reducing the overall scan angle the device could achieve.

The only solution then was to get rid of the mirror and try to polish the steel to a high enough gloss to render a reflection that could approximate the fidelity of mirror-reflected light. Melville spent two months researching methods of polishing steel, then months upon months more of testing various coating and polish combinations. "We had to do a lot of tests," Johnston recalled, "and a lot of things were surprising—things we thought would work a certain way, but didn't." Among the lamentable things they learned was how difficult it was to polish a surface without distorting its shape: "When you polish something, the edges tend to round, and if the edges of the mirror round, and the light hits those, it reflects off at the wrong angle." The set of techniques they eventually settled on—all done by hand—included blackening the edges of the mirror surface so they wouldn't reflect at all.

Johnston and Melville both constantly cautioned me, whenever they described an apparent breakthrough, that their work even when completed was preliminary. Engineering generally is not a passage from question to answer so much as it is a passage from one problem to the next. "Note," Johnston said one day when talking about their polishing travails, "that we're not taking this to the point where it's manufacturable. When that goes into manufacturing, that'll be another engineering task: How do you get this in high volume? All that we've got here is something that works pretty well—now it's time to go on to the next big problem."

By now, Melville had been working on his tiny device for nearly a year and still did not have anything usable.

When Melville finally managed to polish sufficiently the surface of his spring steel, and to get it vibrating happily and reliably enough to display a decent image, he found that after a few minutes of operation the image would begin to distort. He eventually discovered that there was a communication problem between the scanner and the rest of the VRD system.

In order for the system to scan the retina coherently, the display drivers in the computer or television have to know the precise position of the scanner mirror all the time. Melville had decided that the best way to determine the mirror's position was to keep track of the electrical charging system. Every time a charge to the magnets was sent out, the image-generating components were alerted, and thus could calculate the position of the mirror by knowing when and in which direction each end of the mirror was being pulled or pushed.

Unfortunately, the delay between when an electrical charge was sent to the scanner's coils and when the mirror actually moved as a result of the charge proved impossible to measure. "There's a phase delay," Johnston explained, "between when we tell it to move and when it physically moves." Even though the delay was almost immeasurably small, it was enough to distort the image unless it could be measured precisely, so that the appropriate delays could be built into the image-generation end of the system. "You had to figure out where that mirror was in space," Melville said, "to within four nanoseconds. Which is not very much time—it's four times ten to the minus-nine seconds." Melville could measure and compensate for the delay when the VRD was first turned on, but found that after a few minutes of operation the image would begin to break up; the horizontal lines composing it would drift in opposite directions, every other line, the odd-numbered lines drifting right, the even-numbered lines drifting left.

The problem with this infinitesimal phase delay was less the delay itself than the fact that it kept infinitesimally changing. Melville could not build an adjustment into the system for it because the change was constantly inconsistent. No sooner would the image generators compensate for a change in the speed of the scanner than the scanner would change speed again. The slightest deviation in temperature would change the speed of the mirror's response to its charges.

Melville spent months trying different scanner materials and different ways of controlling the machine's operating temperature, to no avail. Given the deadline the VRD team was working under, it was the hardest puzzle he'd ever had to solve. After months of work, all he had managed to determine was that there appeared to be literally no combination of controls and materials in the universe that could eliminate the distortion of the VRD's image.

Finally one morning, in utter disbelief at his own despair, he walked up to Rich Johnston and said flatly, "Rich, I don't think we can solve this problem."

Among the more entertaining aspects of Joey King's sojourn in Japan was the peek at proprietary laboratory research undertaken by large Japanese consumer electronics companies. King's six months were winding down at Advanced Telecommunications Research Institute when he saw a Sony headset, with two LCD panels and lens-and-mirror arrangements that beamed a surprisingly clear image into the wearer's eyes. It appeared that Sony was headed toward the same "eyeglasses paradigm" that was guiding the development effort of Virtual i/O, back in Seattle. The Sony headset was clunky and uncomfortable, but as King well knew, it was an early prototype, and Sony was famous for pouring resources efficiently and effectively into industrial design and engineering.

It was not hard for King to see where the Sony effort was headed. Ever since the 1984 invention of the CD, which stores one thousand times as much information as a conventional floppy diskette, everyone in the computer and electronics industries had been looking ahead to the day when a full-length motion picture could be stored on a CD. Sony, with its enormously successful Discman—a wearable music CD player—had purchased MGM studios in the United States, and was in all likelihood developing a video Discman. With the headset King saw, Sony would someday be able to sell a combined software/hardware package in which the hardware, like Nintendo game machines, would be sold nearly at cost, while the company made huge profits on sales of software from the MGM library.

King, of course, was more interested in the burgeoning potential for VR applications that he saw in the headsets. When he returned to the United States a few weeks later to resume his battles with the University of Washington's psychology department over his interdisciplinary quest for a Ph.D., he tracked down Mike Almquist to brief him on his Japanese adventure. He was eager to resume dreaming, as the two had always been wont to do, about how they would someday launch a VR start-up that would legitimately change the world. Neither of them tended to think small, either: When they thought of their dream start-up, they thought in terms of the Apples or Microsofts of the world rather than the Worldesigns or AutoCADs.

These dreams took on a particularly ludicrous cast when King finally caught up with Almquist, who was still languishing in the basement that was supposed to have been the launching pad for Ambiente after its only client, Kubota Pacific, had gone under. King's friend and collaborator had declined in every way imaginable. With his cofounders gone and his savings draining away, Almquist had moved out of his apartment and into the Ambiente basement/lobby. He could no longer afford his apartment and was stuck with the basement because he had paid a year's rent in advance. He stocked up on rice and canned food from Costco, a discount warehouse where Almquist could use his Discover card one last time, and hunkered down in an effort to figure out what to do next. King found him living in his open basement room with one piece of furniture—a couch—with no shower, no prospects, no plans, and no hope. He was cooking on a hot plate, trying to bathe in the room's tiny sink, and looking a little more each day like the other denizens of the building.

Their conversations, which used to revolve around world domination, now revolved around the unlikely prospects for Almquist's survival.

"I'm going to kill myself," he would say to King.

"Come on, don't talk like that."

"Well, I suppose I could give it all up and go work for Disney."

"That'd be the same as killing yourself."

King finally convinced Almquist that what he had done and seen during his six months in Japan proved that even the established leaders in consumer electronics—people with irrefutable track records—saw the day of the virtual-world interface coming. And if they were getting to the point of developing hardware for it, there had to be a way for people like Almquist and King to help make it happen and to make millions in the process. If we just hang on, King kept telling Almquist, get through this period without giving up, good things will happen.

Almquist was revived enough by King's encouragement to start putting his couch time to good use. He began thinking harder and harder about how to launch a company that not only would make money but also would do something meaningful in the world of computer interfaces. Almquist forced a kind of routine into his life: For the next six months, he would get up, wash as best as he could at his sink, go to a nearby coffeehouse to read, write, and scare people, and "think," as he said, "about how to do all this. And *be successful*. And then I'd go home and cry myself to sleep on my large couch, thinking, 'There's got to be someone out there with lots of money looking for an idea.' "

The Elisha Gray
Memorial Chapter

―――――

WHEN NOT WORKING DIRECTLY on his scanner, David Melville spent a lot of time tinkering with the rest of the VRD and with optical engineer Mike Tidwell's brain. Tidwell, who was far younger and far less experienced than Melville, and infinitely less patient, found himself turning frequently to his elder for advice and comfort, often crying out in frustration, "Why can't I get this to work?"

It fell to Tidwell to design the complex optics of the VRD. The optics had to take three colored beams of light—red, green, and blue—meld them together, pass them through an optical fiber, then bend, reshape, straighten, redirect, and in other ways alter and rearrange these beams, bounce them off the scanner and galvanometer, send them through another set of optics, and direct them carefully into the eye. All of this was to be accomplished over as small an expanse as possible, as the VRD team's overriding goal was to make the device small enough to be worn comfortably on the head.

This looked like a particularly tall order when Tidwell first joined the VRD team, as the prototype at that time was monstrous, stretching circuitously over a table ten feet long. "It wasn't really very good," Tidwell told me. "It was difficult to see things in it, and it wasn't very clear. The problem has always been, 'How the hell do you do this?' And along the way, I was constantly asking myself, 'What's wrong? Why doesn't it work? How can I make it smaller?' "

In some respects, the VRD was not a purely original idea. Most of the first prototype was cannibalized from two previous efforts in optical design: the laser-scanning TV, in which laser beams are bounced off a mirror and galvanometer, then scanned onto a projection TV screen; and the laser-scanning ophthalmoscope, an eye examination device invented by Dr. Robert Webb in the late 1980s. Tidwell regarded the first prototype as a combination of those two systems, with the principal differences being the way the light was projected into the eye by the last lens and the elimination of a lot of parts in Webb's machine that were not needed in the VRD. His view would be borne out two years after he first saw the prototype, when the U.S. Patent Office disallowed, on the grounds of "prior art," several of the claims to originality in the patent Furness and Kollin filed.

Tidwell's essential task was to harness and reshape light, direct it through a maze, then paint the viewer's retina with it.

Light travels in waves, emanating outward from a source the way ripples emanate outward from the point where a rock hits the surface of a pond. By means of lenses of various sizes and shapes, placed in various configurations and in various relationships with one another, an optical engineer can change the size, shape, direction, and behavior of light waves, directing them to hit a designated plane in a designated way at a designated angle. In the case of the VRD, the first version Tidwell worked with had eight different lenses in it along the way from image source to eye.

Once David Melville came up with a mechanical-resonant scanner that could replace the acoustical-optical scanner Joel Kollin had installed, though, Tidwell was able to reduce the number of lenses to three.

Still, the VRD was too big and its image too hard to find with the eye, as the exit pupil—the plane where all of the light was converged down to a point so as to fit through the eye's pupil—was too small. While Melville was hard at work trying to find a way to solve the "phase delay" problem in his scanner, Tidwell worked for months trying to find a way to reduce both the number and the size of "these big, honking pieces of glass," as he called the VRD's lenses.

In this middle manifestation, the VRD worked by taking the light emanating from the light source—in this case, the fiber optic wire in which all three colors of light were combined in a single point—and "collimating" it with the first lens. Collimated light is light whose curves have been straightened out, so it beams straight ahead in a column rather than emanating ever outward in curved waves. This collimated beam eventually hit the scanner, which curved and spread the light outward to dimensions larger than the final image was intended to be. This light then hit another lens, which focused the light down to an "image plane"—a point in space where, if you were to insert a piece of paper, you would see the image, in reverse, appear on it. The light then would pass through this plane—its focal point—and begin spreading again, until it hit a third lens, which focused the light down to the exit pupil point, after which it passed through the pupil of the eye and spread out again, hitting the retina with a focused image of a pre-determined size.

It took Tidwell two years to get the system to this point. It should be noted that each of the three lenses in the VRD was not a single piece of glass but a set of glass pieces—more of a telescope than a magnifying glass. Eventually, Melville realized that he and Tidwell could replace the two-lens telescope after the scanner with a single eyepiece, and move the rest of the system around to adjust the focal length of the light from the optical fiber. The net effect of that last decision, coming on top of Tidwell's previous years of work, was to reduce the eight lenses in the system to two.

A great deal of Tidwell's time and effort went into negotiating what Rich Johnston called the constant "trade-offs" engineers have to endure when designing new systems. The VRD team wanted both to have as small a system as possible and as large a scan angle as possible—a mandate calling for trade-offs between scanner size, size of optics, and distance of the scanner from the eye. The bigger the scanner, the bigger the exit pupil could be; the smaller the scanner, the greater would have to be the angle of scan in order to compensate; the bigger the exit pupil, the lower the angle of scan and thus the smaller the image; and so on. "Name me one thing in life," Johnston often said resignedly, "that isn't a trade-off. Life is nothing but decisions like that: What are the odds? Is it worth taking a risk?"

Tidwell at last came up with a graceful system of mirrors and lenses that did indeed scan a high-resolution color image on the retina. By means of an ingenious arrangement of scanner, galvanometer, mirrors, lens, and a beam splitter—mirrored glass, set at an angle directing light to the eye, that lets a portion of light pass through itself and reflects a portion of light eyeward—the user could look into an eyepiece and see a 40-degree-by-30-degree color image, rendered faithfully enough that he or she could read VRD renditions of agate-type stock market tables printed in *The Wall Street Journal*. And because the beam splitter both reflected light and let light pass through, the user could see through the image to the reality beyond—allowing the VRD to be used for "augmented reality" applications, in which information in the form of words or diagrams could be superimposed on the surrounding real world.

Tidwell next turned his attention to the exit pupil size. Johnston directed him to take an idea of Joel Kollin's—adding a "diffraction grating" to the eyepiece—and "make it real," as Johnston put it. A diffraction grating splits the light hitting it into several beams coming through it at various angles, each beam being an exact duplicate of the others, thus allowing the viewer to see the entire image by lining up with any one of the beams coming through the grating.

This was to prove a nightmarish task, replete with setbacks, and may have accounted in part for Tidwell's even more than characteristically sour mood whenever I approached him to talk about his work.

As time and work wore on, he seemed to grow more and more fixated on the politics swirling around his project, to the point where he spent as much time thinking about intrigue as he did about light waves and lens configurations. It was a particularly sore point with Tidwell that Microvision had awarded "inventor's shares" of stock to Furness and Kollin for work that Tidwell felt was not legitimately inventive, while he and Melville, who were bringing the VRD to the threshold of commercial viability, had gotten none. Diagramming the first prototype for me one day, he threw down his pen after finishing a sketch and said disgustedly, "All this stuff had been done before! Webb essentially did the laser scanning on the eye. This whole system, except for the final lens, was used to build a laser-scanning television. It was all done essentially to paint out an image on the screen. The only thing that was done different here was combining Webb's work where he had already scanned light on the retina and made people see images, with the optical system that had already been designed to do the laser-scanning TV. Yet this was the thing they were granted hundreds of thousands of shares of Microvision stock for! I swear to God!"

It was hard to talk with Tidwell exclusively about his work, as he constantly veered off into diatribes about his distant masters at Microvision. "God, I mean, motivation around the lab has been down for a year!" he exclaimed one day. "Totally downhill! I've been totally demotivated by those Microvision guys, to the point where I want something else to do—something that's fun."

Still, his soul was divided. If he was going to profit from his work as much as he hoped to, he would have to find a way to like and work with Microvision's management. He could see the day coming when his work would have brought the VRD to the point where it could be turned over to private enterprise, and he felt that by then Microvision would be desperate to hire him, as his research would have turned him into the only optical engineer in the world with expertise in retinal-scanning optics.

So whenever I asked him about Microvision, one of two things would happen: Either he would set off on an expletive-laden tirade or he would rhapsodize about how much fun it would be to bring a head-mounted retinal-scanning system to market and get rich on Microvision stock options in the bargain.

Virtual i/O entered 1995 falling behind schedule, the projected ship date for its first product slipping by degrees from March to

September. Given that the company was trying to break particularly challenging new ground, this was a reasonable enough development, and one not entirely unexpected.

More troubling was the likelihood that the company might not be first to market with a head-mounted display for consumers. Two other start-ups—VictorMaxx, in Chicago, and Forte, in Rochester, New York—also were developing wearable displays. Although these two competitors were making headsets exclusively for computer game players, the fact remained that they threatened to seize shares of a market that Virtual i/O had hoped to have all to itself.

Across town at Zombie, the spectacle of three hardware companies lining up at the starting line was bracing, as it presaged a bigger market for Zombie software. It also lent credence to the vision of Zombie cofounders Long and Alexander, who could now cite the emerging three-player hardware arena as proof positive that the head-mounted-display market they kept predicting was actually going to arrive. There was no question in their minds that the three headset companies would compose a great launching pad for immersive VR-game software—a market that figured to be thoroughly owned, in the beginning, by Zombie.

As they worked on their first game, Locus, Long and Alexander kept testing it on prototype headsets from all three hardware companies. They wanted to ensure that their game would run flawlessly on all of them.

Even so, they couldn't help but root for their fellow Seattleites at Virtual i/O—not only because they were from the same city, but because Long and Alexander believed that Virtual i/O's "eyeglasses paradigm" would prove superior to their competitors' offerings. It was going to weigh far less, would be easier to hook up to computers, would have a better image display, and would not shut out the outside world the way the other two products—classic "helmet paradigm" displays—would do.

Thus, while Zombie was developing Locus for all three headsets, the company's engineers were working most closely with Virtual i/O, whose engineers spent a lot of time over at Zombie in the early part of 1995.

However anxious Virtual i/O might have been about its competition, for Zombie these were heady and exciting days, as the company was working in a collegial atmosphere on the launch of a new immersive interface standard. At times, Zombie engineers felt less involved in a business than a cause—the advancement of a world-changing dream.

Long and Alexander had no sooner gotten used to their newfound happiness, however, than the little collaborative bubble they had built around themselves and their allies was abruptly burst. On May 25, Forte filed a lawsuit in federal district court, in Seattle, against Virtual i/O. The lawsuit, charging Virtual i/O with infringement of a Forte head-tracking patent, sought an injunction against the company's first product launch, now scheduled for sometime in the fall.

Forte asked for the injunction because, it said, Virtual i/O enjoyed a number of unfair advantages over Forte. While Forte founder Paul Travers had only one investor, a venture capitalist, Virtual i/O had several, who provided not only cash but also advertising and promotional tie-ins with their own businesses. Combined with the patent infringement, Forte argued, this gave Virtual i/O a market victory before either company had even released a product.

The patent infringement argument was complex. There are essentially six different ways to track movements of a VR user's head so that a computing system can accurately render graphics, constantly updating its display as the user's head moves around. The Polhemus system uses magnetic radiators and receivers; one system connects the helmet to the computer with a boom; another uses ultrasound signals; yet another outfits the VR helmet with a gyroscope; another uses infrared sensors; and one uses magnetic sensors that orient to the earth's magnetic field. This last is the most widely used method—so widely used, in fact, that when Forte applied for a patent on its head tracker, the U.S. Patent Office turned it down, saying that two of ten previously filed patents contained the same technology. Forte appealed to the patent office, showing that its tracker differed in one respect—the way it calculated its position and sent the position information to the

computer—and the patent office eventually agreed. Since Virtual
i/O had relied on the more broadly used and patented technology,
it argued that Forte's patent did not apply to its head tracker, and
that Virtual i/O needed no patent at all, for head tracking had become so well known that the science was no longer proprietary
and patentable.

The district judge assigned to the case, Thomas Zilly, declined
to issue the injunction and tried heroically to understand the competing and overlapping testimony of various engineers, to get the
two sides to negotiate an agreement rather than go to trial, and occasionally to leaven with a laugh the glum and dull proceedings,
which were to drag on for a full year. The testimony, a combination
of complicated engineering and outraged accusation, droned on for
months, with the rare burst of good cheer coming from the frustrated judge.

"Your Honor," thundered Virtual i/O's attorney at one hearing,
complaining about Forte's lawyer, "he's just trying to confuse the
Court!"

"If that is his intention," Zilly answered, "then he has succeeded
admirably, because the Court is thoroughly confused."

While Forte's engineering arguments were rather weak—a circumstance highlighted by the array of engineers lined up on the
Virtual i/O side of the docket—the company did have some compelling arguments on its side. Chief among these was a letter from
Virtual i/O's Greg Amadon offering to license Forte's head tracker
in return for royalty payments. When the two sides could not agree
on a royalty schedule, Forte argued, Virtual i/O decided to steal the
technology rather than pay for it. Virtual i/O's cause was further
set back when it tried to file a head-tracking patent of its own, even
though it had argued in Zilly's court that the technology was too
widely known and used to require patenting. When Zilly learned
of this maneuver, he heatedly accused Virtual i/O "of saying one
thing to the patent office, another to the Court."

Down at Zombie, Long and Alexander watched in dismay as
their fruitful collaborations with Forte and Virtual i/O were
abruptly circumscribed. After reveling in the open, collaborative

atmosphere of the game-engineering world, the two were going through something akin to culture shock. Now they were afraid to talk too much with either hardware company, for fear of being dragged into the lawsuit on one side or the other.

They began wondering how much they could trust their Seattle collaborators, who occasionally exhibited a *Mission Impossible*-esque taste for industrial espionage. One night, shortly after the lawsuit had been filed, a group of Virtual i/O engineers and Zombie programmers were hard at work down at Zombie headquarters. It was nearly midnight when the last of the Zombie engineers called it a night, leaving two Virtual i/O visitors alone in the company's offices. The next morning, when Alexander arrived, she was dismayed to see that the Forte headset her company had been using for the Locus project was ripped apart. Looking at it lying there on the ground, she could see at a glance what the attackers had been up to: "It was obvious that they were looking at the head tracker."

When Dave Melville threw up his hands and told Rich Johnston that he didn't think there was a way to overcome the tendency of the VRD's image to drift apart, the two engineers spent hours talking through the problem, with Johnston peppering Melville with question after question. The more they talked, the more the two realized that Melville was attempting the impossible. Gradually, they talked their way around to trying something completely different: Rather than looking for a way to control the resonance of the scanner in order to make it react to the speed of the image generators, they decided instead to have the image generators react to the scanner. Let the scanner run at whatever speed it wanted; it would be easier to make the system electronics change to accommodate changes in the scanner speed than to keep trying to adjust the vibrations of the mirror.

Melville began trying to devise a way to build a "phase lock loop" into the VRD. This loop would consist of tiny "phase detectors," installed in the scanner and connected by wire to the VRD's electronics, that would constantly signal the positions of the wings on the vibrating spring steel. The VRD then would adjust its signal coming from the computer or television in reaction to changes signaled by the phase detectors.

It was an ingenious solution, but one that proved difficult to implement. Melville's phase detectors were the smallest parts in the scanner, and thus extremely hard to manipulate. It also was hard to install them in a place in the scanner from where he could get accurate enough measurements. After months of trial and error—installing the detectors, testing them, removing them, installing them elsewhere, and testing them again—Melville eventually came up with a way to install them on the underside of the spring steel itself without reducing the performance of the reflecting surface. "Now," Melville said one day, showing me the detectors under a microscope, "we always know exactly where the mirror is. And it becomes the master for the system, telling it what clock frequency everything has to run at."

This proved to be the project's biggest breakthrough. Now, Johnston's team could think in earnest about miniaturizing the display. For the past year, Microvision had been hounding the HIT lab to build portable units that company marketers could take with them in their ceaseless globe-trotting efforts to find new investors or corporate partners. Now that they had a scanner that could reliably and indefinitely deliver light to the retina, Johnston believed that his team could build a display small enough to carry around in a briefcase. It would be monochrome, true—portable display units could not accommodate the large gas lasers needed for green and blue light—but it would be a persuasive proof of concept.

By now, I had seen the VRD grow—or, to be strictly accurate, shrink—from a massive bench-mounted device to something perched on a small table to a set of works Johnston believed could be made to fit in a small suitcase. I had also seen the image change from a red and fuzzy picture that was nearly impossible to find in its lens to a full-color image so sharp that you could effortlessly read agate type from *The Wall Street Journal* in it. Most impressive of all had been the gradual change in the reactions of people ushered in over the years to peer into the VRD's optics. At first, the crowds of visitors had been sparse and bemused, but they had grown gradually more impressed as the VRD improved. By the time Melville's third-generation scanner, with its phase detectors working, had been installed in the device, it was beginning to attract large, credentialed crowds.

It was fun to watch these people come in to view the VRD, which after two years had become a showcase not only for the HIT lab but for the entire Washington Technology Center. People trooped out to Seattle from all over the world to see it. I saw visitors from Disney, various branches of the U.S. military, Thomson Multimedia, Hewlett Packard, Hughes Aircraft, Microsoft, Silicon Graphics, and countless other engineering and entertainment enterprises step up to the VRD, peer in, and step away amazed. "That *is* impressive," said Joel Iseman, a Silicon Graphics representative who visited the lab once a year or more. "When I last saw this, the image was just red, and you sort of had to take it on faith. But this is really something."

Mike Almquist was entering the sixth month of his sojourn in squalor when he ran into an acquaintance named Adam Feuer, a software engineer interested in computer networking. It now was the summer of 1995, and Almquist had revived his spirits to the point of being thoroughly disgusted with himself and the way he was living.

Feuer, who knew of Almquist's obsession with virtual reality, was casting around for business partners, having just fallen out with a group he had joined to start a company providing Internet connectivity services. He dropped by Almquist's basement one day and asked to see what he had in the way of VR software. Almquist showed him his burning building demo and a rough demo he had of some sea-floor mapping he had done while Ambiente was working with the University of Washington oceanography department.

The demo was quite dramatic. It began with a black screen, which filled up at high speed with spidery red lines that formed a compelling pattern of peaks and valleys, the pattern being a visual rendition of sonar data bounced off the ocean floor.

"Whoa!" exclaimed Feuer. "This is really cool stuff. . . . We might be able to turn this into a product." It turned out that Feuer had once worked with someone who did sea-floor surveys, and he knew enough about the onerous expenses and problems involved in mapping the ocean floor to suspect that there was substantial money to be made if the mapping could be done with computers.

Feuer arranged a visit with a maritime surveyor friend who explained to Almquist that sea-floor surveyors had to rent boats, at $60,000 per day, that dragged a sonar buoy around and recorded the sonar data. The data was converted into flat printouts, which were cut up with scissors, stretched, bent, printed, and arranged so that the contiguous sections lined up with one another. A painstaking series of photographs was then taken, with cartographic marks, contours, geological anomalies, and other information superimposed over the data at each stage, until, hundreds of expensive hours later, a two-hundred-page map of a tiny section of ocean floor was finished. "A lot of people," Feuer said, "complain that they have really cool 3D data that they'd rather see in 3D, instead of converted into these stupid flat maps."

Almquist, who is prone to excitement, suddenly saw himself on the threshold of making millions. In the course of their research, he and Feuer had identified some twenty survey companies that they calculated would be willing to pay $1 million each for a software package that would allow them to see and interpret sonar maps of the ocean floor in real time. Because traditional surveying was so costly, Almquist figured, the software would pay for itself after two or three surveys.

Although the demo he had shown Feuer was unfinished and crudely hacked together, Almquist began believing that he could have it working flawlessly with only a few months of work. Sitting in his cold and spare basement, surrounded by refuse, dirty laundry, library books, and dwindling supplies of canned and dried food, he began regaling Feuer with tales of how close his software was to completion, and how they soon would be rendering sonar data in real time and selling high-priced software packages to grateful oceanographers and oil-company explorers. By the time Feuer left, Almquist was dancing around his basement, his arms raised and fingers extended in the Beavis and Butt-head "Cornholio" salute, alternately screaming about world domination and trying to come up with names for the new company they would form.

Feuer came back a few days later with Jeff Hussey, a young investment banker who had turned Feuer down for financing during his previous business venture, but who had told him to keep in touch. Hussey, who no sooner had become an investment banker than he discovered that he hated investment banking, had always been fascinated with technology—particularly Internet technology—and was eager to start a high-tech company that might make him a millionaire and provide him some excitement and challenge in the bargain. Although he found Almquist's surroundings rather unprepossessing, he was nonetheless taken with his energy and apparent vision—particularly when Almquist showed him the seafloor demo.

Hussey is a thin and intense man who wears designer eyeglasses, keeps his hair carefully cut and styled, looks far younger than his thirty-five years, and wears his face set in a permanent scowl, as if expecting a fight from everyone he encounters. When he gets excited, his voice rises, he sneers involuntarily, and he shouts in short, excited bursts, the sentences piling up on top of one another with increasing velocity. No sooner had Almquist shown him his demo and explained how it worked than Hussey started expostulating: "Think of a hardening nipple! The hardening nipple! Okay? All right?"

Bemused, Almquist sat in silence as Hussey raved on. "You probably haven't heard about this. But on Wall Street, everybody gets paid in a bonus. A big chunk of your annual compensation comes in the form of an annual bonus. And the annual bonus is based upon your productivity and profitability over the year, and that of the group and that of the firm. And they all . . . I mean, invariably, at least in the eighties, when trading bonds was a big deal to the firm's profitability, I mean, like, some mortgage trader, some bond trader, some derivatives trader, would like *screw it up for everybody* by doing some *dumb-ass thing* and losing three hundred million dollars! Most of those guys are not smart! I mean, they're not, like, *rocket analytic*. These traders don't necessarily have finely tuned brains. They have finely tuned *intestines*. I mean, it's all visceral. They can play poker with the guy over the phone. And I know this because I used to do it. You can tell just by your data—which is, you know, the bonds that the guys are offering, and the trade you know he did last week, and the tone of the market—whether the guy's long or wrong, or he was short, or whatever, what the deal is, and that's really what you're trying to do, is outsmart the other guy. And so there's lots and lots of data in the market. And the big problem is—and this is one of the problems when I was selling quote machines—*screen real estate* is a very valuable asset, because it basically, there is a field of view, and depending upon the guy's *visual acuity*, you can have the font so small and therefore fit so much information on the screen. But most guys, even the best guys, can't really keep track of like a hundred things. That's for, like, pretty much an *above-average guy*. So you got all this data up here. And what you need to do is you really need to convert all of that data into what I call like *a feel for the market*. What's really going on? And that's why I say, 'the case of the hardening nipple.' Because if a guy walks into the bar, and a gal is sitting over there, I mean, there's *lots and lots* of data going on there. And it can all be, like, boiled down to like that one little piece of data! That a guy can like *totally* understand! And if you can take all of that data, all of that tabular, numeric data, and like boil it into a . . . *little nipple*, and watch that nipple, you know what's going on. You've got a feel for the market!"

Almquist sat there trying to figure out whether he was learning more about the stock market or Hussey himself as Hussey ranted. "I mean, that would be like a Holy Grail on Wall Street! You create all this visual representation of something that a guy, a trader, who's responsible for a million, ten million, a hundred million dollars' worth of inventory in firm capital, can tell him exactly what's going on! You gotta take all this data and get it into . . . and create a *visual representation* that a human can like get *meaning* from. And Wall Street is where it can happen, because you get a lot of leverage on that. So I think that's really the future of VR, is to basically take mass amounts of amorphous data and turn it into meaning that a human can understand. And so I think that ideas and technology that move in that direction are *bankable*. Because somebody will pay for it. Because they can make *money* off it."

When the smoke cleared, the three had formed a loose partnership of sorts, with the idea that Almquist would finish the sea-floor visualization software, Feuer would work at setting up their business, and Hussey eventually would be the company salesman.

Almquist, of course, having been an acolyte of Furness's, had never been good at realistic planning or realistically assessing the state of his rough drafts. For money, he had taken a sixty-hour-per-week job as a systems administrator, and he hammered away at the sea-floor product for months in his spare time. He found that he was digging himself deeper and deeper into a hole of code, and he finally had to admit that what he thought would take a few months would take more than a year to complete. At a loss as to how on earth to explain things to his partners—who seemed to be growing increasingly skeptical about him as the months wore on—he saw his HIT lab experience looming up before him again, and he began to wonder about his own abilities. Finally, after five months of fruitless work, Almquist broke the news to Hussey and Feuer that he wasn't getting anywhere, and that he was beginning to have doubts about the worth of their idea. The market, he decided, was going to be tiny—maybe less than five customers or so—because software systems developed in academic labs and given away for free were being improved to the point where few surveyors would be willing to pay for something only marginally better than a program they could get for nothing.

The confession led to a long conversation, far into the night, about Almquist's visions for virtual reality in general. His months of research and thinking had led him to the conclusion that he had been hopelessly naïve in his HIT lab days, and that the virtual-world interface of his dreams was years—and generations of products—away from being realized. "In the first place," he said, "VR is incredibly boring unless you have multiple people collaborating. And there's probably like thirty products or milestones that have to be developed before you can even think about distributing environments and having people—"

"What are these thirty products?" Hussey asked.

Almquist started rambling about everything from graphics boards to high-bandwidth fiber-optic cable to methods of rendering and distributing graphics that were similar to the Virtual Space Teleconferencing experiments his friend Joey King had seen and done in Japan. "To have the kind of collaboration you need, you need to build an incredibly huge server," he continued, "which means that you either need to build an incredibly monstrous computer or have the ability to make a bunch of small computers look like one big computer—"

"Wait!" Hussey suddenly shouted. "Wait a minute—that could make us money!"

For all of the torment Johnston, Melville, Tidwell, and their teammates on the VRD project endured in the course of their research, their life in the lab looked like a productive sojourn in Paradise compared with what Microvision was enduring in the infernal commercial sector. Even as the technology moved forward steadily, the technology's owner showed increasing signs of faltering, possibly dying.

It had taken Furness scarcely more than a year from the time he signed the Microvision contract to all but give up on the company. In retrospect, he felt that Microvision had been doomed, and now he felt trapped in a partnership with people who were destroying his dreams. "These guys are messing with my life's work," he said the first time I asked him about his corporate partners. He was utterly downcast. "I mean, this is a nightmare."

He felt that he and the university had been naïve in signing on with businessmen who were proving to be inept. "Nobody here really had ever done anything like this before. The university has been successful in transitioning technology, but not to the point where it has remained intimately involved in the development of the technology it licensed to somebody else. Usually, what they've done is license it and the company goes off and develops it. But in this case, it's not only licensed, but we're continuing the work. So the university is sort of laying down the track as the locomotive is coming."

When Furness had signed the Microvision deal, he envisioned a partnership in which the company's money bought research from the HIT lab that created the seeds of a technology that Microvision could turn into products in its own labs and manufacturing facilities. Furness expected that at first the two would work in parallel, the lab moving the technology forward while Microvision built its own lab and hired its own scientists, to whom Furness's engineers in due course would turn over research results that Microvision's engineers could then productize. Furness believed that Microvision should begin by developing products for limited industrial and military use—for clients, in other words, who were used to paying thousands of dollars per device, who understood the high costs and long time lines of cutting-edge product development, and who were thus willing to subsidize a company's work as it developed new products and refined its production procedures.

Rick Rutkowski and Steve Willey, though, seemed intent on going directly to the mass market with some kind of display that would be universally used in a consumer application. Although not often willing to talk specifically with lab researchers about their plans, the two did talk quite often about a cellular phone that could receive faxes and scan them into the user's eye. Furness and his VRD team alternately laughed and cried among themselves over that idea, which they regarded as useless and unworkable.

Despite his lack of faith in Microvision's managers, Furness felt he had no choice but to help them court established companies. He worked tirelessly at gaining entry for Rutkowski and Willey to make presentations to executives of the leading display manufacturers in the world, often at great risk to his own reputation.

The presentations never went well. Typical was a meeting Furness arranged with the heads of Fujitsu's display division. Fujitsu, through a friendship Furness had struck years before with one of the company's research directors, Dr. Masahiro Kawahata, had been one of the earliest and most devoted supporters of the HIT lab, and Furness was able to parlay his relationship with Kawahata into a Microvision presentation in Tokyo.

Rutkowski spent well over an hour explaining how the VRD would work and detailing how a partnership between Microvision and Fujitsu might take shape. Microvision, he said, would someday be taking the HIT lab's VRD technology and collaborating with Fujitsu and others in making various retinal-scanning display devices, with Microvision giving preference in its selection of partners to companies willing to invest in retinal-scanning development now. Finally, he was asked, "How long before we start seeing usable technology from Microvision?"

"Two years."

"We'll wait."

The problem, of course, was that Microvision couldn't afford to wait. Its money was draining away faster than the technology was moving forward.

Rich Johnston felt that reactions like Fujitsu's were to be expected, since the Microvision "product" was little more than a package of risks. "There's no established market for these things," he said, "so you've got a huge market risk. You've also got a technology risk. Will the technology work? You can sit here in a lab and make a system, but can you make a product? And will it be the best solution on the market?" Add it all up, he continued, and "there's risk, risk, risk. Would you be willing to give these guys a bunch of money up front to do their work? If you're one of these companies, you're going to say, 'Why don't I wait? Is there any advantage to me giving them money now instead of a year or two from now?' As you wait, all you're doing is removing risk. The technology will move forward, and the question of whether there is a market will be closer to answered. There's just no incentive for a corporation to put money up front right now."

Moreover, Microvision's strenuous selling efforts were creating more competitors than partners. Johnston chortled over a discovery he made one day on the Internet of a Dutch graduate student's web site. The student, an optical engineer, was building a retinal scanner, his effort funded by a hefty grant from Philips Research. "This is one of the companies that at one point Steve and Rick said they had a deal with," Johnston said. "It never materialized. Now Philips is funding somebody else to do VRD work." The circumstance struck him as particularly ironic because Steve Willey was constantly haranguing the lab about its open, collaborative environment and the risk Microvision endured that another lab underwriter—Texas Instruments, say, or Hewlett Packard—might steal Microvision-funded ideas. "Yet here it's these guys they spent all this time in a 'close partnership' with who have now decided to fund not them but somebody else."

It was not just the time factor and murky terms of the partnership agreement that scared off the Fujitsus of the world. Masahiro Kawahata told me during one of his visits to the lab that his company basically didn't trust Rutkowski and Willey because they didn't seem to know what they were doing. He was particularly perplexed by their plan to operate exclusively as a licensing company and do no manufacturing of their own. "They're a *virtual company*," he liked to say, relishing the opportunity to pun in a foreign language.

The Microvision grand plan was a source of considerable vexation for Furness. "We were concerned all along about the business model of the company, and one of the things that we said up front was that this company had to *make* something. They weren't just going to be a broker for a license, a sublicense. Now they don't have to make it themselves, they can source it out, somebody else could make it, but they have to control it, because if you don't control the hardware, you lose it. You basically give it away to somebody else. You have to be part of that manufacturing process because that's the only way you find out how it works, and how to improve it. It's just like cutting off a feedback loop if you don't have that involvement."

Rich Johnston felt that the Microvision model was suicidal. "You learn more about what you're doing by doing it," he said. "Believe me, when you build the first hundred or first thousand of something, you learn *a lot*. When you get those in somebody's hands who's using them, and they feed back the issues and the problems, you learn so much more about how to improve the product. Now, if they're not the ones doing that, if it's some other company, who's gaining that knowledge? Who's going to very soon know more about the product than you do? Do you want your customer knowing more about your product than you do? How long will it take them to figure out that they don't need you any longer?"

It was easy to understand Furness's distress. His emotional invest-ment in the VRD was immeasurable, and his impatience to realize his dream made it impossible for him to approve of any business plan, however ingenious or certain of success. His temperament was such that had he developed MS-DOS and turned it over to Bill Gates, he would have been gnashing his teeth over Gates's slow-ness and ineptitude in using it to take over the world.

Rich Johnston's disdain for Microvision, though, was more in-teresting—and more telling, I think, about the attitude of the generic engineer toward the nature and importance of his role in the forward motion of technological progress. Astonishing as their achievements might seem to outsiders, hardware engineers in general seem rather resistant to feelings of triumph and self-congratulation. And Johnston certainly never believed as much in the uniqueness and power of the VRD as Microvision apparently did.

I noticed this resistance surfacing over and over again in con-nection with Melville's scanner. Johnston, who was not given to su-perlatives, often cited it as the single ingeniously conceived component in the VRD system, the key to its potential success. I watched him give hundreds of demonstrations to visitors from labs and engineering companies, and often he would be asked, "Why are you the only people who have this technology?" By way of an answer, he would hold up one of Melville's scanners and say, "This thing here—this is what makes it all possible."

Yet any time I professed astonishment or admiration either to Johnston or to Melville, they would be quick to deflate my enthu-siasm. "You're always chasing your tail on this thing, but it works pretty good," Melville said one day. It was the closest he ever came to an outright boast.

No matter how many times visitors would come through and express astonishment at the VRD, Johnston was always turning back attempts to find his team's work remarkable. He seemed to believe less in human ingenuity than in the inevitability of technological progress. "Well, again, what's clever?" he said one day, when I asked him if Melville's scanner was a "clever" invention. "There's lots of clever stuff. There's hundreds of clever things in here, right? *It's just a job.* You know, that's our job, to come up with clever ideas to solve problems. I mean, this scanner is a pretty big breakthrough. You can't find anything like it; people have worked on this problem for a long time, okay? It is a *good device.* And it is clever and it's interesting and it's what we're paid to do. Without Dave . . . I mean, it's a problem we would have solved. If there's a solution, we would have found it. It might have been totally different, it might have been one of the other solutions, it might not have been this one. It was part of Dave's expertise and his desires that led us down this path. But in engineering, everybody's replaceable. You're parts in a machine as a engineer. A designing machine. And it will get invented eventually by somebody else if you don't invent it. I mean, *the constant is invention.* The inventor is irrelevant to the process. People are going to invent, and it will move forward, and, you know, you will solve problems."

He consistently deflected praise directed at him personally, or at Melville and Tidwell. "The technology has a life of its own," he said. "It's going to move forward. Edison developed the first good lightbulb, but there was a whole pile full of people working on it. If he hadn't, somebody else would've, eventually. The problems are going to get solved. And invention will continue. There may be some specific things that never get invented, because these are some guy's dreams, but in general invention will continue. It's a process that's going on because of the mass of people working on it. And any one individual is fairly unimportant to the whole process. Whether I'm here or not here, whether Dave's here or not here, the technology . . . I mean, it may move faster or slower, depending on who's here, or we may come to slightly different solutions, or maybe some that aren't as good, but eventually, if it's a problem, and if it's viewed as a problem by the world in general, somebody's going to solve it. That's the nature of technology. I mean, it's like the telephone: Two guys filed patents for the telephone, about an hour apart. It's just that nobody remembers the other guy's name."

Paradigm Downshift

NEAR THE END of 1995, Tom Furness entered a long crisis period brought on by the rapidly increasing distance between his vision and his reality. In the eyes of his disciples in the lab, his dreams were growing increasingly outlandish even as his tangible efforts—as measured, at least, by their visible results—grew more and more futile.

That September, on the HIT lab's sixth anniversary, Furness delivered a speech that his engineering colleagues regarded as particularly symptomatic. "I have long held the belief that humans have unlimited potential," the director began. He went on to describe the lab's ultimate mission as being a search for ways to ease or eliminate "hunger in the world, and wars and crime and places where our children are not safe. . . . I believe that we can solve these problems. That we can go where no man or woman has gone before. That we can soar by spreading wings we don't know we have. And that we can do this by creating new tools which tap that incredible resource of our minds, allowing us to amplify our intelligence, much as the pulley or level amplifies torque, giving us a new strength and empowerment to address contemporary issues and the frontiers of our existence. . . . In the end, perhaps we are not too different from our early ancestors, when the invention of the wheel provided a new kind of mobility. We, too, are dedicated to a new kind of mobility—mind moving—but with the end goal of making our lives, and those of future generations, more complete and fulfilling. For as we move here, a candle flickers in Tibet. . . ."

Rich Johnston was driven to near apoplexy by Furness's speech, which he was to talk about for years afterward, always with exaggerated and exasperated rolling of his eyes. "My job is *not* to solve world hunger," he would insist whenever the speech was mentioned. "My job is to solve specific engineering problems!"

Mike Tidwell, Johnston's optical engineer on the VRD project, was similarly confused. "Tom gets carried away sometimes, I think, in trying to impart his moral beliefs into his lab work," he said after hearing the speech. "That thing was very ethereal. A lot of that's a little much for some of the people in the lab, when you start talking about solving world hunger, and moving minds instead of mass. . . . I don't think VR's going to solve hunger, sorry. VR's cool . . . but it won't make you warm and fuzzy."

Where Furness was a classic visionary, Tidwell and Johnston were classic antivisionaries. A good hardware engineer, they believed, never advanced a proposition that couldn't be proven, and they were particularly leery of making promises they might not be able to keep.

When it came to the VRD, then, both men found themselves incessantly disavowing their visionary director's hopes and promises. Remarkable as their progress was on the VRD, Tidwell and Johnston knew that the device was years away from being a product, and even more years away from having the kinds of uses Furness envisioned for it. Neither one liked being in the position of having to deliver on Furness's dreams. "I have a problem with that kind of stuff," Tidwell said one day, when I asked him about the rising hopes for the VRD outside the lab. He was particularly vexed about the expectation that it would "cure" blindness. "Even if you're not saying it directly, implying it is not really that moral. Here's what it can do: If somebody has some optical abnormality with their lens or their cornea, some deformation, or even possibly cataracts, cloudiness, because it's such a small beam, you get this pinhole camera effect, and if you look into it you can read it. It won't help anybody with macular degeneration, someone who doesn't have an optic nerve, someone who doesn't have a connection between the retina and the optic nerve, people who are born blind or something like that. One of the problems is that we don't know how many people it can help, and Tom talks about it as if it's going to cure hundreds of millions of people. Well, for one thing, it does not *cure* anything, it's just an aid. Maybe it *could* help a lot of people, but that doesn't mean you go out and get the whole world excited. If you can help five million people, that's amazing, that's great, but you don't go out and get the hopes up of the other ninety-five million people that you're not going to help. That's the part that I have a problem with."

Of course, the biggest problem for Tidwell, as for Johnston, was the reaction from media and public alike to any news about the VRD. Inevitably, the two would receive telephone calls or e-mail from people who had read or heard a story occasioned by a Microvision presentation or a Furness speaking engagement. Johnston frequently received telephone calls in the lab from blind people asking when his vision-restoring device would be finished. This sort of question infuriated Tidwell. "I've even gotten e-mail saying, 'Is it really true that your lab is going to produce a two-thousand-line full-color display that weighs twelve ounces for under one hundred dollars in two years?' " he shouted one day. "*I've* gotten that e-mail!"

To be fair to Furness, much of this outsized speculation was due more to misunderstanding on the part of press and public than to deviousness on his part. But to engineers like Johnston and Tidwell, who were incapable of even imagining something whose viability was unproven, Furness was careless at best, often impossible to understand, and sometimes genuinely dangerous.

Across town at Virtual i/O, Linden Rhoads was grinding her teeth in rage at Furness's powers of promotion. With the release of her company's first product only a month away, she had come to regard him as more a competitor than a collaborator, and she began haranguing anyone who would listen about what she saw as Furness's conflicts of interest. She was particularly upset about Furness's connections with Virtual Vision and Microvision, which she felt caused him to have a "fiduciary interest" in their success. "I just think that the structure there is an awkward one that leaves too much room for conflicts of interest and strange situations," she said. She also found the lab's avowed mission to do academic research more or less worthless to a company intent on beating competitors to today's marketplace. "I don't see the lab as being practical enough, and it seems to me that they're always in some sort of a funding emergency, which is sort of causing them to be too reactionary in terms of what they have to do." Although Virtual i/O belonged to the HIT lab's Virtual Worlds Consortium, Rhoads had joined reluctantly and considered dropping out every year, as she worried about competitors using the lab's more or less open environment to steal Virtual i/O trade secrets. "I keep thinking, 'My God, do I want intellectual property going between here and there?' Because I think we have a whole lot more going on here, to be blunt."

Still, there were advantages to belonging to the consortium, and Rhoads's relationship with the HIT lab was complicated, to say the least. Her membership entitled her to close looks at the VRD, which she regarded as a competitor in the present for attention from press and potential corporate partners, and a competitor in the future for customers. She liked to mine the HIT lab for engineering talent—including Rich Johnston, who turned down a job offer from Virtual i/O out of distaste, he told me, for Rhoads. And she knew that the perception of a relationship between her company and the lab enhanced Virtual i/O's credibility. Few outside the lab, after all, knew about its tumultuous inner workings, and the reputation of Furness, along with the lab's academic publications, public presentations, and adorable image in the media—whose reporters generally were wowed by the gee-whiz stuff Furness and his researchers were studying—all helped improve the reputation of any VR company that could demonstrate some kind of connection with the HIT lab.

Furness, who encouraged anyone who tried to make head-mounted displays commercially viable, nevertheless held out little hope for Virtual i/O's prospects, and he over-ruefully described his lab's troubled relationship with the company as "sordid."

The relationship hit bottom when Rhoads heard about a comment Furness made to *Electrical Engineering Times* magazine about the possibility that users of head-mounted displays might experience nausea, disorientation, or "flashbacks" after doffing the headgear. The aftereffects, Furness said, possibly could appear not only immediately after a VR experience, but hours later, too. Furness's comment was part of a long statement on the need for research in this area, as he had himself experienced what he called flashbacks from using flight simulators, and because no research had been done on such side effects and aftereffects of head-mounted-display usage.

By "flashback," Furness meant that the body's visual and vestibular organs—which combine to orient the brain to the world and keep us from falling over—appeared sometimes to be slow in readjusting to the real world after being immersed in the virtual world, and might "flash back" to the orientation data from the virtual world even hours after a user had removed his or her headset. The result, he said, could be disequilibrium and nausea.

This did not strike me as a particularly controversial notion, since I had taken part in experiments in the HIT lab designed to study just such side effects, and had walked around mildly dizzy and nauseated once for nearly four hours after wearing a VR helmet for half an hour.

Once this quote circulated beyond the engineering audience that reads *EE Times*, however, the word "flashback" was immediately transmogrified into "LSD-type flashbacks," as Furness's statement moved into the context of virtual reality's unsavory reputation among a public indoctrinated by Hollywood (particularly by the horror movie *Lawnmower Man*) and by Timothy Leary and his adepts, who liked to call virtual reality "electronic LSD." Rhoads and other entrepreneurs with an interest in cleaning up virtual reality's image were irate. "When Tom Furness was quoted as having said that the virtual reality head-mounted displays could produce, among other symptoms, LSD-like flashbacks, I was extremely irked," Rhoads said. "I really was offended. I felt like manufacturers and businesses who supported the HIT lab were doing so with the recognition that there was a good chance that the lab would be taken by outsiders to be a spokesperson for the industry in some ways, and that to make such a flagrantly untrue and titillating comment was inappropriate." She took the opportunity to get in a dig at Furness's religious beliefs. "I sort of sarcastically wondered how a Mormon bishop understood what LSD-like flashbacks were." Even when shown the actual quote, which did not include the term "LSD-like," and hearing what the term "flashback" actually means to VR engineers, Rhoads was unmollified. "His experience came not from any clinical data, but from two experiences that he had himself. So how much more can it be unprovable and unrepeatable, if it's not someone even saying, 'X told me that this happened,' but 'I experienced it myself, in the sixties, twice'? And at Wright-Patterson Air Force Base, in a simulator. And you know, we can't give people that kind of effect if we want to, for $799 or $399."

I found this last assertion odd, as Virtual i/O had, much to its own misfortune, delivered precisely that effect in a series of tests at the David Sarnoff Research Center, in Princeton, New Jersey. The company was trying to work out a partnership agreement with Sega—manufacturer of a video-game player that for a time challenged Nintendo for market leadership in the United States—in which Virtual i/O headsets would be bundled and sold with Sega machines. Zombie's Mark Long, formerly from Sarnoff, had heard from old friends about the experiments. "People put these headsets on," he said, "and the world just sloshed around like water. Everyone got sicker than a dog." Although everyone connected with the project knew that the problem was not with the headsets but with Sega's hardware, which couldn't render the environments fast enough to keep up with a user's head movements, Sega had no choice but to kill the Virtual i/O deal.

The Sega near-deal was to be the first of several bundling deals that would fall through over the next few months, proving, disappointment by disappointment, that Virtual i/O's vision was out of synch with the state of the installed base of computer hardware in the gaming market. It was beginning to look as if the

door to the fastest-growing portion of the computer industry—
the gaming segment—was being slammed shut in Virtual i/O's
face.

Down in Seattle's Pioneer Square, Zombie Virtual Reality Entertainment was also entering a season of disillusionment and chagrin.
Long, like Rhoads, found the HIT lab to be overly academic in its
orientation, and disinterested in the problems of commercial ventures, which are beset with competition and deadline pressures.
Two or three Zombie initiatives to work in concert with the lab
had fallen through, and Long now felt that the HIT lab was not
"the hotbed of VR talent that we had expected." Furness's lab suffered, Long believed, from many of the same problems that had
frustrated him at Sarnoff. "I've seen these kinds of labs before," he
said. "They're academic, they're always scrambling for money, the
directors have to be in a million places at once, they struggle to survive, and they never really get anything done." Since he and
Alexander were in essentially the same predicament as were
Rhoads and Amadon at Virtual i/O—having to force their way into
profitability before they ran out of their investors' money and patience—they had no time for the deliberate, relatively directionless
pace of work in academe.

Long and Alexander also were struggling with disappointment
in the marketplace. The release of Zombie's first game, Locus—a
game designed for use with head-mounted displays—had been
timed both for Christmas 1995 and to follow the release of Virtual
i/O's Gamer!, the HMD with head tracking built into it. Since
there were also two other tracking-equipped head-mounted displays on the market—one from Forte, the other from Victor-
Maxx—the Zombie cofounders were expecting Locus both to be
a best-seller and to help launch the market for head-mounted displays and their applications.

Instead, it turned out that they had developed, in Locus, a game
targeted toward a nonexistent—and possibly nonemerging—market. Developed at a cost of $975,167, Locus was underwritten by
a $785,300 advance from GT Interactive, its publisher (game pub-
lishers contract with development houses in much the same way

that book publishers contract with authors), and sold just over 18,000 copies, for total sales of $300,755.

The dismal sales forced Long and Alexander to step back from the HMD market. Although Locus could be played either with or without a head-mounted display, at least 30 percent of Zombie's development costs went into writing code for the game's interface with an HMD. "For a small company," Alexander said, "we've found that we just can't afford to put ourselves out on a limb too much to create a game that won't sell that much but is really great to play on a head-mounted display. So we're going to concentrate more on 3D environments for the screen."

In doing so, Zombie dropped one challenge and took up another, since the technological step backward put them in a far more competitive environment—particularly as the tools for creating three-dimensional worlds on computer became more widely available and easier to use. Faster microprocessors and better video cards had made computers capable of rendering three-dimensional worlds in "real time," so when a character in a game turned around quickly, the surrounding environment changed as fast as it does when you turn your head around in the real world. "Everyone's doing 3D now," Long said, "and although we have particular expertise in the psychophysics of virtual reality, the tools are rapidly evolving to where anybody can do it. So to a degree, our technical expertise is getting less and less relevant, and more of our survival will have to do with our art direction and the story behind what you're given in the environment you create."

The computer game engineering world is an odd amalgam of research and development, daring, caution, technology, art, pop culture, and the hit-and-miss guesswork that characterizes the American entertainment and publishing businesses. As Long had observed before, some of the most able and imaginative software engineers in the world had gravitated to the game market, where they were encouraged to keep expanding the boundaries and capabilities of computer performance. Yet game developers not only are constantly pushing the technological envelope, trying to be first to market with a breakthrough; they also must be careful not to get too far out in front of the curve. As Zombie's experience with Locus proved, a technological breakthrough is worthless if it breaks through to a feature that the computers it is designed to play on cannot exploit or display.

Games also must appeal to consumers not simply on technical merit but on aesthetic merit—a point that is lost on the vast majority of programmers, who tend to focus on the underlying algorithms and overriding gore in a game rather than on such refinements as narrative, level of social commentary, and quality of dialog. This can be particularly frustrating for those designing and developing games, as the aesthetic criteria seem, particularly to the engineering mind, to be indecipherable and random. Game publishing, like music or movies, has evolved essentially into a hits business, in which publishers pump out as many titles as they can afford to produce in the hopes that one of them will sell enough copies to pay for development of all the rest. Since it is all but impossible to predict which particular game in a publisher's repertoire will be a best-seller, or why, it can be difficult to figure out exactly what a publisher wants from a developer.

Thus the publishers' approach is to sign up as many development houses, like Zombie, as possible, and flood the market with different kinds of game titles in the hope that one will ascend to best-sellerdom. The game business is very much like the movie, book publishing, and music businesses, in that publishers sign contracts with game developers, pay them advances against royalties, market their games, and hope for the best. There is very little marketing "science" behind a given publisher's decision to finance the development of a given game.

The guesswork component—a major factor in all publishing, whether of books, movies, or music—is greatly magnified in the games world by a tremendous lack of data. Because the genre is so new, there is no artistic tradition or history of consumer behavior for publishers to research when developing new titles. This problem is made astronomically worse by the constantly shifting nature of the computer hardware world. Game developers always risk either manufacturing an outdated title (one lacking a compelling new software feature, for example, like three-dimensional graphics or 32-bit color, that is available in a new competing game) or bringing out a title so innovative that consumers lack hardware powerful enough to play it.

Considering all this in the wake of the Locus fiasco, Long started thinking more and more about the role and value of narrative, verisimilitude, and exposition in games. This artistic dimension in gaming was largely ignored by the rest of the industry. Most games were simply walking puzzles, in which the player navigated through a landscape mined with traps and opponents in search of a treasure to find or a woman to rescue. The most popular games were of the "first-person shooter" genre, in which the player's point of view is that of the main character, who must make his or her way through treacherous environments (caves, jungles, tunnels, buildings, cityscapes, etc.), employing a variety of weapons, available at the touch of a key, in a quest to destroy the creatures who come looming and darting out of hiding places along the way.

Long liked to think of games more in terms of novels or movies, with both human players and artificial-intelligence-endowed, computer-generated creatures as their characters. When he thought about a new game's look and feel, he was more prone to borrow from traditional media than from other games. He was particularly taken with the narrative structure of myth, where a hero sets off on a peril-ridden quest for victory over a foe, eventually gaining self-discovery and an understanding of his place in the universe. "With its struggle, its conquests, its battles, its accumulation of knowledge, myth is just so compelling," he said one day, during a discussion of a new Zombie project called Zero Population Control. In that game, the player was to be "Arman, the last of the Warrior Messiahs," who is returned to Earth from deep space—where he had been sent as an infant in order to save him from the monsters taking over the planet—to rescue Earth from from the rule of the evil robot-creatures who have instituted a post-apocalyptic, totalitarian social order that enslaves humans. Arman knows nothing at first about who he is or why he has been sent to Earth. He knows only that he is under constant attack.

As he works his way through the game's highly stylized landscape—the game would have the look of early Soviet Futurist and Constructivist art—the player/Arman deciphers clues he finds in the form of pictograms and other messages that gradually elucidate his identity and mission. Once the player ascends to the final level of play, and wins there, he is treated to a ceremony of disclosure and celebration that rewards him for his heroic efforts and bestows upon him, at last, full understanding and self-knowledge.

Looking at Long's plans for the game and listening to him discourse on mythic narrative, it was hard not to look back at the classics of myth—*The Epic of Gilgamesh, The Odyssey, The Aeneid, The Song of Roland*, to name a few—and think of them as . . . well, as first-person shooters, and to think of computer gaming as a new literary genre in its earliest stages. Just as previous narrative forms in theater, writing, and film went through their first-person-shooter stage, I thought, so will this new, interactive art form progress from the crude combat saga to richer narratives elucidating more diverse experiences and ways of life. It is only a matter of building tradition, making the art form's tools easier to use and more accessible, and bringing more and more imaginations into the business of composing these fictions.

This is, of course, not as easy as it sounds, as modern literary forms took hundreds of years to emerge, and the computer platform presents special problems of exposition and direction. In this connection, Long and Alexander were at work on an interesting essay on the problem of narrating through the interface of a computer program that was to be published in the 1996 Computer Game Developers' Conference *Proceedings*. Entitled "The Emerging Design Grammar of VR," the essay looks ahead to the problems game composers will encounter as they try to move beyond the current state of the art, in which games are "primarily simulations," to a "hybrid design grammar that will allow designers to create compelling narratives in realtime games."

The primary obstacle, of course, is the computer itself, which is a binary calculating machine—too primitive a sort of brain to handle matters of exposition, psychology, and plot in an art form in which the reader is both spectator and character. Alexander and Long tried to illustrate the obstacles facing the narrative composer by showing how a computer might handle a simple expositive device in *The Wizard of Oz*—getting Dorothy to notice and pay attention to the Munchkins:

> The player is Dorothy. She opens the door to the house. The Door_object sends message to color all polygons that are not inside the house_object. The Dorothy_object sends message to Munchkin_objects - Dorothy_object is in walking state. Munchkin_objects check their tables:
>
> If Dorothy_object is walking, and no collision detection, count 12 secs then go to Dorothy_object.
>
> If Dorothy_object collides, change to giggle state.
>
> If giggle, remain in that state.

Not exactly "Stately, plump Buck Mulligan came from the stairhead. . . ."

When not spinning their fantasies about the artistic possibilities of virtual reality, Long and Alexander spent a lot of their time figuring out how to stay in business long enough for virtual reality to grow into a paying proposition. Looking ahead to Christmas 1996, Long saw a bloodbath coming. "A lot of companies have gone under over the last two Christmases, and I think there's going to be further consolidation, to the point where there's just going to be seven major publishers, just like there's seven major movie studios or really seven major publishers of anything, music or whatever." Zombie's strategy, he explained, was to find a way to survive through 1997, on the theory that if they could stay in business that long, they would be home free.

The lesson Virtual i/O was learning about the head-mounted-display market was proving far harder to absorb than Zombie's. For one thing, the company did not have a fall-back position in the hardware world the way Zombie did in the software world. For another, Virtual i/O's founders were inexperienced, none of them ever before having tried to compete in the consumer electronics hardware market. And for yet another, they were unwilling to hear the hard truths being shouted at them from every corner.

When Virtual i/O's first two products—dubbed i-Glasses! (a

headset that could be hooked up to a TV receiver or VCR) and the Gamer! (a headset, with head tracking and a PC connection, for playing computer games)—were released in late spring 1995, it was obvious that the company had a tremendous winner. Virtual i/O's products enjoyed unmistakable advantages at every point of comparison over products from the company's only two competitors, VictorMaxx and Forte. Where the other manufacturers' headsets each weighed more than two pounds, Virtual i/O's weighed less than seven ounces. VictorMaxx's headset, the Cybermaxx, sold for $1,000, Forte's VFX 1 sold for $895, and Virtual i/O's Gamer! was first announced at $799 and its i-Glasses! for $599, with prices of both dropping month by month, eventually settling (as near as I could tell, at any rate, the company's pricing announcements being frequent and conflicting), at $299 and $399 respectively. Virtual i/O's units also were far easier to hook up to PCs, requiring little more than the plugging in of some components to the PC box, while their competitors required users to take their computers apart and install interface cards in them. These advantages drew raves from newspapers and magazines all over the country, and visitors to trade shows lined up for hours to try on the headsets. To judge from the rather clever design of the displays and the reaction of focus groups and the press, it looked as if, after years of unrealized promise, the dream of bringing VR technology to the consumer market had finally been realized.

By the end of the Christmas season, however, it was clear that the company had a problem: No one was buying the headsets, and many of those who did buy them eventually brought them back. (Some at Virtual i/O pegged the return rate at higher than 50 percent.) While Virtual i/O carefully guarded its sales figures, news leaked out that the company was selling only a few hundred displays a month, at most, rather than the twenty thousand per month that investors had been led to expect.

Inside the company, theories abounded as to what was wrong. Some believed that the products were not ready for the mass market, since they kept breaking down. Consumers returning them claimed variously that they couldn't get the displays to work at all or that they worked only a short time before failing. Some headsets would come on oddly, with one lens lighting up several minutes ahead of the other; others would overheat; and in others, the image would suddenly freeze if the viewer moved his or her head too rapidly. Some in the company—including Amadon and Rhoads—held that there was nothing wrong with the headsets and that customers were lying when they claimed they wouldn't work. Many in this faction believed that once the "wow factor" wore off, customers realized that there wasn't much they could do with their expensive new toys, and they wanted their money back. We don't need to refine the product we have so much as we need to give customers a use for it—a killer app—this faction said. They argued strenuously that Virtual i/O should either buy or develop stereo three-dimensional content in order to take advantage of the i-Glasses!'s ability to display in stereo 3D, and to evangelize more effectively with game companies so that video game players would have more reasons to buy the Gamer!, with its head-tracking function.

Amadon and Rhoads, however, apparently decided that their company's problem was essentially one of marketing and sales, and they turned a deaf ear to anyone proposing that they spend money on applications and compelling content or that they refine the design and manufacture of their headsets.

By the end of 1995, Virtual i/O had split into roughly two factions—one led by Wolfgang Mack, the other by Amadon and Rhoads. Mack fell into the killer app group, Amadon and Rhoads into the marketing and public-relations group. Matters came to a head just before New Year's Day 1996, when Mack and Amadon had a violent argument in front of the rest of company management. Mack left in a rage, and Amadon called him that night—New Year's Eve—demanding that he come in to work the next day. When Mack showed up, Amadon fired him.

The firing of Mack created an immense morale problem at Virtual i/O. As the only one of the three company founders with an engineering background, he took much of the faith in Virtual i/O on the part of the company's engineers with him. Amadon had hoped that firing Mack would heal a growing and demoralizing company rift; instead, the firing made the rift irreparable.

Mack's departure also created problems for Virtual i/O in the courtroom, where its lawsuit—which up until his firing had been largely Mack's responsibility—was still dragging on, with no end in sight and less and less likelihood of a clear victory for Virtual i/O. The lawsuit had devolved into a long mutual siege, with the two sides trying to starve each other out. Every step, however small, brought both parties back into the courtroom to argue over minute details. Virtual i/O's lawyers wanted Forte witnesses to fly from Rochester, New York, to Seattle for their depositions, while Forte insisted that the Virtual i/O lawyers fly to Rochester; Forte's lawyers wanted Virtual i/O's witnesses to fly to Rochester, while Virtual i/O wanted Forte's lawyers to fly to Seattle. Each company bombarded the other with expensive discovery demands, and each tried to disqualify the other's expert witnesses. By January, the case file, which now filled eight huge expandable binders, was packed with arguments over hundreds of immensely insignificant details.

For a while, Mack became the central bone of contention, as he proved adept at evading the attempts of Virtual i/O's lawyers to get him into court. Reading the voluminous files on the dispute, it seemed at times that it was a lawsuit over Mack, who no longer had any interest in defending Virtual i/O's interests but who was apparently barred from going over to the other side by onerous nondisclosure documents he had signed in return for a generous severance package. For months, he proved improbably ingenious at evading the courtroom, primarily by not answering his telephone, by claiming that he was too busy looking for work to find the time to schedule a deposition, or by arguing that he couldn't commit to a deposition time too far in advance because he might find a job in the interim that would prevent him from being deposed as scheduled.

Mack emerged in the court documents as a compelling figure who illustrated the essential charm of the American legal system, where any argument, however absurd on its face, is given its deliberate and expensive day in court.

Linden Rhoads began pleading with Judge Thomas Zilly for mercy. She told the judge that her company's second round of fund-raising was being held back by Virtual i/O's investors until the lawsuit could be settled, that the Gamer! alone had cost $5.5 million to bring to market, and that the lawsuit threatened to put her and Amadon out of business. She asked that the trial date, now scheduled for May 22, be delayed, that Zilly force Forte to turn over more company documents, and that Forte's expert witness on head tracking be disqualified. Zilly's answers—no, no, and no—were followed by his order that Virtual i/O turn over all of its patent application materials, which the company had been desperately trying to keep out of the courtroom.

With the lawsuit spinning out of control in unexpected directions, with its product stagnating on the company's shelves, with its investors' faith wavering, and with its management in turmoil, Virtual i/O entered 1996 on the brink of collapse. In response, Amadon and Rhoads launched an epic PR offensive that resulted in stories appearing in *Broadcasting & Cable, CyberEdge Journal, Aviation Week and Space Technology, Wall Street Journal–Japan, VR News, PC Magazine, Entertainment Weekly, USA Today, Newsweek,* and countless other trade magazines and daily newspapers. Amadon decreed that all requests to the company for information be referred to Rhoads and that Rhoads be the only company employee allowed to be photographed for stories about Virtual i/O. Employees leaving the company were made to sign agreements preventing them from discussing anything about Virtual i/O with anyone from the press for years, with the penalties for violating the agreement heavy enough to cow departed employees into frightened and determined silence.

Thus I entered 1996 subjected to an odd stereophonic experience when it came to conducting research on Virtual i/O. In one ear, I heard the constant, optimistic shrieks of Rhoads, detailing corporate partnership deals in the making, array upon array of retailers lining up to sell her headsets, fantastic sales figures, growth almost too rapid to manage, and a wave of new Virtual i/O products under development in 1996. "Our company has to be a pioneer," she said in one typical monologue, "which is an aggravating situation to have to be in. But at least we're doing what you should do, which is that if you're in the beginning of a burgeoning industry, you have a market lead, which we do, we do have the lion's share of the market right now, such as it is, that at least we are going out there and positioning ourselves for future glory, to look for all kinds of technology, and to either own or lead the standard."

In the other ear, meanwhile, came insistent whispers from a collective source I came to call Deep Bile: a chorus of voices owned by people in whose hearts raged a constant war between fear and outrage. Departed Virtual i/O employees, they described a failing company run by lunatics. "It's like *The Caine Mutiny*," one of them said, "where it really wasn't about the strawberries at all, it was about something else." For this group, whose legions were to grow astronomically during the coming year, 1996 was a death watch; for Amadon and Rhoads, it was a private fight for survival and a public declaration of Homeric success; for me, it was to be an engrossing stereopsychodrama.

When not gazing rapturously up at the big picture, Tom Furness spent the lion's share of his time dealing with what he saw as unreasonable and self-destructive paranoia on the part of Microvision's Steve Willey and Rick Rutkowski. In his increasingly desperate desire to see the company get some kind of deal off the ground somewhere, Furness kept trying to put together research partnerships between Microvision and established companies interested in the VRD. But he was constantly thwarted by Willey, who apparently believed that all interested parties were thieves rather than potential partners. "I went through this with a company years ago, where we had a new technology," Willey said to me once, characteristically declining to name the company. "And it was so clear to us that you didn't speak to *anybody*. We didn't dream of telling our friends, our colleagues, the press, publications, nothing. Because we knew that when we came out of the chute our only chance was to get in front of a wide audience of prospective partners with a complete package."

This argument only added to Furness's mystification, as Microvision still was not doing anything by way of putting together any kind of manufactured "package." The company remained intent on being a broker rather than a builder—a course of inaction that Furness had come to regard as an outright assault on his efforts.

Furness's deepening depression over Microvision took on the dimension of heartbreak over an opportunity he saw to take a giant step toward realizing his dream of recapturing "lost world citizens"—people prevented by disability from partaking fully in life and society. Fujitsu Research Institute, one of the biggest companies in the Virtual Worlds Consortium and one of the earliest to sign on with the HIT lab, decided, after a series of meetings with Furness, that it wanted to conduct a year-long series of studies of the VRD and blindness, to see what forms of vision impairment the display might be able to alleviate. An ecstatic Furness began putting together a research agreement only to have Microvision's Willey step in and try to stop the project just as Furness was ready to sign the agreement. (Microvision's contract with the University of Washington stated that any company working with HIT lab VRD researchers had first to reach agreement with Microvision.) Fujitsu wanted to buy a portable VRD prototype—the lab now had built three of them, which could show a monocular image, and had a system in place for building more—take it to Japan, and have ophthalmologists conduct careful studies of its possible uses in relieving vision problems. While the HIT lab was eager to give a VRD unit to Fujitsu because Furness was willing to do nearly anything to find useful applications for it, Microvision wanted to have nothing to do with the company. For months, Furness tried finding common ground for the two companies, but was rebuffed every time by Willey. In one meeting that Furness found particularly frustrating, Willey, Furness, and lawyers from Microvision, Fujitsu, and the Washington Technology Center sat for six hours in a room trying without success to hammer out an agreement. As time wore on, Furness saw his best chance at finding an application for the VRD slipping away. Even worse, his long and close relationship with Fujitsu appeared in danger of eroding, as the company was growing tired of the HIT lab and its intransigent partners at Microvision.

Another deal the lab tried to put together with Microvision graphically illustrated for Furness and Rich Johnston why Microvision was finding corporate partnerships unobtainable. A Seattle start-up, Advanced Marine Technology (AMT), had come to the lab looking for help in developing an augmented reality display that would superimpose geographic and navigational information on the seascape sailors would be studying through binoculars. The company wanted to develop binoculars that could be hooked up with trackers and input-output cables to the ship's computer and navigation systems. Sailors looking through the binoculars would see, superimposed over the outside world, data about heading, geographic location, weather, water depth, and so on. Furness showed AMT executives the VRD and explained how it might be used as an augmented reality application, and Advanced Marine signed a contract with the lab to conduct an $80,000 feasibility study on use of the VRD in an Advanced Marine system.

The deal hit rough water, though, when Advanced Marine tried to contract with Microvision for the rights to incorporate VRD technology into its prototype. Microvision refused to allow the HIT lab to use the VRD in any of its Advanced Marine work. Advanced Marine, still hoping to strike a deal, asked Steve Willey if he would allow the company to buy VRD display hardware in a year or two, when Microvision had gotten to the point of manufacturing devices. No, answered Willey, but we will sell you designs for our devices, and you will pay us both for the designs and a royalty fee for every device you build yourselves.

Rich Johnston came out of that meeting with his eyes cast heavenward, his hands extended palms up, his face set in his favorite "What can you do?" expression. For weeks afterward, he regaled his fellow researchers with what he called his "Nordstrom analogy"—an allusion to the famous Seattle family business whose progenitor, John Nordstrom, parlayed a small Alaska gold rush claim into the world's leading clothing retailer. "Imagine," Johnston would say, "that you went to Nordstrom to buy a suit, and they said, 'Well, no, we won't sell you a suit, but we will sell you the *plans* for a suit that you can make yourself. And moreover, you have to pay us more money for every suit you actually make from the plans we sell you.'"

Later, I asked Microvision CEO Rick Rutkowski about the Fujitsu and Advanced Marine negotiations. "The deals are not happening," he said shortly. "How can we prevent some sort of accidental transfer of our intellectual property?"

Tom Furness entered 1996 feeling that defeat was closing in on him from nearly every quarter. The lawsuit between Forte and Virtual i/O struck him as a depressing and destructive waste of time and money that ultimately would destroy not only both head-mounted-display companies, but the overall advance of the technology as well. Microvision, the company he had joined forces with to advance his invention, had instead turned into a company intent, as far as he could see, on stopping it in its tracks. He had come to believe that Microvision would find a way to destroy the fruits of his VRD team's laboratory research no matter how good the work turned out to be.

Furness fell more and more to sitting in his office and lamenting the mysterious workings of human nature—particularly the nature of humans in the business world. It seemed that whenever he got involved with businesspeople, he found himself adrift and helpless, a babe in the woods. He was utterly unable to tell the good from the bad among them. Again and again he would put his head in his hands and mutter, "These businesspeople—these *ruthless* people—I just can't understand them!"

It was with considerable surprise, delight, and relief, then, that he picked up the telephone one day to hear the voice of his erstwhile protégé, Mike Almquist—who had angrily dropped out of sight nearly two years before—on the other end. "Tom," Almquist said, "I've started a new company, we've just raised $1 million . . . and I'd like you to sit on the board."

Almquist's call to Furness was the culmination of a long rethinking of his strategy for bringing virtual reality to the masses. A combination of his soul-searching, reading, conversations with Adam Feuer and Jeff Hussey, Joey King's encouragement, and his own hard thinking on the evolution of the Internet had led him to scale back his grandiose dreams. He decided he must work first on the world's information-delivery infrastructure, making it into something that could handle fully three-dimensional content, before working on his real dream: the tools and content for creating immersive virtual-world interfaces. When his plans had advanced to the point of thinking about a corporate structure and a board that would be attractive to future investors, he realized that the presence of the well-known Furness on the new company's board would considerably enhance the company's prospects.

During the months Almquist had spent fighting off depression and premature death in his desolate basement, he watched the world begin hitching its ride on the Internet. He noticed people subscribing by the millions to services providing them Internet access even though the Net essentially had nothing to offer them. This led Almquist to two conclusions: The urge to interact with other people and with media over the Internet was clearly irresistible; and the Net was about to collapse under the sudden surge in demand.

The problem, Almquist knew, was not the Internet itself, which was built to handle high-speed, high-bandwidth transmission and could carry loads far heavier than anything likely to be thrown at it in the foreseeable future. As more and more users signed on, though, and as more and more web sites were created, the information being sent back and forth was getting stuck in a bottleneck at either end of the connection between a user and a web site. TV cable modems and improved telephone and modem technology would solve the problem at the user's end. It was the problem at the web site end that led Almquist to say to Hussey that people either would have to buy monstrous, expensive servers for their web sites or find a way to make several small computers look like a single huge one. He had figured out a way to make web sites cheaper to set up and operate, and almost infinitely faster.

In order to understand why Almquist's declaration so excited Hussey, it is necessary to understand how information travels back and forth between the Internet and a given web site. When someone sitting at his or her desktop sends a message out over the Internet, it is broken up into small "packets," which are routed through various routers and networks in the system. These packets have two "headers" on them: an "IP header," which might be likened to an address on an envelope, and a "TCP header," which allows the addressee's server eventually to reconnect the packets back into a single message.

These packets are received at a web site's door by a router. The router looks at the IP portion of the packet's TCP/IP address, then delivers it to the appropriate destination within the server, which looks at the TCP portion of the address before translating the address from Internet "language" to the language of Ethernet—the hardware infrastructure of your garden-variety web site or office network—and reassembling all the packets in a given message. As a web site becomes more and more popular, this router-to-server-to-sub-address connection gets overwhelmed, and the whole delivery-and-response system slows down, sometimes coming to a halt entirely.

Two things contribute to slowdowns in this bottleneck. One is the hardware that comprises the web site—the server or servers storing the data that visitors to a web site are trying to access. Servers can handle only so much traffic at once, and if a web site becomes too popular, visitors have to queue up in the bottleneck and wait for a server to be free to receive their request. This server hardware can consist of anything from a single server or set of servers manufactured by Sun Microsystems or SGI, to a more complicated and high-powered server at the highest end, or a single PC or group of PCs at the lowest end. At the beginning of 1996, cost of the more expensive servers ranged from $8,000 to $30,000 or more per box; cost of a PC was less than $3,000 per box, and dropping.

The second factor contributing to the bottleneck problem was the way routers connect with servers. A router connected with a group of servers is programmed to study server traffic and performance and make guesses as to which server will be free at any given time. Because routers do not know at the precise moment they are sending information on to the servers at a web site which servers are least busy, the sites often are inefficient, with one server overworked while another sits idle.

What Almquist proposed to Hussey and Feuer was development of a device that could speed up delivery from the Internet to the web server, dramatically lessen the cost of maintaining a web site, and help make web sites almost infinitely extendible. This device, as Almquist envisioned it, would essentially be a high-speed, intelligent "load-balancing" switch that could look at both the TCP and IP portions of a packet's address, instantaneously survey a network of web site servers to see which one was least busy, then deliver the package of packets to that destination. This device would allow a web site owner to use cheap PCs rather than expensive servers or workstations, and to simply add PCs to the web site as it grew more popular. The cost of operating a web site and growing it to keep up with demand would be driven downward drastically, and the web site would become far more efficient and reliable in the bargain.

The more he, Feuer, and Hussey talked about this idea, the more excited they became. To Almquist, it was a chance to make the world of the Internet capable of handling the data loads required for his vision of legitimate VR applications; for Feuer, it was a chance to work on Net communications, his passion; and for Hussey, it was a chance to hit a "home run"—make himself an instant millionaire. The three set up a company with Hussey as the CEO, Feuer as VP of engineering, and Almquist as the chief technology officer (CTO), talked about how to divide the company's stock, and began planning their fund-raising effort.

What happened next is the stuff of old Mickey Rooney–Judy Garland movies. The three put together a business plan, gave their product a name—BIG/ip—dubbed their company Virtual Softworks (later they would change it to F5 Labs, the term "F5" being the highest rating on the scale measuring the power of tornadoes), and went off to raise money. It took them all of two presentations—one in downtown Seattle, the other across Lake Washington, in Bellevue—to raise just over $1 million less than two weeks after starting their company. The only challenging part of the whole exercise was figuring out how to dress Almquist like an adult.

With Hussey speaking from out of an appropriately pin-striped suit, and with Almquist—wearing a broad, outdated tie and an ill-fitting Brooks Brothers suit—showing and manipulating his burning building and sea-floor visualization demos on a huge overhead screen, the pair wowed the Seattle financial community. "Their solution matched pretty much what we were looking at in the marketplace," said venture capitalist Richard Novotny, who invested in F5 and was named to the company's board. "You could see out in the Internet, the number of servers going up and up, and the backbone not keeping up. And I liked how Hussey was a little bit on the cocky side, confident, how he knew what he wanted and knew where he was going with the thing. Almquist, their technical guy, really knows what he's doing. And they knew what the product was *now*. They looked at a wider product line, and they were willing to change as the market changed. They had it very well thought out. They're going to have a nice, solid base where they can add value—standard components with unique software. It just adapts itself very well to the market."

Almquist had a somewhat less businesslike analysis of his success. "Woo-HOO!" he shouted, safely out on the street after the second presentation. "Woo-HOO! They bought my Godzilla dance! I romped! I stomped! I devoured small planetoids!" Then he made, with his mouth, a muted, menacing sound meant to imitate the sound of a monster breathing fire: "WHOOF. . . ."

Money in hand, the three young captains of industry leased office space in downtown Seattle a block away from Hussey's day job at A.H. Capital, began moving equipment in, hired a few of their friends, and immediately started building BIG/ip. Almquist moved out of his basement lair and rented, with King, a large, splendid house on Seattle's Queen Anne Hill, with a view of Elliott Bay. It was, he said, a way of forcing himself to succeed: "To keep the house, I would have to *do* this, and do it right." Having emerged from his basement and his depression with renewed and vengeful energy, Almquist was ready to devour small planetoids with reckless abandon. Looking out at the months ahead, he saw himself doing nothing but writing splendid code, spending money, seducing customers, and unleashing his will upon the world.

A Hole in the Ground
Surrounded by Liars

———

YOU COULD NEVER DECIDE, when regarding Jeff Hussey and Mike Almquist, whether theirs was a marriage made in heaven or hell. Their partnership either was a perfect blend of complementary skills and attributes or a perverse meeting of opposites and incompatibilities. Almquist was irreverent, mischievous, sloppy, plump, grizzled, and almost suicidally playful. Hussey was thin, intense, tidy, serious to the point of humorlessness, impeccably groomed and coifed, and given to bluster. Almquist looked like a chronically childish adult; Hussey looked like an overserious child who liked to dress up and play at being grown up.

The pair came across as a stereotypical high-tech start-up duo: one a manager of money, process, and people, the other a manager of technology. Almquist gave F5 Labs technological credibility; Hussey made the company look businesslike. They gave the impression that Hussey would keep a tight fiscal rein on the company, thereby keeping Almquist, the eccentric genius, on track and under budget.

Moreover, each was well connected in his particular world: Almquist with the society of programmers, Hussey with the investor community. Potential investors looking at F5 Labs were assured, by Almquist's apparent grasp of technical issues and by Hussey's CEO-ish look and feel, that the company was technologically onto something and had its business house in order. Theirs looked like the kind of magical combination that investors craved and start-ups generally lacked.

Hussey and Almquist were careful to keep projecting this image of businesslike responsibility and relative probity by keeping their ultimate ambitions secret from the company's board of directors, most of whom were appointed by their investors. While their board saw F5 as Hussey and Almquist's life's work, the two regarded the company as a mere stepping-stone to their real dream. They wanted to build F5 to the point where it could carry on without them more or less as a service and sales company, turn it over to successors, and start a full-blown VR company that built tools and applications. Hussey wanted the new company to get to work as soon as possible on what he persistently called "the nipple"—the stock market visualization tool built on Almquist's sea-floor visualization code—while Almquist had grander ambitions: He and Joey King wanted to start a VR company on the scale, it seemed from his energetic monologues, of Nintendo.

Both Hussey and Almquist hoped to have BIG/ip finished and selling by the end of 1996; Almquist estimated that it would take him and one or two other programmers no longer than six months to build.

Talking alternately with Almquist and Hussey about their ambitions when one or the other was not present, it soon was apparent to me that neither wanted the other to know exactly what he was up to, and that each felt he was exploiting the abilities of a less clever partner in the service of his particular dream. While I could not tell at first how much either of them trusted or respected the abilities of his accomplice, or which of them would prove more adept at Machiavellianism, I could see that they were headed for a showdown.

It was clear from the outset of the F5 adventure that both Hussey and Almquist were essentially ungovernable, and that when it came time for one or the other to take a subordinate role in the company, neither would be able to do so. Neither one had

ever managed to work for more than a few months under supervision without coming to blows with his superiors or finding a way
to work on his own, free of guidance or restriction. Almquist's
longest stint in any one place was at the HIT lab, where he was remembered for his brashness, his hostile takeover of the lab's software group, and his forced march out the lab door. Hussey's
résumé consisted of a four-year sojourn as a bond trader with Kid-
der Peabody, the launch in 1986 of a magazine-publishing venture
that failed in short order, the attainment of an MBA degree from
the University of Washington, three years as a salesman for Reuters
Information Services, a short time selling stock-quote machines for
ILX Systems, and then self-employment—first as an Internet access provider, then, at age thirty-five, as cofounder of F5 Labs. The
consistent theme throughout Hussey's career was his inability to
work with other people—an incapacity that he cited more with
pride than regret. What he liked best about his sales positions, he
said, was the capability of working for months at a time without
having to report to superiors. Whenever his job called for him to
interact with fellow employees, it seemed, it got him in trouble.
Thus the recitation of his employment history is peppered with
such asides as, "My direct style pissed off a couple people, so we
parted ways," "A personality style like mine is kind of an acquired
taste," and "How I got here at F5 is I'm not a very good employee."

No one worried more about Hussey's ability to run a company
and manage people than Hussey himself. "I'm not sure that managing a bunch of people is what I want to do," he often said. "I
mean, you can see the problem going back to my third-grade report cards: *'Has a problem getting along with other people.'* I have to
hope that in the long run people here are more interested in what
I do for their net worth than in what I do for their psyche on a day-
to-day basis. That's the thing about management that I struggle
with. Good managers are more concerned about the psyches of
their employees than they are about the bottom line. But I never
said I was a good manager."

His inexperience and acknowledged ineptitude as a manager
were compounded by the intense pressure brought on by F5's
market potential. Use of the Internet was exploding, and the Net

was breaking down from the overload. Any product offering a solution to that problem was regarded in the financial community as invaluable. This led Hussey, Almquist, and the company's board to believe that their collective investment of $1.2 million could be worth anywhere from $40 million to $200 million within a year or two, and the possibility made for an excruciating fear that something might go wrong.

This sense that F5 had a precarious hold on vast potential wealth also made the principals immensely suspicious of one another. After only a few months of work, Hussey and Almquist looked with increasing skepticism on the work of Adam Feuer and of Ross Morris, who had been hired as the company's VP of sales and who was working at lining up potential customers and partnership deals some six months before July 1996, when the first version of BIG/ip was scheduled to be finished. Hussey in particular kept looking at the work everyone was doing and calculating its worth against the shares of stock each held—a morbid exercise that inevitably left him convinced he was doing more work per share than his collaborators were. His suspicion and anger zeroed in first on Feuer, who was finding it hard to work on code with Almquist, and who, Almquist told Hussey, "cannot deal with stress, and he keeps getting slower and slower and slower in his coding, and more and more emotionally reclusive." The two finally tried to negotiate a reduction in Feuer's stock allocation and salary, and Feuer walked out. When Almquist and Hussey tried to pay him $210,000—or $.70 per share for his stock, as agreed to in the buy-sell agreement the three founders had negotiated when they started F5—Feuer, looking at the stock's potential worth, refused to accept the buyout, claiming that Hussey had coerced him into signing the agreement. His erstwhile partners filed suit against him.

Morris left soon after, returned, and left again for good after a final blowup with Hussey.

Almquist and Hussey tried in the midst of this upheaval to keep company productivity on track by hastily hiring friends and acquaintances without taking much time to assess their skills or interest in advancing the F5 agenda. By the beginning of summer

1996, they had hired two programmers, a system administrator to set up and maintain F5's internal computer network, a new VP of sales who was a friend of one of the company's board members, a business manager who was a friend of Hussey's, and a chief scientist—Joey King, who was to work for F5 part-time while finishing his Ph.D.

With Almquist parceling out tasks and writing code; with Hussey trying to learn enough about software to assess the group's performance and keep it to some kind of schedule; with King designing BIG/ip's interface, writing specifications and technical papers, and researching competitive technologies; and with Hussey and the new sales VP trying to evangelize for the upcoming product in the marketplace, the group sailed into summer expecting to write BIG/ip's code in a matter of months and to be selling units in large enough numbers by November to have recouped their investors' money before the end of the year.

To anyone familiar with software development and not named Mike Almquist, this seemed improbable, to put it mildly. Yet this formidable schedule was the least ambitious of Almquist's plans. In addition to BIG/ip, he wanted to complete what he called the "BIG product line," consisting of BIG/ip, a web site security system called BIG/Firewall, a router, a multiple-processor server, and four more BIG boxes, all installed on a BIG rack and sold as a single unit. Almquist hoped to have one of these "BIG 19-inch racks" deployed at each of the six network access points (known as NAPs) linking the various networks that comprised the Internet. Once these racks were deployed—Almquist and Hussey referred to the deployment as the "VR Sandbox"—the Internet would be ready for immersive three-dimensional applications. "After that," Almquist liked to say, "it'll all be software and content." With the BIG system in place, the Internet would be capable of delivering truly compelling VR applications—the sort of things Almquist and King wanted to make their life's work.

F5 Labs, then, was simply a passage to the paramount Almquist/King dream—and, for that matter, the Furness dream—of bringing the virtual-world interface to the world. "This whole technology is something that ultimately we'll need down the road," Almquist would say to King during their excited conversations about the future. "By January, the BIG line will be done, we'll have tons of cash, and we can start doing our real VR stuff."

I found it incredible that Almquist actually believed what he was saying, and even more incredible that King believed it, too. I would walk through F5's offices, which consisted of six unfinished—and largely unfurnished—rooms in an old, declining downtown Seattle office building, and look at crates full of computer hardware, a CEO who worked at a conference room table because he had no desk, an empty receptionist's station, windows with metal frames that had been crudely painted a garish purple, three programmers alternately playing networked Duke Nukem games and working on separate parts of BIG/ip without doing much in the way of consulting one another, and wonder how on earth Almquist and King could actually think they were only months away from taking over the Internet.

Yet everyone at F5 was wildly excited, convinced that by year's end they would all be rich, powerful titans of the Net. Even King, whose stature in the research community gave him entrée to all the best and most secretive industrial and academic laboratories in the United States and Japan, believed that his and Almquist's grand plan was eminently reasonable. King was, among other things, a member of the DARPA group that evaluated research proposals for that agency's funding, and in that capacity he saw everything of importance on the leading edge of Internet and VR research. "I sit there with my government badge on," he said one day, laughing, "and listen to everyone tell me what they're up to. I know most of the VR work going on in the country. Silicon Graphics is a leader, but they won't ever get their cost per unit down. Microsoft's not a factor—I know everybody in the group working on VR stuff over there. And there isn't much else going on. So what we're doing is incredibly timely, and incredibly well thought out."

As summer 1996 shaded into fall, there was a great deal of excitement in the air at Zombie. Every time I visited there, I felt as if I were dropping in on some unknown young rock band on the verge of breaking into stardom. The long, narrow rooms at Zombie, jam-packed with noise, nose rings, computers, sound and video equipment, wall decorations ranging from campy calendars to animal skulls, and purposeful kids running around with purple hair and artfully torn clothing, were being rearranged to accommodate an influx of even more employees and equipment. Zombie was nearing completion of its newest game—ZPC ("No Flesh Shall Be Spared")—and the company had secured funding for two new games that Mark Long brashly predicted would forever change the definition of computer gaming.

It was not uncommon during those days to hear in various rooms at Zombie the sounds of ZPC—explosions, loud gunshots, suspense-evoking musical riffs, crescendos, screams, sadistic laughter—as various Zombies brought the latest version of the game up on their screens to test or try out.

Long loved looking at ZPC, which had grown into a lavish blend of first-person shooter and rather moving depiction of a world and state of mind. Its game play was more or less identical to the classic Doom, the famous id software offering that had defined the first-person shooter, but its 'art direction set it apart entirely from everything else on the gaming market. The face of Arman, the last of the Warrior Messiahs, for example, was an expressive mix of anger, brooding, confusion, and haplessness. With long black hair and an unkempt beard, a heavily lined forehead, and a quizzical and sorrowful facial expression, he looked like Rasputin played by Nicholas Cage. It was hard not to identify—or at least sympathize—with him when his face first came up on the screen.

The game also had powerful, movielike sequences in which the player heard soaring music and moved with Arman to a new level of combat, attained by dint of the player's skill. Use of the traditional sound track and art-direction devices that invest a filmgoer in the emotion and action of a movie, combined with the emotional investment of a player competing in a game, made for a powerful effect on the player/viewer of ZPC. All of this was considerably heightened by the lush, apocalyptic tone of the land- and cityscapes created by British artist Aidan Hughes. The aesthetics of the game set it dramatically apart from traditional first-person shooters, where the art direction tends to look like something hacked together by computer programmers who care and know nothing about aesthetics.

For all of his excitement about ZPC, Long knew that it was a long shot on the game market. He was betting that the game-buying population would be expanding beyond the hard-core gamer—who cared only about technological advances—into the general population, where people would be driven to buy a game more for its artistry and story line than for its breakthrough engineering.

This is not to say, however, that he and Alexander had decided to devote their company to writing Doom-engine games forever. Zombie's next two projects—dubbed Spearhead and SpecOps—were gigantic leaps forward for the company in both art and engineering. Long and Alexander had decided to build the games from scratch, creating their own game engine—eventually, it would be called "Viper"—that would allow for a legitimately three-dimensional game and that would dramatically raise the level of complexity in gaming. Both titles would move beyond the simple first-person shooter standard to a new paradigm, in which the user not only would do battle against computer-generated creatures but also would have to collaborate with them. In these next two games, the player would be part of a team of soldiers sent on missions against enemies in various parts of the world.

Long also wanted to move out of the more or less unreal worlds of traditional games into a realm where games depicted real-world situations enhanced with exaggerated special effects, thereby both entertaining and educating the player. Both new games would be informed largely by his own experience as an army Ranger and by his and Alexander's prior work as builders of military simulation systems. After assembling his game-building teams for both titles, he gathered them together for a meeting and soon found himself ranting about "a game where we can use all of what we know to create a sense of presence. I want to give players a really compelling environment. Action movies—in particular military action movies—I think they target the audience real well . . . male, single, lots of disposable income . . . so we want to be the James Cameron of these 3D action games. I want to see cars flip over, I want spe-

cial effects where you go, 'Whoa! That was really cool!' We're taking state-of-the-art military technology and making a game out of
it, a tech game based on SIMNET technology . . . we're going to
do some cool stuff!"

Long's B-movie vision was inspired in part by technological advances that allowed him to bring unprecedented production values to his new games. Two new technologies—motion capture and
texture mapping—combined with faster microprocessors and new,
high-speed graphics boards for PCs—made possible a new kind of
photorealism for computer gaming. Producers using motion-
capture technology could fit actors and actresses in suits covered
with sensors, have them perform various motions, record the data
from the sensors on computer, and end up with data consisting of
what looked like wire-frame human forms moving through space.
(Among the first uses of motion capture was the recording of gym-
nasts' and martial artists' leaps, tumbles, kicks, and punches for use
in first-person shooters and hand-to-hand combat games.) Producers then could take photographs of actors in costume and "texture map" the photos over the skeletal data, with the result that a
figure somewhere between a videotaped live actor and a cartoon
character came to life on the computer screen.

It was not particularly easy to make all this work. Among the
problems that Long's developers would face in the months ahead
was the tendency of their figures to literally jump out of their
skins, as it proved extremely difficult to make the mapped textures
and the figures they were supposed to be covering move in perfect
concert all over the screen.

A fair amount of the excitement at Zombie was occasioned by
the steady stream of visitors from bigger companies who came
trooping through the company's warren. Alexander and Long took
calls from three larger, established companies per week, on average, with one or more of them eventually sending representatives
out to Seattle to look Zombie over. Sierra On-Line, Seattle's
biggest and best-known computer game company, and Microsoft
had each been through Zombie several times. Sierra in particular
was aggressively acquiring smaller companies, having bought nine
over the previous twelve months. Long and Alexander, who were

growing tired of living the hand-to-mouth existence of game de-velopers trying to survive on publishers' advances, saw only three ways to better their lot: sell a percentage of Zombie to an investor, hold an IPO, or sell the company outright. The two were hoping to avoid an IPO; it would be, in Long's words, "a huge pain in the ass," subject to the unpredictable whims of the market, and it would in-troduce the risk of an investor lawsuit afterward. They were reluc-tant to bring in new investors because they did not want to dilute their equity and the equity of employees who would be getting Zombie stock options. "So," Long explained at one of Zombie's in-frequent company meetings, "we want people to be thinking of us as a company to be acquired. Zombie was structured from the be-ginning with that in mind. We're really only one hit away from being a good acquisition. A hit would bring in about $15 million, and if we get one, publishers will be lining up to buy us. We'll be able to ask for two to four times sales to be bought out."

One of the longer dances with bigger companies took an unex-pected turn late that summer. Walt Disney Imagineering had sent an engineer, Avi Bar-Zeev, up to Zombie during the winter to look the company over. Bar-Zeev had graduated from Ohio State University in 1992, worked at Seattle's Worldesign, a company founded by former HIT lab associate director Bob Jacobson, until 1994, then had gone to work for Disney. He worked on Disney's first forays into virtual reality, serving as lead engineer on the com-pany's *Aladdin* ride—a "ride" in which the Disney "guest" (as the company calls its visitors) puts on a huge VR helmet (suspended from cables, it looked rather like the primitive, monstrous helmet designed by Tom Furness's team in the VCASS system), grips tracker-equipped controls that look like bicycle handles, then nav-igates through the world of the movie *Aladdin*, encountering three-dimensional characters along the way. (The user also flies past a bar at one point, its sign alternately flashing the words "Bar" and "Zeev.")

Bar-Zeev was eager to visit Seattle again, as he and F5's Mike Almquist were friends, having dreamed and brainstormed together during Bar-Zeev's time at Worldesign. The two had been discussing for months the possibility either of Bar-Zeev hiring Almquist at

Disney or of Almquist hiring Bar-Zeev if he secured funding for F5 Labs.

In any event, Bar-Zeev went back to Disney with a hearty endorsement for Zombie, and Disney accordingly called Alexander the following June, swore her to secrecy, then asked if Zombie would be willing to work on a VR ride that the company wanted to include in a new Disney location-based entertainment venture. To be called DisneyQuest, the venture was to launch simultaneously in eight different U.S. cities in the spring of 1998. The Disney outlets were to be glorified video arcades, with a variety of games, including one in which the player would step into a booth, design his or her own roller-coaster ride, store the ride on a card, then climb into a "motion pod" and "ride" the roller coaster he or she had just designed. The pod would be capable of turning 360 degrees, horizontally and vertically, and the rider would fly through a world, or worlds, that had been selected in the composition booth.

For Long and Alexander, the Disney offer was a colossal break. "I mean, we're doing a *ride for Disney*," Long said at a meeting announcing the deal. "It's a huge breakthrough for us." He was less excited over the money the contract would bring—although, at more than $1 million over the course of the next twelve months, it was far and away Zombie's biggest and best contract—than he was by the meaning of Disney's faith in Zombie. "The buzz on our company right now is pretty good," he said excitedly to his troops. "We're becoming known for good engineering and innovative work. You should just be proud of what we're doing. Most companies are dominated by men—we're more representative, and I honestly think that's why we're better. As long as we keep doing what we want, we'll be great!"

When the HIT lab's Rich Johnston checked his e-mail one morning in June 1996, he found a detailed missive from Microvision's Steve Willey outlining the elements of an impending deal with Microsoft. It was the first Johnston had heard of any Microvision dealings with Microsoft, and he was strangely unexcited. Anyone else looking at the mail would have thought the company had finally gotten a long-sought break—part of every Seattle start-up's secret dream plan, after all, is to make a deal with, or be bought out by, Microsoft—but Johnston saw it as yet another example of Willey's rich and confusing fantasy life. Willey apparently believed he could build a head-mounted display in eighteen months without benefit of an engineering and manufacturing facility of his own. "I don't know what this is about," Johnston said, looking the mail over and tossing it aside dismissively. "Probably doesn't mean a thing."

Indeed, Microsoft never showed up for a VRD demonstration, and Johnston was never to hear from Willey about the "work" in connection with Microsoft again.

It now was near the end of the third year of Microvision's contract with the HIT lab, and the company's business operations consisted entirely of such false leads. For all of Willey's hints, boasts, and pronouncements that one deal or another was in the offing, Microvision had yet to sign a corporate partner or deal of any kind with anyone, and Furness and the VRD team had lost all faith in the company's ability ever to do so. Furness, Johnston, and Mike Tidwell had heard Willey talk at various times about pending deals with nearly every big electronics company in the world, and by now Willey's pronouncements had become the group's favorite running joke.

Not that the joke always elicited laughter. Assertions like those in Willey's e-mail generally sent Mike Tidwell into fits of apoplexy. "They've got this pattern," he said when I showed him the message. "They say they're going to do something, and they get all excited about it, and they say it's going really well, and they say it's a done deal, and then they say, 'Oh, well, there's one catch.' Then they say, 'It's not going too great.' Then it doesn't happen. They've done that a million times. There was a Korean investor, a semiconductor company, Philips, Sony, military contracts that they said were in the bag. . . . 'We're gonna do this contract! We're gonna do this at this show! We've been told by Colonel So-and-So that it's going to happen! We've got the money . . . it's on the way . . . well, there's this one hitch . . . we can't make this deadline . . . oh, it won't happen. . . .' These guys the whole time we've been here have not pulled one thing off. It's just fucking pathetic."

Tidwell had other reasons to be angry at Microvision. He had been asking for months for their permission to allow him to publish his master's thesis—entitled "A Virtual Retinal Display for Augmenting Ambient Visual Environments," it was a scientific description of the VRD color system he had worked on with Melville and the rest of Johnston's team—on the World Wide Web. At first Willey had refused permission, then said he would discuss it further, then stopped returning Tidwell's calls and e-mail messages. "Our culture," said a sympathetic Tom Furness, "is that you get things published, out in the open, and your professional reputation is based on your publications. But companies want to keep everything secret. They want to be close to the vest, do the trade secret bit, and so that causes tension."

In the case of Tidwell, it caused not only tension but rage. Adhering to the letter of his contract with Microvision and counting on Willey's inability to follow through on negotiations, he had sent Willey a letter telling him he intended to publish his thesis in thirty days. If Willey did not answer, he believed, he had the right to go ahead and publish it. "I'm going to publish it as soon as the time runs out," he said. "And that's not going to be the half of it. A lot of what I'm going to do over the next year while I'm at the university is publish everything I know about the VRD. They're not going to like it, but tough shit for them—it's their choice. I'm going to get some professional advantage out of the work that I've done. I'm not going to let it go undone."

He was coming unhinged not only over the company's attempt to censor him but also at the increasing number of distressing signs that Microvision was running out of money and might not be able to continue funding his position. For the past year, Microvision routinely had been late with its quarterly payments, often rushing to the lab with a check on the twenty-ninth day past the payment due date—one day before full-fledged default, which would have resulted in the voiding of the Microvision-HIT lab contract. Each late payment left those living on Microvision's money anxious about their future. Each late payment also set off a series of reactions from the university hierarchy, including letters sent to Microvision notifying the company that it was on the verge of breaching its contract; calls to Furness from university administrators and lawyers demanding an explanation; and increasing unhappiness from Furness's landlord, the Washington Technology Center, which was growing more and more disenchanted not only with Microvision but with the researcher and lab that had brought the company into contact with the university. "Now the university has decided that these guys don't know what they're doing," Furness said. "Before, the university was letting us go on our merry way and do our work and things like that. But now Microvision has awakened a sleeping giant. Now all these people up and down the chain of command are looking at us, and the more Microvision tries to explain itself to everybody, the more everybody just thinks they're incompetent."

This was proving to be doubly depressing for Furness. Not only was the company all but destroying his chances of moving what he called his "life's work" into the mainstream, but Microvision also was destroying his reputation at the University of Washington. More and more often, his superiors at the Washington Technology Center and at the University of Washington's executive offices were asking pointed questions about the HIT lab and Microvision, and it was clear to Furness that he was growing tainted by his association with the company.

Occasionally, in my largely futile attempts to learn from Willey and Rutkowski why they kept proceeding in such an apparently suicidal fashion, I would manage to break through their paranoia and cadge a strategic observation or two from them. These grudging glimpses into the Microvision world usually were afforded me in the context of allusions to pending "deals" with investors or corporate partners, followed by apologies from Willey and Rutkowski for their inability to be more forthcoming.

From what I could tell, their mandate was a muddled mix of seeking publicity and maintaining secrecy. On the one hand, Willey professed to want no one anywhere to know what Microvision had in the works. Ideally, he and Rutkowski would work in secret for years, then suddenly would leap into the market with, Willey said, "the patents in place, with the prototypes not only working but tested, and third party independent tested, and so on, and you put it on the table in front of these very large entities that would like nothing more than to eat you alive and take your patents, and you say, 'Well, you've got a decision to make. We're either going to compete with you in the market, we're a company of twenty to thirty people, but guess what? We've got seven patents, we've got something that's working today, we will be in the market within a year, with any one of your competitors or with you. Or, more likely, with you *and* one of your competitors.' "

This was not the scenario the company had been living, however. Years in advance of the day when they would have a workforce that large, a product working and tested, and any patents at all, Willey and Rutkowski were making presentations to anyone who would sign a nondisclosure form and listen to their spiel. By mid-1996, they had made presentations to Sony, Fujitsu, Sharp, Thomson Multimedia, and hundreds of other companies—nearly everyone in the world, in other words, that could conceivably mount a competitive threat.

This risk of exposure brought them absolutely nothing by way of financial return. Their fund-raising history was a grim tale of rejection and descent through various levels of investor, from the most preferable to the least preferable.

Objections from sought-after investors fell into three categories. Many venture capitalists refused to invest in hardware enterprises of any kind, as the manufacturing costs were too high, the time between investment and market return—should there ever be any—too long, and the chance of any legitimately viable hardware market being taken over by Japanese conglomerates too certain. Thus Richard Novotny, the EnCompass Group investment officer who sat on the board of F5 Labs, barely gave the Microvision proposal a look, saying, "I try to stay away from the hardware side." Jim Bromley, from Dain Bosworth, Inc., gave voice to an attitude typical among investors: "The technology just looks to be too far out there. VCs usually want to turn their investment around more quickly."

Others felt that the Microvision business model was untenable and too vaguely defined. The company business plan presented to prospective investors in 1996 was full of holes and warning signs, not the least of which was an "Organization Chart," entitled "The Product Development/Management Structure," with twenty-two slots in it. Only two of the slots—"R. Rutkowski, CEO," and "S. Willey, Executive VP"—were occupied by humans. The rest, from "VP Operations" to "Sales Engineer 2" were empty. "I looked at their business plan and declined," said a terse Tom Alberg, a VP at McCaw Cellular who had retired when that company was bought out by AT&T, then gone on to found the Madrona Group, a venture capital firm in Seattle. He was particularly dubious about Microvision's intent to serve as a licensing rather than a manufacturing company.

Many financiers, particularly in Seattle, were more leery of Microvision's people than of its technology, noting that the "management" of the company didn't seem to know what it was doing. Jeff Hussey, the investment banker from A.H. Capital who cofounded F5 Labs with Mike Almquist, also gave a characteristically hyperbolic expression to a widely held stateside bias: "You know what the definition of a Canadian stock is, don't you?" he asked rhetorically when I asked him about Microvision. He was referring to the rather rich history of fraud in the Canadian oil and mineral mining markets. "It's a hole in the ground surrounded by liars!"

Willey, Rutkowski, and Todd McIntyre, who joined the company in 1996 as its "Vice President of Business Development and Director of Marketing," circled the globe in search of money, making pitches in the United States, Europe, Taiwan, Korea, Japan, and a host of other places. They started out courting venture capitalists, then smaller private investors, all the while seeking out electronics hardware and software companies, agencies of the U.S. Defense Department, and various American defense contractors in search of licensing agreements and research contracts.

Finally, in mid-1996, after three years of almost nonstop fundraising attempts, Rutkowski, traveling with McIntyre, hit what he saw as the end of the road. The two had just finished a futile pitch to an investor in New York City, and they returned to their hotel suite to mull over their lack of options. After having exhausted every investment avenue in the world, their company had turned up not a single investor or partner; having spent $7.7 million over the last three years, they were down to their last $500,000.

Rutkowski turned to McIntyre and told him that the company had only one option left: to try an IPO.

If a company's stature were measured by the number of deals it had pending that ultimately fell through, Microvision would have been looking with immeasurable envy at Virtual i/O. The best thing that happened to Virtual i/O in 1996 was the settlement of its lawsuit with Forte—and even that was a mixed blessing. While terms of the settlement—which was reached early in May, the day before the trial proper was to begin—were sealed by the court, which also enjoined the participants from discussing it with any-one, they did include onerous royalty payments by Virtual i/O to Forte. And with the course its business was taking, Virtual i/O had no cash to spare. The lawsuit had racked up legal bills totaling more than $500,000, the market for its product was shrinking rather than growing, and the company's investors were loath to ad-vance Amadon and Rhoads any more money.

In a series of press releases over the latter half of 1995, Virtual i/O had announced distribution deal after distribution deal for its headsets. By year's end, the Gamer! and i-Glasses! were being sold in seven national retail outlets, including Egghead Software, In-credible Universe, Circuit City, and FAO Schwarz, at seven other regional outlets, through three different catalog companies, and were being distributed by two companies in the United States, three more in Canada, and by industry giant Escom AG in Europe. One by one, though, the retailers dropped the headsets, as the ef-fort involved in selling them was too high, sales were too low, and return rates, at 50 percent, were unacceptably high. By March 1996, Virtual i/O had no remaining contracts with retailers, and was trying desperately to put together a deal with Blockbuster Video to rent headsets through Blockbuster outlets; even worse, Escom AG, which had ordered thousands of i-Glasses! with the in-tention of bundling them with personal computers sold in Europe, entered bankruptcy reorganization, owing Virtual i/O hundreds of thousands of dollars.

Virtual i/O fared just as dismally on the corporate partnership front. In addition to the failed Sega partnership, deals with Microsoft, Time Warner, and Sony all failed to materialize. Company president Linden Rhoads had been particularly excited about the possibility of a deal with Sony that would bundle the Gamer! with Sony's PlayStation, and it was a source of considerable—if unacknowledged—frustration for her that Virtual i/O could not get Sony to finalize a contract.

By spring of 1996, Virtual i/O management had shifted, however unconsciously, from trying to create and dominate a new market to trying desperately to come up with a miracle that would turn the company fortunes around. Instead of gradually growing the head-mounted-display market, Rhoads and Amadon started looking for a quick hit—a deal or discovery that would reverse the company's fortunes overnight.

This search was advanced on two fronts, one being the search for a partnership or distribution deal that would turn Virtual i/O's headsets into immediate best-sellers. The second front involved the search for a killer app or new product that would instantaneously make the head-mounted display a mainstream device.

I took it as a sign of Virtual i/O's growing desperation that the technologies Rhoads was pinning her hopes on seemed rather implausible. Early in 1996, in her conversations with me, she enthusiastically detailed two vehicles toward salvation, the first being a killer app that Rhoads described as "a way of stereo-izing content much the same way that Ted Turner colorized content." This application was a near-miraculous method of turning standard video images into three-dimensional images like those viewers see through two-colored 3D glasses. "We've found a really effective 3D TV conversion technology, which in real time could convert anything you put through it to 3D," Rhoads said excitedly. This technology apparently worked by simultaneously displaying adjacent frames in a video strip to different eyes, with the result that the viewer saw a three-dimensional image. "It looks about eighty percent as good as real 3D," Rhoads continued. "And to some extent, it *is* real 3D. It's a technique that takes advantage, sort of harvests out the naturally occurring stereo pairs in video, so you're not seeing the frames in sequence, but together, in naturally occurring stereo pairs. It's kind of 'pseudoscopic.' You have to have technology that knows which way the motion is going so that it knows how to do things to maintain the stereo illusion. A very large Japanese electronics company came up with a box that does this very, very well. They can get eighty percent of the 3D effect that you would get in natural stereo."

Her company's plan, she said, was to work in partnership with TCI and Thomson Multimedia, who would install these boxes at the broadcast end of the broadcaster-viewer connection, making it possible for viewers with i-Glasses! to watch standard programming in 3D. The existence of 3D channels would create an insatiable demand for Virtual i/O's head-mounted displays. "So our two biggest investors are also the biggest cable and satellite content distribution providers, which means that if they hook up this box at the head end, at what you call the point of origin, or the point of origination of content, basically they can have 3D channels immediately, and if you have glasses, then you can get the channels in 3D. And you take away the chicken and egg problem because you instantaneously have a very large base of, library of 3D content that you can use, anything in fact, and that will encourage people like the Discovery channel, whose CEO had already decided that they should go gung ho on this, to start doing true 3D on the channel. And so it looks like we're going to be able to do that, and everyone's very much on board, because it really looks amazing."

I kept trying to imagine the consuming masses going bonkers over 3D television, but couldn't quite conjure up the image. Not only did it seem to me that changing the look of television's "stage" would hardly drive millions to buy head-mounted displays, it also seemed to me that Rhoads's vagueness—she tended not to name collaborators, and it was always impossible to verify from companies she did name that the partnership deals she was hyping were actually in the works—was the classic imprecision of a common figure in the high-tech world: the relentless promoter whose success stories are more wishful than real.

Rhoads was similarly obscure and ecstatic about a product under development that she expected to be coming on the market in November 1996: a portable computer with goggles in place of a screen, and with a foldable keyboard, CPU, and cellular phone attachment. This machine, she said, would be small enough to be carried in the user's pocket, would run on standard AA batteries, would be wirelessly connected to the Internet, and would weigh only a few ounces. Virtual i/O, she said, was working in partnership with several large PC manufacturers who had been persuaded by company focus-group tests that business travelers wanted a lightweight, cellular, portable PC that could afford the user greater privacy in public places than could a standard laptop. She showed me a prototype of the device: A pair of eyeglasses with tiny optics attached, it displayed a large, if faint, image of a computer screen, and it was surprisingly easy to look through this image while typing on its keyboard.

As 1996 wore on, though, Rhoads grew more and more evasive whenever I asked her about progress on the "screenless portable." Originally scheduled to be announced at the November COMDEX—the computer industry's huge biannual trade show—it was, she said at various times, "a little behind schedule," "probably going to be delayed," "being slipped back to early next year. . . ."

Finally, I asked Deep Bile about the gadget, and got a scornful reply: "It's a wank." The computer project proved to be plagued with problems, ranging from the near impossibility of moving beyond the crude prototype stage to increasingly violent disputes between Rhoads and Amadon and the project's lead engineer, ex-Apple engineer Steve Bailey. There proved to be hundreds of issues, both large and small, that stood in the way of developing the company prototype into a reliable and useful product. New inventions were required everywhere along the line, from optics that could deliver a VGA-quality image to wireless electrical connections to integrated circuits and cell phone/computer linkages. Bailey kept trying to explain that the project was unrealistic—the display issues alone, he insisted, were more than Virtual i/O could manage, and it was more or less insane to expect a display company to take on all these other problems and solve them in a matter of months.

Finally, Bailey grew weary of fighting Amadon and Rhoads, and left the company.

While Rhoads kept breezily assuring me that Virtual i/O was thriving, there were clear indications that it was floundering. The HIT lab's engineers, who seemed constantly to have one eye on job postings in Seattle newspapers, noticed a definite pattern to the listings: Every three months or so, Virtual i/O would be advertising for the same engineering posts it had advertised and filled three months before. Bailey, it was apparent, was part of a general, recurring series of exoduses from the company. Rumors kept surfacing that whole shifts of contract laborers hired to assemble headsets were being laid off, and each time I visited company headquarters, I could see that more and more space had been vacated. At its height, Virtual i/O employed 120 and had two shifts of contractors assembling headsets; now, it seemed, all the contractors had been laid off, and it looked to me as if the full-time workforce was down to fifty or fewer.

At the same time, the voice of Deep Bile grew louder and louder as the chorus of ex-employees grew in size. The more dire company sales and balance sheets looked, the more panicked company management grew. "The panic was there from day one," Deep Bile said. "It's one thing to be in panic at the tail end of the company, where it's like, 'Holy shit, we have to bring in two million bucks or the door's gonna close!' But this constant panic . . . they seemed to live on it, to *like* it whenever a project was behind schedule. People are working long hours, there's that adrenaline rush, 'I'm getting as much as I can out of my employees, look how hard they're working, it's two o'clock in the morning and they're still here!' "

The panic manifested itself not only in the constant demands made on employees to work longer and harder, but in the constant indecision and changes in strategic direction. As soon as sales of a given product fell below projections—and they always did, as the projections were based on how much money the company needed rather than on how much it could be expected to make, given a realistic assessment of the market—Rhoads and Amadon would abandon it and lead their employees in a different direction. "If you believe in the product," said Deep Bile, "you need to stick with it for a while, because it's a new market and a new concept. But every month there would be a new product that would attempt to be introduced. And so you would have people rush at a breakneck pace, put in tons of hours to come up with a new product that was not feasible or was flawed. And it would be the same thing on the sales path. One month we'd be going to go retail, retail, retail! It can take close to six months to get good relationships with retailers. But it would be one month into that effort and they'd say, 'Close down all the retail, we're going to go direct sales, set up a bunch of phone lines, eight-hundred numbers. . . .' And that wouldn't work because you have to submit your eight-hundred number ads to magazines three months in advance, so a month later they'd be screaming, 'Nobody's calling the phones—we're going to go back to retail!' That went on forever, every month."

It seemed that no decision at Virtual i/O came easily, and every layer of complication brought with it layer upon layer of added expense. "They wanted to meet with some distributors in Singapore once," one Deep Bile story went. It was cited as a typical example of how company decisions were made. "But they changed their minds at the last minute, decided they weren't going to go. But then an hour later, they decided they *were* going to go. Now instead of calling up the guy in Singapore and saying, 'We're going to be a day late because we have to rebook our flights because we missed them,' they flew from here to Vancouver to Chicago to New York to England to Cairo to Hong Kong to Singapore to get there. That was more enjoyable to them because that was the big panic rush, 'We have to get it done!' It was a buzz that they would get, always running around in a big panic. They were addicted to the panic, the rush, that adrenaline of people running around. They kept trying to walk that line between being really aggressive and trying to get things done, and being fucking wacko."

Savvy employees learned to evade Rhoads and Amadon's last-minute requests for trips to far-off ports of call. One unlucky middle manager was sent to Paris on a day's notice, then forced to cool his heels there for a week because Virtual i/O couldn't, or wouldn't, arrange for his flight home. After that, a favorite tactic among Rhoads and Amadon's subordinates was to let their passports lapse. "I can't go!" they would say in mock sorrow when asked to fly to Europe or Asia on a few hours' notice. "I don't have a passport!"

With sales at a standstill and product development spinning its wheels, Rhoads and Amadon decided that the key to turning Virtual i/O's fortunes around was to get their employees to work harder. One e-mail memo defined the Virtual i/O workday as running from eight A.M. to six P.M. at a minimum, and the workweek as being six or seven days long. Rhoads and Amadon insisted that people work on holidays in return for added vacation days that somehow never materialized. Engineers and product leads would get calls from a panicked Amadon at two or three in the morning, demanding answers to questions.

Rhoads and Amadon tried compensating their employees for this treatment in odd, short-lived ways. They would print T-shirts with motivational slogans, the slogans directed at particular projects or departments ("Operations—Summer '96: QSC—Meet the Goal!"). "There was the Employee of the Month program," Deep Bile recalled, "which was literally *the* Employee of *the* Month. It was never repeated. There were a lot of things like that. One time there was a bounty—if you got somebody hired you would get a bounty—but that only lasted for a month. Friday-night beer parties would come and go. One month, it would be, 'We're going to have a Friday-night beer thing at the office.' That would start at four, and everybody would go home by four-thirty. They just didn't want to be there. So that would happen once every two or three months. And there was the bagels-with-the-president initiative. If you wanted to meet with Linden in an informal way but not have to make an appointment, every Monday morning she would have bagels and we could go in her office and eat bagels and talk. That happened twice."

Bagels, for some reason, emerged as a kind of precious currency at Virtual i/O. In an attempt to get employees to put in ever-longer hours, Rhoads and Amadon instituted a "free bagels" policy for anyone who would arrive for work at seven A.M. This actually worked for a while—until company managers started telephoning ahead to "reserve" a bagel rather than coming in on time to claim one. Before long, employees would arrive at seven, ask for one of the bagels they could see sitting under watchful guard on the table in the company lunchroom, only to be told that the remaining bagels were all reserved for managers who would be coming in later.

Summer 1996 saw Tom Furness begin a long psychological and physical decline. It seemed that defeat was beginning to close in on him from every direction, and he often found himself contemplating the unthinkable—closing down his lab and giving up his lifelong quest. "There are days when I say, 'Why am I doing this?' " he would suddenly say. "I can do fine at the university by just doing what other professors do and get paid the same amount and that kind of thing. Why am I doing this?" Other times, visibly depressed, his voice barely audible, he would mutter, more in anger than resignation, "Maybe there's a useful lifetime, half-life, of the HIT lab. At which point it's time to move on and do some other things."

The truth was, Furness was exhausted. Nearly seven years after having opened his lab, he was beginning to realize that he had been working from the start more or less around the clock, with most of his time spent trying to raise money. Now he was being forced to face the fact that he was no more financially secure than he had been the day he first opened his doors. It had been a struggle from the beginning to keep his lab operating, but the struggle had been made to seem deceptively easy for the past four years because of two large contracts—one from the Air Force Office of Strategic Research, the other from Microvision—that underwrote almost his entire operation. Now both of those contracts were due to run out during the next year, and Furness had no big moneymakers lined up to replace them.

This is not to say that the lab's reputation was declining. Both the VRD and AFOSR projects were generating scores of research papers by graduate students and other researchers that heightened interest in the lab around the world. Lab scientist Suzanne Weghorst and her group were drawing attention from doctors and medical equipment companies to her research into interfaces for "virtual emergency rooms" and "surgical simulators" that someday would allow doctors to diagnose injuries and illnesses, and even operate surgical robots, from remote locations through virtual-world interfaces. Another graduate student, Dace Campbell, was drawing attention to his Blocksmith project, with which an architect wearing a data glove and head-mounted display could enter a "virtual design studio," where he or she could build virtual structures from which computers extrapolated blueprints for construction of physical buildings.

None of these things could draw big money, however, and Furness felt that his lab was on the verge of bankruptcy. Then his resultant depression was deepened by a decision, made by the Washington Technology Center board, that he regarded as a nearly fatal stab in the back. Every year, the WTC had budgeted $250,000 or so in discretionary money for Furness to use on experimental projects—ideas that had no corporate funding but that he believed showed promise. Because money given to the lab by corporations was allotted to specific projects showing some promise of short-term profitable return, the WTC money was the only money Furness had available each year for his true love: pure research into high-risk notions whose payoff might be years or decades away. Now the WTC, in decreeing that the HIT lab had had more than its share of such gifts and must survive on its own from now on, was taking away the care and feeding of his best and most visionary projects. "My Lord," Furness said when he first heard the news, "this is the money that funds our best work!" Over the years, he had funded Hunter Hoffman's acrophobia project, Dace Campbell's Blocksmith project, Mike Almquist's burning-building demo, the VRD project, the Parkinson's disease treatment, and countless other experiments with this money. "The VRD would never have been started if it hadn't been for this seed money."

He saw the board's decision as a sign that the world in general was losing interest in virtual reality. More and more, it seemed, funding decisions were a matter of fashion, with the people who controlled purse strings constantly chasing after new trends in research before old ones were given a chance to produce results. "What do I do now?" Furness asked. "What's next? It'd be so easy to just go where the money is. I mean, we could continue to sell ourselves as a warm-body operation to various government clients, do a little piece of work here, a little piece of work there, but we'd be selling ourselves short. Where we can really make a contribution is with an agenda, where we can see this next wave and start work preparing for it. But we need to have people to buy into that kind of vision. And if they don't buy into it, you have your own funding that you take the risk and invest anyhow."

For years now, he had been dreaming of beginning work on a full-blown "VR workstation," and had been hoping to begin soon on preliminary research funded with WTC seed money. "If I could, I would be working on this VR workstation that would involve hardware technology that would let you interact intuitively with this three-dimensional surround world, but also with the software tool kits that would let you author worlds rapidly as well as distribute them efficiently, communicate between distributed virtual worlds, and in the process do the human-factors work, make sure it doesn't get people sick. I think that a virtual terminal is going to be the future. One that is intuitive and easy for people to make use of. It would sort of be a multimedia version of my supercockpit program that I did at Wright-Patterson. It would be the thing after multimedia—*Supermedia*. We'd have this collection, this family of modules that would basically elevate us to another realm substantially in terms of, 'How do you get in and out of the brain?' That's what I'd really like to work on."

There would be no chance of that, though, without his seed funding, as no corporation responsible to its investors could afford the luxury of a twenty-year-long project with an uncertain outcome. "The problem is that companies that fund hardware development are so short term," Furness lamented, "and their margins are getting much smaller. Compaq, for example, is not going to invest in something that takes years to produce results."

Furness's summer was spent largely in meetings where he labored to stretch smaller and smaller dollar amounts further and further. Whenever I dropped into his office, it seemed that I heard variations on the same theme:

"Okay, Jon's going to have to hustle some of that money up himself. . . . So . . . thirty K . . . that's twenty percent of Suzanne for six months, three months for Paul. . . . That'll buy us a little time. And I can fund Sisinio by taking a little bit of our WTC money from our infrastructure pot and fund him half time for the summer. . . . I'm worried about all the students we're losing because we don't have funding to keep them. . . ."

The financial stress might have been bearable had Furness been able to see that his work in the lab was beginning to make a difference outside of it. But whenever he looked for signs of a HIT lab legacy in the industrial sector, he saw only failure. Every one of the state's VR businesses—some of which Furness had directly helped start, others of which were indirectly trying to help carry on his dream—was either a flop or on the brink of becoming one. There were days now when the vision he had brought with him to Seattle seemed laughable when measured against its results. Furness fell to brooding more and more about his disappointment, with his moods occasionally lapsing into uncharacteristic, outright bitterness. "Virtual Vision," he said one day, as if looking back over a quest he had abandoned, "was our 'great white hope,' so to speak, to really launch the industry in Washington. They were gonna crank those displays out like crazy, people were just going to buy 'em like crazy . . . and we ran into this classical problem that Virtual i/O and others are finding: *that you have to have something to do with it.*" He was particularly depressed to see that his Virtual Vision experience, rather than being an anomaly by virtue of having failed, was emerging as one of his more successful adventures—especially when measured against his ongoing Microvision travails.

It was proving impossible to have a conversation with Furness without his digressing into lamentations about Microvision. "They don't have a clue how to do anything," he said after one particularly infuriating meeting with Steve Willey. "It seems like they just bounce from one thing to another. For example, this whole business about . . . they've been encouraging us to build a see-through helmet-mounted display. But they keep changing the design specifications! The problem is they don't understand what the trade-off issues are. It's like they're shooting from the hip all the time. And I think that basically it's just that they don't know! They don't have any experience!"

Now that Microvision was beginning to plan an IPO, Furness had begun allowing himself to think that stock in the company might actually be worth something—at least until the investment community began finding out the horrible truth about Microvision and its management—and the possibility had him fixating on his belief that Steve Willey and Rick Rutkowski had cheated him out of equity in the company.

When Microvision was first set up and its founders were trying to find more investors, the H Group had enlisted the aid of Furness in making presentations to potential sources of money. In return for his work, they had split the company stock four ways—25 percent each for the three members of the H Group, and 25 percent for Furness. "It was a handshake deal," Furness said. "Then, after a while, I sort of asked them about this, and they'd say, 'Oh, don't worry—it's gonna happen soon.' They just kept promising to put it in writing." Eventually, Rutkowski took over control of the company, and the three original investors were shunted aside. "And here those shares are sitting there and Rick Rutkowski can't stand my guts," Furness said. "And he isn't going to do anything to get those shares to me." As more time went on, and as it became undeniably clear that Rutkowski and Willey were determined not to give him his stock, Furness grew more bitter. Even if the shares proved to be worth only a few dollars each, they figured to add up to a substantial dollar amount coming to him, as he was supposed to have been given them for free. "These were *shares*, not options." The more he pondered the slight, the more valuable the shares grew in his mind, and the more outraged he felt. "So here I am, after all this time, and I'm going to come out with *zero shares*. And I see all these clowns that are on the board of directors—where do all these guys come from? I mean, I see another one of my babies going to the dogs."

Furness's feeling about this stock were complicated. On the one hand, his religion taught him to be indifferent to material wealth. On the other, he had put more into the company than had all sorts of "freeloaders"—as he had come to call the investors who had been granted substantial shares of stock for their money but who had put no work into the invention or the company—and he felt on principle that he should be rewarded for his ingenuity, his labors, his faith, and his generosity. It was as if someone had sneaked into his head and stolen his life's work, and with each passing day the situation seemed to eat away at him even more. "Microvision," he said heatedly one day, "is probably the worst experience of my life."

He alternated between brooding about the company and fighting off panic about the future of the HIT lab. He had no deals in the offing on the scale of the two that were winding down. Whenever he sat down with the lab's executive committee to go over future projects, he would find himself listing an array of "warmbody-operation" projects, none for more than $50,000, and none lasting longer than one year. And many of those were uncertain enough to shake even Furness's inveterate optimism. At one meeting, he wrote out a list of twenty pending projects, until someone interrupted with a question:

"These are done deals, right?"

"Well . . ."

In the midst of all this turmoil came a final and crushing development: Max Wells, the lab's associate director, announced that he wanted to launch a start-up company. Although Wells also wanted to hedge his bets by staying on at the HIT lab, Furness was sure that university rules would not permit him to remain in the lab if he intended to spin off lab technology into a private venture. Furness had brought Wells to Seattle a few years after he established the HIT lab, and he had always hoped that someday Wells would succeed him as lab director. "Max is a dear friend, a soul brother," he said, "and I've invested in him as associate director of the lab. He's *my guy;* I brought him in. I had high hopes that he would really get into this and enjoy it, basically take over for me when I leave, so that there would be a legacy here that can continue on, rather than just be a professor's lab. Now, when I leave, it's sort of all over."

Looking back over the lab's history in light of Wells's announcement, it seemed to Furness that he was always being abandoned by people he had invested in emotionally, worked together with, and turned on to VR technology. Part of the problem, he thought, was the entrepreneurial spirit in the lab, which seemed to infect people with a powerful start-up virus. But a bigger part was the lab's lack of money, which prevented him from setting people up in career-track research positions. "It seems like everything we do here is a new journey. Typically what happens is we have a group of people come into the lab, get excited about the technology, then look around, thinking, 'You know, there's probably not a whole lot of future here for me.' These people get all turned on, and we've got this entrepreneurial spirit, we've got folks coming in, talking deals all the time with them, and it pervades the whole lab. There's this spirit that's in the lab of an industrial connection and going out and seeking your fortune. I think we accept the fact that we're a breeding ground for these kinds of entrepreneurs."

He saw Wells's decision as the latest and most devastating in a series of similar events that stretched back over his entire career. He had been betrayed when politics had taken his beloved Wright-Patterson laboratory away from him; he had been betrayed by William Bricken; a number of beloved students and researchers— Mike Almquist, in particular—had left the lab furious at him (although he and Almquist had effected a reconciliation of sorts, and Furness now sat on the board of Almquist's new company); his overseers at the Washington Technology Center now were betraying him by taking away the sole source of seed funding for his grandest visions; and now he felt deserted by the man he had groomed to stand shoulder to shoulder with him, share his dreams, and eventually succeed him and carry his vision on to fulfillment.

Furness was sitting at a small table in the university's faculty club when he was ruminating about all this. His monologue was punctuated by long, emotional silences, during which he stared down at the table, slowly stirring his raspberry seltzer, the ice cubes in it having long since melted away. The club was empty save for a waiter leaning against the bar, reading a newspaper, and one old man sitting on a couch nursing a midday Scotch and water.

"So you know what will happen here," Furness said at last, as if picking up the predominant theme in his professional life, "is that I will be out there all by myself again. It's really lonely."

The Visionary Position

IN MAY 1996, Microvision began its arduous forced march toward a late-August IPO on the NASDAQ Stock Exchange. The effort called for Rutkowski, Willey, and McIntyre to make yet another round of presentations, this time to stock portfolio managers, investment houses, market analysts, and others in the financial-markets industry. Among the points they had to cover in their presentations were the likely first products in the retinal-scanning markets, the overall market potential for that category of products, who would buy them, and how much intellectual property (the patents, for example, on Melville's scanner) the company had locked up. Their audiences also expected to be able to examine a working prototype. "Among the typical questions," a laughing Todd McIntyre said to me one day, "is, 'How do you evaluate a company with no meaningful earnings stream?' "

Indeed, at nearly any other time in history it would have seemed an insane notion to believe that a company with no product, no manufacturing plant, and virtually no employees could declare a dollar value for itself, set a price for its stock, and start trading on the market. But the stock market at the time was breaking every rule that had forever governed investor behavior. The market in 1996 would see 244 high-tech IPOs, raising $13 billion. Investors and speculators were bidding the price of technology stocks so high in proportion to their company's assets that there seemed no longer to be any caution, skepticism, or care holding these gamblers back from placing irrational and extravagant bets. Initial public offerings—the introduction to public trading of a privately held company's shares—seemed particularly prone to outrageously high valuations, turning those who held shares before trading began into instant millionaires.

Of course, McIntyre's question was easy for the HIT lab's VRD researchers to answer. The more they learned about Microvision's plans—and information was hard to come by, as the company's managers communicated with the lab as little as possible—the more jaundiced they grew. Mike Tidwell in particular was incensed at the inability of Rutkowski and Willey to understand the technical limitations of the VRD, particularly as they related to the size of any potential product's display system. Rutkowski had decided that one of Microvision's first products should be a "video-fax" display built into a cellular telephone, so that business travelers could receive faxes wherever they were, through their cell phone, without having to hook it up to a computer or fax machine. Tidwell tried to explain to Rutkowski that it would be impossible to put a VRD inside a cell phone. The VRD's intermediate image plane, various other tricks required to increase the scan angle, and the diffusion grating that had to be incorporated into the optics in order to expand the exit pupil all made that optical system so large that it would probably double the size of a cell phone. No one, he argued, would prefer a huge cellular telephone over a pocket-sized one for the ability, which they would rarely need, to read a fax on it. Better, he said, to make the display unit a separate, detachable component that could be plugged into the phone as needed, particularly as a cellular phone user would get no more than one call out of ten requiring fax attachment.

"Mike," Rutkowski said condescendingly, "your arguments are way off base. We have information from cellular phone marketing people saying that forty percent of wireless transmission five years from now is going to be data communication, not voice. And we think our model is right on. It makes a lot more sense for us to capture that early adopter market." By 2001, he believed—and this belief was faithfully recorded in the Microvision business plan—the early adopter market would amount to 125,000 such phones sold, at $600 each.

Recalling the conversation later, a livid Tidwell said, "I'm thinking, 'Oh, that's great! Unless you develop a new scanner in the next two years, that's all you're going to get—early adopters.' He's telling me that for every 1.5 times you make a telephone call on a cell phone, you're going to get a video fax on your VRD cell phone. It's bullshit—it isn't going to happen! I'm just suggesting that it would be better to have something you pull out of your briefcase and plug in. But, of course, it just pissed him off, because I'm not the businessman, I'm not the marketer, I'm just the engineer! Just because they hadn't thought of it—that was the main problem with the idea. I can't work for somebody like that! Fuck him!"

Unfortunately, Tidwell desperately wanted to be able to work for Rutkowski, and a great deal of his anger was due to the troubled negotiations he and others had had with Rutkowski and Willey over the potential shift of the VRD team from the HIT lab to Microvision as the lab began "handing off" technology to the company. Having invested three years of his life in developing VRD optics, Tidwell was loath to let it go. He wanted to take the technology as far as it could be taken, and the only way he could do that was to follow it to Microvision. Steve Willey had let it be known in mid-1995 that he wanted to start transferring lab researchers to Microvision as soon as the company could raise more money to fund the building of lab facilities and the hiring of engineers, and Tidwell had been waiting for an offer ever since.

Willey had first broached the subject with Tidwell of moving to Microvision in September 1995, when he sent Tidwell e-mail saying he wanted to hire him "right away." Months passed before Tidwell heard from Willey again, and this time it was to discuss having Tidwell work 60 percent of his time at Microvision, and 40 percent at the HIT lab. Furness and Willey negotiated that arrangement for a few weeks, then the subject was dropped, until

Rutkowski contacted Tidwell in mid-1996 to reopen negotiations for a full-time job at Microvision. Tidwell said then that he wanted to be paid at least what the HIT lab was paying him, and wanted stock options as well. He and Rutkowski reached verbal agreement on the terms of a deal, with Rutkowski saying he would send him an agreement letter in a few days.

When the letter came, though, it was for a lower salary—lower even than he was paid at the HIT lab—and fewer options than Tidwell had agreed to in their conversation. There followed weeks of talking, during which it would seem from time to time either that they were on the verge of an agreement or that Willey and Rutkowski never talked with each other about Tidwell, since whenever one of them promised the optical engineer something, the other professed to know nothing about the promise. Finally, when the parties had closed to within $500 per year and twenty-five thousand shares' worth of options, Willey said he would consult one last time with Rutkowski and call Tidwell back "later that day" with a final offer. "It was pathetic," Tidwell said later, "like a used-car salesman constantly saying he has to go talk with his manager." Willey didn't call until the next day, and the conversation was short. "Mike," he said, "I'm sorry, but what you were asking for was just too high, so I'm afraid it's just not going to happen." Just when Tidwell thought they were on the verge of deal, then, Microvision abruptly cut off talks.

Melville, meanwhile, had a far easier time. While Tidwell was important to the VRD's future, Melville was indispensable—a circumstance obvious even to Microvision's managers, who tended to look down on the HIT lab scientists. In order to lend any credibility at all to their offering memorandum—the document describing Microvision and its future to potential investors—Microvision needed to have genuine engineers on staff. Moreover, the company would be helpless without Melville's continued work on scanner technology, as the scanner was one of the genuinely new inventions in the VRD, and the key to its future as a product. "Dave's in a unique position—the only time he'll ever have it," Rich Johnston said. "Because of the work he's done and the background he has, he is the only person in the world that Microvision *has* to hire. He has a chance to command a high salary—probably thirty percent higher than he could get anywhere else—and get a bunch of stock. And who knows? It could really take off."

Thus Melville was able to negotiate a $90,000 annual salary—a massive raise from his HIT lab pay—a $35,000 signing bonus, and a generous package of options. And whether out of esteem for Melville or simple carelessness, Microvision gave him the bonus without any conditions. He could have walked off the job the day after collecting it and not have had to give it back. "Dave was able to cut a very good deal with them because they had to have him for the IPO," Johnston said. "He had 'em by the balls—it was smart of him to squeeze a little bit." He was also convinced that Microvision hired Melville and not Tidwell because Melville tended not to ask questions and raise arguments. "They want a yes man. They can't stand people who question their methods."

Melville was indeed the only remaining lab researcher willing to believe in Microvision's managers, but his determined optimism about them came more in spite of what he saw them doing than because he believed they were making smart, ethical, or generous moves. On the one hand, Melville had been eager to move over to Microvision when the time came because he was desperate to keep developing his scanner. "I'm kind of going with the technology," he said. "I want to make sure it's done correctly. I'm going there to guard my interests as much as anything else. When you think up things like this, it's like a baby of yours, this thing that you want to care for and feed and nurture so that it matures into all it can be. I feel like if I let this out of my hands, it's not going to be all it could be."

He also had been something of a determined underachiever, putting aside career advancement for the sake of working on interesting problems, and now he felt the need to make up the income he had lost as a result of pursuing dreams for their own sake. "Money's involved, too. I've got a family, mortgage, daughter starting college in two years. And there's the possibility of the company really pulling it through, and my options really being worth something."

Those attractions aside, he was deeply troubled by the way the relationship between Furness, his teammates, and Microvision had deteriorated. Although Johnston and Tidwell tried to comfort Melville by joking affectionately that he had gone over to the "Dark Side" in moving to Microvision, and by making it clear that their esteem for him was undiminished by his change in employers, he couldn't help but feel that his relationship with them, and with Furness, had been fundamentally changed. Furness, for example, believed that Willey and Rutkowski would eventually try to patent Melville's work under the company's name rather than the university's in order to avoid making royalty payments on future products and licensing deals. So no sooner did Melville reach agreement with Microvision than Furness had him sit down and write more than twenty "disclosures" on various aspects of his work at the lab, in order to forestall Microvision from future attempts at trying to secure patents for itself on those parts of Melville's work. And Furness constantly reminded Melville that he was essentially going to work for an enemy by telling him, only half jokingly, that he—Furness—was sending Melville on a "mission," in the Mormon sense of the word, the implication being that Melville's job was to convert Microvision's evil managers into decent, ethical human beings.

Melville spent a lot of time agonizing over his move. While he felt he had no choice but to carry on his work, he also felt in some ways that he was betraying Furness. "I feel a lot of loyalty to Tom. He put a lot of faith in me at the beginning, and I feel I owe him for that." He also was more tormented than he let on by the ribbing Rich Johnston and Mike Tidwell gave him. "They razz on me, and I kind of go along with it, but in a way it will be nice to get over there and get away from all of this negative energy. Especially from Mike—he's really down on them. One thing he's got to learn is that there's no perfect situation." He also kept looking across the battle lines at Microvision and trying without success to see his new employers in a good light. "I really try to go, 'Okay, what do I see?' It's really hard to tell whether they are really trying to pull a fast one or if they're just not swift. Are they really trying their best? I think you have to assume that they're trying their best. Why would they want to sabotage things?"

Melville's ease in reaching agreement only exacerbated Tidwell's already considerable anger, and the younger engineer seemed to grow increasingly obsessed with what he saw as evergreater deviousness on the part of Microvision. Thus it was with some satisfaction that he was able to point out to another engineer—a materials scientist named Dan Bertolet, who reached an agreement with Microvision at about the same time that Melville did—that he had been greatly deceived.

Microvision offered Bertolet a low salary and large options package—a classic offer in the Pacific Northwest's post-Microsoft era. In the wake of Microsoft's outsized success, every new employee of every Northwest high-tech start-up was at first giddy with visions of instant millionairism, and the allure of options had new employees willing to work long hours for low salaries on the theory that they would be enriched overnight when their options vested and their company went public.

It seemed to Bertolet that the options were generous—he was to pay $2 to $2.75 per share for 48,000 shares, and the stock would be valued at $9 per share when the company went public. Factoring in the three years Bertolet would have to wait until he was vested and could sell his shares, and the likelihood that the shares would increase in price, he felt he had been made rich before even starting work.

When he told Tidwell about his deal, though, Bertolet learned that Willey had disingenuously described the options package when he offered it to him. Before going public, Microvision intended to do a "3.2-to-1 reverse split" of its shares, reducing the total number of shares in Microvision to slightly less than one-third of what it had been prior to the split, and multiplying the price per share by 3.2. Bertolet had not understood that his options deal, as described to him by Willey, was a combination of pre- and post-split numbers, making the deal look far more attractive than it really was.

"Dan," said Tidwell, "you can't have before *and* after numbers in the same calculations." Then, in a gesture graphically illustrating how engineers talk with one another, he turned to the white board in his office and wrote:

Reverse split 3.2–1
option price: $3.2 \times 2 = \$6.40$

post-split shares is /3.2

Let:

$\times$ = option price you think you're getting
$\times^1$ = actual option price
y = IPO price you think is going to happen
y^1 = actual IPO price
N = # shares you think you're getting
N^1 = # shares you actually are getting

True Value = $(y^1 - x^1) \bullet N^1$
Your Expected Value = $(y - x) \bullet N$
Ratio = True Value/Your Expected Value

$$\frac{(y^1 - x^1) \bullet N^1}{(y - x) \bullet N}$$

$x^1 =$
$3.2 \bullet x$
$y^1 = y$
$N^1 = N/3.2$

So now,
Ratio =
$(y - 3.2 \bullet x) \bullet (N/3.2)$

$(y - x) \bullet N$
$= y -$
$$\frac{3.2 \bullet x}{3.2 \bullet (y - x)}$$

$= (9 - 6.40)$
.... $(x = 2$ and $y = 9)$
$3.2(9 - 2)$

$= 11.6\%$

Bertolet looked at the calculations for a moment. "Oh, shit," he muttered.

After he left, I asked Tidwell for an explanation in English. "Dan's option price today is two dollars, times the number of options," he said. "The money he would make is the difference between the share price and the option price times the number of shares. Dan thought the shares were nine dollars each and his option price was two dollars per share. But the nine dollars a share was the post-split price [the price after the company reduced the number of its shares by a factor of 3.2], and the two dollars per share option price was the price *before* the split. You have to multiply his option price by 3.2, and divide the number of shares by 3.2. So the difference between his price and the actual share price is only eighty-one cents, rather than seven dollars."

In other words, Bertolet was being offered stock not at a fraction of its market rate, as was standard, but at a price that was so close to the market price that it was more generous of him to buy his options than it was of the company to offer them.

Now Tidwell felt fortunate to have avoided reaching agreement with Rutkowski and Willey. "It's bad investment—that's all there is to it," he said. "That's what working for a start-up company is, whenever equity is part of the compensation package. You become an investor whether you like it or not. And Dan is not a very sophisticated investor. I know enough to ask questions to find out what's going on, and only because the stock market's been a hobby for me since I was ten years old."

Once the news of what had happened to Bertolet circulated around the HIT lab, any doubts that anyone other than Melville had entertained about their apparent dishonesty were forever removed. "See," said Rich Johnston when I told him about it, "this is where in my mind they're being slimy. Level with the guy: 'This is how we're doing our options, take it or leave it.' You don't have to be slimy! Especially when somebody's making a decision based on their life. A job is a life decision—don't screw a guy when it comes to life decisions. It's really stupid. Why be in a position where your employee is going to be hacked at you?" He paused, then asked, "What's Dan going to do, anyway?"

"I don't know," I answered. "He had already accepted the job when he found out."

"Oh, that's funny!"

There was at Virtual i/O a small room with a glass wall facing out at the rest of the company. This room housed two young women—Kristen Schurr and Dawn Elliott—who served as the company's canaries in the coal mine. It was Schurr's job to deal with Virtual i/O's creditors, and Elliott's to do the company payroll. Not a moment passed without at least one Virtual i/O employee looking through the glass wall, trying to divine the company's fortunes. "Everybody was watching them," Deep Bile said, "because we knew that the day the payroll department walked off the job, the rest of us could walk, too."

Out of solicitude for their fellow employees, Schurr and Elliott kept their door closed and a Soundgarden CD playing at full volume in their CD-ROM drive. Both were devotees of the Seattle music scene, and they played the band's music partly to keep themselves sane and partly to keep coworkers from overhearing their conversations.

Elliott's job was to scrape together money from wherever she could find it and cover the company's paychecks. Schurr's was considerably more stressful—not only did she have to tell outraged creditors that the payment they expected to receive would not be forthcoming; she also had to beg and charm them into sending more supplies on credit.

As time went on, Schurr's conversations tended to follow the same pattern. A supplier would call, she would look up the balance due him or her, and see that it was in the hundreds of thousands—sometimes millions—of dollars. Virtual i/O might on that day have $200,000 or so in the bank—having cadged yet another bridge loan out of TCI—with the bulk of it needed for payroll. Schurr would be looking at these dismal numbers while the creditor was shrieking, "But Greg promised me I'd get paid today!"

Schurr had an uncanny ability to fend these people off and get them to send still more supplies to Virtual i/O. Since some of these creditors let her seduce them into extending more credit even after Virtual i/O owed them more than $1 million, Schurr became something of a legend to those who knew how she spent her days. It was undoubtedly this amazing skill that led to her being designated the company's one and only Employee of the Month.

The reward proved to be of typically dubious merit. The prize was a round-trip ticket to anywhere in the United States, and it was only after Schurr won it that she discovered the prize was not the straightforward purchase of an airline ticket for her but the problematic transfer of company frequent-flier miles to her. This, of course, proved impossible to orchestrate, and the resulting fiasco turned into a months-long saga that became for company employees both a form of entertainment and the archetypal illustration of the sort of promises made by Rhoads and Amadon. Schurr found herself—unofficially, at least—still on the roster of unpaid Virtual i/O creditors when she finally left the company.

The mood among the Virtual i/O workforce during the latter part of 1996 was a complicated mix of fear, unrealistic optimism, anger at Rhoads and Amadon, eagerness to believe Rhoads and Amadon, and denial of the painfully obvious. Although Rhoads and Amadon kept sales figures secret from as many of their employees as possible, it was obvious to everyone that the headsets weren't selling—particularly when the marketing department shrank to a single VP to whom no one reported. Even the din in Schurr and Elliot's office wasn't enough to camouflage the company's desperation. Moreover, angry suppliers occasionally would show up in the Virtual i/O lobby demanding money, and the number of employees who ran afoul of the company's president or CEO and got themselves fired was growing ever larger.

Two things kept a number of important engineers at the company working well past the time when Virtual i/O's hopelessness and the worsening abuse at the hands of Rhoads and Amadon should have driven them out the door. One was a passionate belief in their technology; the other was the hope that Virtual i/O would go public, taking advantage of the markets' thrall to technology companies. The fatal allure of stock options kept people in and around the Seattle technology start-up culture believing in wildly fantastic business plans and possibilities, and Virtual i/O proved a classic case study in the epidemic of digital gold rush fever. "That's what you're putting in a lot of those hours for, is that hope of the options," said Deep Bile. "And so people would put up with it, because the work environment isn't too much different from Microsoft—you work long hours and you're told that you suck. So people were holding out for a while, thinking they could cash in their options and not have to work for two or three years." This hope that their options might magically have a moment of worth kept some of Virtual i/O's critical talent hanging on until autumn, when finally it became clear even to the most inveterate optimists that the company could never launch an IPO. Once that news sunk in, there was a mass exodus of engineering talent.

Meanwhile, TCI, which had been keeping Virtual i/O alive for months with a series of bridge loans, was running out of resources of its own. TCI was racking up significant losses, partly as a result of CEO John Malone's attempt to move into multimedia through the purchase of several smaller companies and an interactive television experiment with Microsoft that went nowhere. In an attempt to shore up its bottom line, TCI laid off 6.2 percent of its workforce in late 1996, sold half of its Netscape stock, its 20 percent stake in the Microsoft Network, and its 30 percent share of the @Home Network, and closed down two of its wholly owned subsidiaries. News reports pegged TCI's debt at $15 billion, and company officials were quoted as saying they hoped to drop $1 billion in expenses during the coming year.

This was not the best of times, in other words, to depend on TCI's largesse. Indeed, the company, which now owned 37 percent of Virtual i/O, turned its budget cutters loose on Amadon and Rhoads's dream.

By this time, my sole official contact with Virtual i/O—conversations with Linden Rhoads, who had barred anyone else at the company from talking with me—had ceased. Rhoads either would cancel at the last minute an appointment I had with her or would not show up for it. Finally, she simply stopped returning my calls. I now depended solely upon Deep Bile for information, and was to grow more and more astonished during the fall months of 1996 at the amount of e-mailed news that circulated through the Deep Bile network for former Virtual i/O employees, at the presence of one or more Deep Bile moles inside the company, and, most of all, at the boundless anger that kept bubbling furiously to the surface whenever members of the group exchanged information among themselves.

One message that crossed my screen included an attempt at explaining the group's collective obsession with the misfortunes of Rhoads and Amadon: "By way of explanation of our apparent fixation," it began, "everyone needs some source of drama in their life. And VIO has it all, sex . . . office politics, backstabbing, power struggles, conflict between good and evil, money, set in a hi-tech world. 'Dallas' with Circuit Boards."

That didn't account, though, for the tone of eager and gleeful vengeance that kept coming through in other messages that circulated through the group. These were some of the most bitter human beings I had ever encountered. For them, the end of 1996 turned into a countdown toward the most eagerly anticipated event of the millennium—the firing of Rhoads and Amadon. News of virtually every potentially significant company event in this regard spread instantly. Mid-December saw a message circulate that read, "it looks as if the holiday bonus this year at Virtual i/O will be layoffs," followed a week later by mail listing the laid off and their total salaries. Then came a coded message to the group from inside Virtual i/O:

```
Princess Leia has escaped the Death Star and is
heading back to Alderaan, but the Rebel Alliance
has taken serious hits. I, Wedge Antilles, remain
as one of the last of the rebel spies not to be
found out by the Emperor. Today Darth Vader
remains surveying the Emperor's battle plan.
Yesterday he enlisted Grand Moff Tarkin to monitor
all communications from the sector in search of
escaping rebel spies. Thus, this will be the
```

newest secure transmission source until the
Empire finds out.

An escape plan for one of the few remaining
spies has been attached to this communication.
Please review and pass along to all those who
can help. I will keep the Alliance up to date on
the progress of the Empire. Over and out.

By the time this message was copied to me, it included a trans-
lation for the uninitiated:

Darth Vader is Linden (and sometimes Greg). One
of her weirder management phases was a Star Wars
theme. She wanted to intimidate us all and felt
the reason we didn't respect her was not because
she was an idiot, but because she was a woman.
So she decked out her office with Star Wars
crap, including a device that would play the
"Darth Vader" theme whenever you opened her door
and microphone/mask that would make her voice
sound like Darth's.

Grand Moff Tarkin is the sys admin, who has
changed the email privileges so that they can
read any email going into and out of VIO. While
this has been upheld as legal, it doesn't
exactly improve morale. And don't even get me
started on the possibility of the place being
"bugged."

They've done this email thing in the past, but
with 100 employees sending 10-20 emails it was
impractical. Needless to say, we used the fact
that they were listening/reading our email to
our advantage by placing information we wanted
them to know. Now with fewer employees and a

```
smaller number of "suspects" it is possible to
monitor email for "evidence" or "subversive
conduct." Just like Burma.

So our source is using an outside email account,
which cannot be monitored internally. Do they
think we're stupid?

The "escape plan" was a copy of someone's
resume.
```

The year ended for Deep Bile on a note of almost unbearably high expectation. Rhoads, they all believed, was to be fired any day, with Amadon not far behind. By Christmas 1996, it was clear that the two were being forced out. Group members spent the holiday regaling themselves with a copy of an e-mail message that was said to be Amadon's plea for mercy. "G&L are apparently in deep doodoo with the board members," the missive began, "and have been asked to go away ASAP. This is their counteroffer." There followed a message addressed "to: tci" listing financial terms of an Amadon agreement to surrender much of his authority as CEO.

Deep Bile was unmoved. "This is NOT a joke or a parody," read the rest of the Deep Bile message. "This is what they really sent. Read it and try really hard not to laugh. Remember they have burned through 30 million on gross sales of maybe 5 million. Also keep in mind, they were asked to get the hell out of Dodge and this is their counteroffer. Not a very firm grasp on reality." As for how Deep Bile came to be in possession of the plea: "Let's just say that if you print out a memo where you are asking for a raise while all the managers are in a meeting picking people to lay off because you've managed to plow 30+ million into the ground, employee loyalty isn't very big."

Dramatic as the intrigue and chaos were at Virtual i/O, they were more than rivaled—for entertainment value, at least—by the nonstop contretemps and high jinx at F5 Labs. The place in short order took on the look and feel of a demented *Upstairs, Downstairs* story.

"Upstairs" was the domain of the investors, company CEO Jeff Hussey, three sales and marketing employees, and F5's chief financial officer; "downstairs" was the domain of Mike Almquist and his four fellow programmers. The more you saw of the downstairs, the less sense you could make of what the people upstairs were telling you.

Upstairs, all was optimism and arrogance. Richard Novotny, an investment officer in the EnCompass Group, the Japanese-owned venture capital firm that was F5's biggest investor, was serenely confident in F5, which he described affectionately as a company full of "kids too young to know it can't be done." Hussey held court every day in the small conference room at the front of F5's down-at-the-heels downtown Seattle office suite. He sat at the head of an oblong table, papers and a speaker phone arrayed in front of him, alternately making telephone calls and talking with great bluster about his company's extremely high chances of success. F5's ease in raising money, he liked to say, was attributable both to the timeliness of its product and to Hussey's savvy. "Raising money is really just advanced storytelling," went one of his favorite lines. "And the story line is simple: 'A, B, C, D . . . rich!' "

He felt it was important to think of F5 not as a technology story but as a business and financial story. "What we are, what we want to be, we just want to be a *money printing press*. I mean, I would hope that no one would ever walk out of here and think that we're more about technology than we are about business. Because that is the thing that everybody makes mistakes about! I mean, when people get more jazzed about, you know, about ones and zeroes than they do about dollar signs, that's the beginning of the end. And that's the problem with most of the 'VR companies,' is that they're way more excited about ones and zeros than they are about dollars!" In this respect, he felt wary and frustrated about the denizens of F5's downstairs. "I mean, most of them are far more motivated about being able to sit around and think great thoughts. That's what they want to do—sit around and think great thoughts . . . and, 'Oh, by the way—making a few million bucks would be cool, too.' "

In this respect, he felt he was the key to F5's success. Hussey liked to refer to himself as an "oil refinery" for the crude aspirations of his company's software engineers. Almquist and his programmers had a timely idea that could be made to make a lot of money if someone with proper business thinking were guiding them— holding them to a production schedule and tailoring the product's set of features for the present-day marketplace. It was Hussey's job to funnel their "great thoughts"—the desire to build an innovative, powerful, clever piece of software—into something practical that customers would need and want to buy in large volume.

For all of Hussey's bluster, I always came away from our conversations with the impression that he was in over his head. His sole value to Almquist had been his connections in the financial community. His short career had consisted entirely of sales, stock trading, and fund-raising, and he had no experience managing people, running a company, or working with software developers. I generally left his conference room with the same vivid picture indelibly printed in my mind: Hussey, crisp and confident, sitting at the head of that long table, shouting and gesticulating energetically, dressed in a shirt that—to judge from its telltale pattern of creases—he had just purchased, taken out of its package, and put on. That grid pattern made him look as if *he* had just been taken off the shelf and unwrapped: a brand-new company's brand-new CEO, his inexperience there for all to see.

I would walk from the CEO's office down a hallway to an L-shaped room that served as home to Almquist, Joey King, and three other software engineers. The contrast was jarring enough to make you wonder if this room was an asylum and Hussey the jailer. The floor was coated with rubber, giving you the sense that you had entered a padded cell. Almquist sat facing a blank wall in one corner, his computer labeled "bungholio"—a tribute to *Beavis and Butt-head*. The computer next to his, operated by programmer Dave Olafson, had atop it a huge, horned Viking helmet. Facing the wall opposite Almquist sat F5 systems administrator Matt Sommer, who growled rather than spoke and who ended nearly all of his conversations with his arms upraised, his forefingers and little fingers extended, while his mouth roared, "Goat's blood!"

Almquist, Olafson, and Sommer spent months of fourteen-hour days in this room, their time a weird stew of "coding like the wind"—as Almquist liked to say—playing networked Duke Nukem, banter, screams, roars, laughter, e-mailing, and planning sessions at the white board. They grew a culture in the room strange enough to keep the company's nonengineers from entering unless they had no choice. Their play devolved primarily around two motifs: the "pirate" motif, and the "goat's blood" motif.

Thus, any conversation on any topic was apt to lapse into one of these themes. Almquist and Sommer, watching one of their computers crash one night, surveyed the code scrolling by on the screen and delivered themselves of the following commentary:

"Avast ye, matey, the BIOS looks like she be takin' on water!"

"Aye . . . she be goin' down fer sure. . . ."

"Arrrggghhh . . ."

"The ol' rustbucket . . ."

"Arrrggghhh . . ."

"Arrrggghhh . . ."

Similarly, the engineers frequently ranted about their lust for goat's blood, the importance of the ritual sacrifice of goats, and the need for abundant supplies of goat's blood to make their computers run faster and stronger.

"I want this to run one hundred megabit . . ."

"Oooohh . . . much goat's blood!"

Visitors from Sprint Communications, who spent a day at F5 learning about BIG/ip, undoubtedly were bemused by the writing on the white board behind Mike Almquist as he stood there going through the technical arcana of a BIG/ip-fitted web site. In madly clearing the conference room of its discarded food wrappers, half-full bags of corn chips, crumpled Wendy's Big Gulp cups, and various papers and other garbage in advance of the Sprint team's visit, someone had forgotten to wipe the white board clean of this code:

```
ip = forward ( , cache)
            if (! Dst:VIP) first_OK
                    do another lookup
        .            big_ip (mbuf, ip . dir = OUT)


        .
```

goatsblood( )

The sole serious note in the programmers' lair—aside from the occasional visits from Joey King, who divided his time between there and the HIT lab—was afforded by the arrival in August of Avi Bar-Zeev, who quit his job at Walt Disney Imagineering to hitch a ride on Almquist's dream. Tall, gaunt, and goateed, Bar-Zeev looked like an ascetic who had wandered in from fasting in the desert to work on programming. This impression was oddly heightened by his penchant for wearing a T-shirt labeled, "I Flew the Magic Carpet"—a commemoration of his work on the Disney *Aladdin* ride.

Bar-Zeev, like Almquist, had all but grown up with a passion for doing virtual reality and his life after college had been a restless search for the best milieu in which to pursue his goal of working on VR tool kits. His previous move to Disney from Worldesign had been less out of love for Disney than from lack of viable alternatives. "I didn't want to go to work for a corporation," he said. "I didn't think about joining SGI or any other computer companies. But I thought Disney might be cool because this is an *art* company, it's a company that gets the whole picture, not just the technology."

It seemed at first that he had found a visionary's paradise. Disney not only wanted to push the boundaries of virtual reality, it had more or less infinite resources to put at its dreamers' disposal. Bar-Zeev went to work immediately on the *Aladdin* VR ride, which proved to be the best virtual-world experience ever built and implemented anywhere in the world—testament not only to Bar-Zeev's abilities, but to the resources Disney put at his disposal. "At Disney's R and D lab, I was really happy," he says. "It was great—it was an environment where you pretty much can do what you want, you get a lot of resources and lots of people who are there to assist. You have tools, you have computers, you have what you need, pretty much. I had a lot of fun there, working on stuff that was really interesting. It was the opposite of Worldesign, where there was, like, no hope, ever."

Unfortunately, at Disney there was also, like, no excitement, ever. This was due not only to the lack of a fight for survival to make things interesting, but also to the lack of anything genuinely thrilling to work on. Bar-Zeev wanted to work further out on the edge of what was possible. "There's a lot of people at Disney, like at a lot of big companies, whose sole function is to slow things down. You're spending hundreds of millions of dollars, you want to make sure you're doing the right thing, you really want to be careful about it. They have evaluations all the time, they want to make sure this is really what they want to do. 'Show me a model. Let me buy off on this.' The buy-off process there is amazing." It was clear to Bar-Zeev that his future at Disney would be assured not by "technology smarts" but by "an entire political game. If I were to stay there and try to do what I want to do, it would be by moving up the management chain, getting allies, getting resources, hiring people, and selling ideas. That's not what I'm good at. I hate the politics, really, I just am not cut out for it. The place for me to succeed is where it's just smarts—and in the start-up, even if you have to have the marketing and everything else, to a great extent, *smart wins*." In leaving Disney for F5, then, he was banking on smarts— his, Almquist's, and Joey King's. Almquist persuaded him that he would only have to put in a few months' work on the niggling little cash cow that was BIG/ip (Bar-Zeev was given options on 3 percent of the company's shares) before they all could set off on the project they were born to do—launch a genuine VR company.

The high spirits at F5 were a function of pressure, stakes, excitement over pending success—this idea that a bunch of young hackers could take the world by storm simply by virtue of smarts and greed—and the way Almquist had of turning every one of his enterprises into a form of personal expression. There were days when I thought the whole F5 adventure—including my role as the chronicler of its beginnings—was all something being dreamed up in Almquist's unquiet mind.

Almquist has a peculiar magnetic quality that attracts the surprised and bemused attention of everyone whenever he enters a room. He looks like the incarnation of mischief. His grooming is uncertain, his diet is frightening, and his wardrobe looks streetish. He favors a worn-out, mildly garish blue-and-yellow polar fleece pullover—which he wears both indoors and out, day after day, whatever the weather—threadbare T-shirts, baggy jeans, and ragged shoes with holes in both the soles and uppers. He lives on doughnuts, Wendy's bacon cheeseburgers, Taco Time carryout, pizza, massive doses of Cherry Coke, iced tea, and—on health-conscious days—Kickass Chicken Chili from Seattle's Art Bar, a tavern located a few blocks' walk from F5 headquarters. Between meals, Almquist generally carries a Gatorade squeeze bottle wherever he goes. He likes to pour Cherry Coke into it, sucking on the bottle until it is drained, then neurotically chewing on the mouthpiece until he gets around to a refill.

It often seemed to me that Almquist was not so much an entrepreneur or software engineer as he was a performance artist, his role of the moment being that of the founder of a high-tech startup. He had an odd kind of frenetic energy—if you looked closely enough, you could see little lightning bolts constantly crackling off of him. He referred to any event, however traumatic, disastrous, strange, unexpected, or distressing, as "the usual madness," and he could not keep himself from incessant play, no matter what purportedly serious task might be occupying him at the moment.

Thus Almquist's e-mail to his fellows invariably was peppered with manic asides. The first draft of BIG/ip was first installed at the busy web site in California of an Internet service provider and web tool-kit maker called Focalink, partly to test it and partly to see if Focalink would buy it, and when Almquist traveled down there to install and tweak the box late in October, then went on to visit Tower Records, which also was installing a test version of BIG/ip, his postmortem was a characteristically colorful mix of technical language and expressive commentary:

```
Some things I noticed in my fun trip to
California!

-root need to start em off with either: bash,
```

tcsh, or "STTY TERM PC3"! Otherwise blood will shoot out of my eyes and fingertips! Damn TTY was DRIVING ME, GILL, OWEN, EVERYONE BATTY! This needs to be fixed.

-WE NEED to put PORTMAP(?) and INETD(?) on BIG/IP cause Tower doesn't need to deal with the SSH nonsense. There are going to be sites that WON'T need ssh and DON'T WANT TO DEAL WITH IT! This merits some documentation and perhaps a "install script"?! Something - blah blah blah!

-we need to ship 19" rack screws with the product AND LOCK NUTS! Lock nuts are cheap and our customers would LOVE US TO DEATH! Adds about $0.50 to the product. . . . .

-one of their BIG/ips went GUMBY due to "BIG BAD BIGD!". This is DIRECTLY related to "tcpkill". I need to make it so it allocates the kernel socket ONLY once and we need to fix the "reverse" kill (kill between BIG/ip and user). Under Focalink's testing, it caused BIGD to have a heartattack and generate a 128MB log file. Jeesh - if they didn't take the box down it would've eaten the filesystem. . . . .

ALL of this PLUS the following are "ACTION ITEMS" that Sally and I are negotiating. When we've come to an agreement we'll DEFINITELY LET YOU GUYS KNOW! The pressure is BIG and so are the payoffs! ACK ICK OOK OCK! Please let me know if I've missed something. . . .

These exclamatory asides that Almquist could never keep out of his mail were equivalent to the facial expressions he employed when taking conference calls from potential partners and customers. I watched him one day negotiating a deal worth potentially hundreds of thousands of dollars to F5 over a speaker phone. Almquist was kneeling on a chair, his elbows resting on the conference table, while he leaned toward the phone. His polite and patient "tech speak" was accompanied by a constant stream of facial contortions, rolling of the eyes, exasperated grasping at his hair, and the occasional widening of his mouth into a silent scream. When the call was finally finished after some twenty minutes, he got up from the chair with a piratical "Arrrrgggghhhhh . . . that place is IQ-bound!"

He could never resist lapses into wisecrack mode, whatever the circumstances. Often, Almquist's jokes came out of nowhere, catching his interlocutor unawares and bringing otherwise serious discussion to a halt. Discussing the hiring of a new developer, he said, emphatically, "We are *not* going to hire any dweeboids. And I don't want to hire a 'Unix bigot' [his term for a developer who disdains the Windows and Macintosh operating systems in favor of the more exotic and less user-friendly Unix operating system]—we do that and we'll end up with a wacky, insane, sagelike individual."

He still, apparently, had not recovered from his time under William Bricken.

"We don't really need a senior person, we need a junior person who's competent," answered Bar-Zeev. "Maybe one senior and one junior . . ."

"What about fifth-year seniors—is that a good or a bad thing?" interrupted Almquist. While Bar-Zeev looked at him in confusion, he growled, "Nah . . . Matt's bad enough."

"Shit, man!" Matt Sommer—the goat's blood fetishist—retorted. "I got more degrees than you do!"

"Pedigrees don't count!" Almquist answered. Then he made a series of weird, apparently mocking noises before blurting out, "Is that your face or did your neck throw up?"

The question of how to subject BIG/ip to as strenuous testing as possible was resolved in classic Almquist fashion. Since it was well known that virtually the sole business making money on the Internet was pornography, he decided that he and his cohorts should "harvest" as many pornographic images as they could find on the Internet, collect them on a web server, then see if BIG/ip could take the punishment it was sure to receive. After collecting thousands of images, F5 posted notices on a few computer bulletin boards devoted to erotica, inviting interested readers to "check out an underground porn site" at http://206.16.117.1.

Even Almquist was surprised by the results. Within days, the site was being hit constantly by visitors; within weeks, it was, to judge from web site statistics Jeff Hussey dredged up from industry newsletters, one of the world's top ten sites when measured by the number of visitors per day it received. I walked across downtown Seattle one day with Almquist to visit the room where F5's web servers were located, in an office tower suite filled with racks and servers. Almquist was replacing the version of BIG/ip that was working at the "alpha site," as they called the pornography server (this was to distinguish it from the "beta site," which housed F5's official web site), with an updated version. He disconnected BIG/ip from its router, installed the new version, reconnected the boxes, then sat back to watch.

There is a panel of lights on the router that shows how heavy the traffic is to its web site. On the other routers in the room— there were seventy-five different web sites installed there—one or more lights might be blinking on and off as visitors trickled in. On the F5 site, as soon as Almquist reconnected, all the lights on the router's panel instantly flipped on and stayed on, steadily. "Look at that," Almquist said, amazed. "They're like frenzied rats at the feeding bar."

The porn site's performance proved to be something of a mixed blessing for F5. On the one hand, the statistics were proof positive of the power of BIG/ip. On the other hand, Almquist and Hussey couldn't tell anyone about the results for fear of creating a reputation- and business-killing scandal. The two didn't even feel they could tell F5's board members about the content on the site—a circumstance that made for some peculiar reports to the board.

"Our subsite is probably one of the top ten in number of hits in the country," Hussey said at one board meeting. "We're doing a gigabyte [one billion bytes] an hour, we're getting half a million hits a day, doing twenty-four gigabytes of throughput a day. All on three twenty-five-hundred-dollar boxes."

"How on earth are you generating that much traffic?"

"Well . . . I can't really say."

"Why not?"

"It's . . . er . . . a secret web site."

"What the hell is a 'secret' web site?"

Silence. Nervous laughter. Change of subject.

F5 planned to release the first official version of its product on November 1, 1996, and projected sales—at $25,000 per unit—of nearly $1 million by January, with the opportunity shortly after that to spin off its VR company. Almquist had assigned different portions of the coding to himself, Olafson, and Bar-Zeev, and had expected that the three would meet frequently to review one another's code. It became apparent early on, however, that Olafson did not like anyone looking at his work, so the three fell into a habit of working for weeks at a time without doing any real consulting among themselves. This was an odd way of writing software—particularly on such a complicated project—but it struck no one as being especially troublesome until the November 1 deadline approached and BIG/ip began acting in strange and unexpected ways.

The main problem was the alpha site, which would perform heroically for more than two days, then would begin arbitrarily terminating connections until finally it crashed, the crashes coming every three days. As near as Almquist and Olafson could determine, BIG/ip had a "memory leak" causing it to run out of memory and finally just to shut itself down. Olafson's approach to this problem was to keep patching in new chunks of code—"putting a Band-Aid on it"—every time he encountered a new problem. Almquist persistently begged, cajoled, and commanded him not to take that approach, as it not only did not identify and permanently correct the root of the problem, but tended to introduce new bugs into the product. As weeks went by in this fashion, and as the November 1 deadline drew nearer, tensions between the two grew ever greater.

The tensions were made worse by Olafson's occasional insistence that the problems were in Almquist's code rather than in his, and that Almquist was causing the project to fall behind schedule both by his careless work and the amount of time he spent doing things other than coding—building boxes, spending time in meetings and on the telephone, fooling around, and being witty. Almquist, for his part, began ridiculing and deriding Olafson behind his back, telling Bar-Zeev and Sommer that Olafson's brain was full of monkeys randomly pounding away at terminals, that he "works like an R and D guy rather than a product-oriented guy," and that "Dave has a graduate student mind-set: You just get something to work so you can get a grade, and you don't have to worry about reliability or supporting all these different uses over the long term."

Olafson, for his part, complained to Sommer that Almquist didn't respect him or his work, and he withdrew deeper into a shell of secrecy. Almquist would give him specific portions or features in BIG/ip to finish, and he would ignore him and work on different features without telling anyone. Then, when Hussey asked if the desired feature was ready, or when Almquist asked to test it, it would turn out not to have been done.

Anger between the two escalated to the point where Hussey grew increasingly frustrated and angry, Almquist felt helpless, Olafson constantly felt under unwarranted attack, and Sommer said that his job description now read, "Keep these two guys from killing each other."

It was obvious that in starting F5, Almquist and Hussey had vastly underestimated the importance of wetware in the production of hardware and software. The two figured that their product would be so easy to build that they could ignore the mundane details of establishing and running a business, and hiring and supervising employees. Now, with an intractable employee and no manager who knew enough about software engineering and human psychology to act as a persuasive arbiter, all meaningful work on BIG/ip ceased, as Almquist and Olafson, like two goats in a Warner Bros. cartoon, locked horns and ran in place, their spinning legs digging holes in the ground, neither combatant making progress against the other.

It began to dawn on Almquist that he and Hussey had deluded themselves by thinking that there was no difference between dreaming something up and making the dream come true. Commiserating one night in a Seattle tavern with Sandra Smith, the producer at Zombie in charge of SpecOps, Almquist listened in rapture as Smith discussed the procedures at Zombie for hiring, supervising, and disciplining employees.

"You have a *process?*" Almquist shouted, in mock shock. "You have *procedures?* How daring! How novel!" Then he went on to detail his travails with Olafson, ending with a mournful invocation of his helplessness: "We put him on double-dare, super-duper, secret probation."

When the November 1 deadline came and BIG/ip was nowhere near ready for the build that was to have incorporated nearly all of its Version 1.0 features, Hussey, who had been persuaded to leave supervision of the programming to Almquist, came unglued. "They had the opportunity to have their job and do their work the way they wanted it," he said, "or at least the way they expressed that they wanted it, and they were unsuccessful. So now, we're going to do it *my way.* There are going to be milestones, and if they don't get that done, they will have decided for themselves that this is the wrong place for them!" He was particularly furious at Almquist. "Squish blew it!" he screamed. "He blew it! He is *totally* responsible for not looking at anything for that whole time! Now he wants to absolve himself of this responsibility, and he's trying to skate like all get-out, and he is unabsolved! It was a bunch of wishful thinking on my part to think he could manage a product into existence through other people. I'm just going to have to get my hands a lot more dirty on management issues, *which I detest.*"

For all his arrogance, Hussey was forthright in acknowledging that he was ill suited to manage people directly. He was the first to admit that people found him hard to understand or like. "I'm getting my head handed to me because of my need to have as few people working here as possible," he said. "Because of my *personality problem.* With each person I add here, that just increases the problem factorially."

He was to demonstrate the truth of that proposition in a meeting held later that day to upbraid his programmers for missing their deadline. Intending to motivate them, he frightened them instead. Hussey started out by explaining that the company was spending $100,000 a month, and had only six months' worth of money left. "But money is less of a problem than time," he said. "We have competitors coming on-line that we have to worry about. I can get you more money—money is easy to raise—but I can't get you more time." He wanted them to think in terms of customers waiting at the door rather than of a start-up working in a void. "We're no longer a start-up," he said, "we're a small company selling *products to customers* instead of a story to media and investors."

Hussey was particularly preoccupied with customers because F5 already had two, even though BIG/ip was not genuinely dependable and salable. Focalink had one box, which it could not get to work, and another was being installed at Tower Records, which was one of the world's leading Internet retailers.

The Tower Records project had everyone at F5 in a panic. Matt Sommer had gone down to Tower the previous day to install a BIG/ip upgrade, and came back terrified. "Just so everybody knows," he said, "they've got like fourteen million dollars of inventory gathering dust in a factory waiting for BIG/ip to go on-line. That scared the shit out of me. . . ."

It infuriated Hussey. "Okay," he hissed, his face set in a ferocious sneer, "so we have a little problem set here. The problem set being, these guys think that we're bringing them a new BIG/ip that's even bigger and stronger than the one we had before, and in fact BIG/ip is not big and strong. Big/ip is small and weak!" The November 1 build, expected to be robust and bug-free, instead was crippled by the same problem as its predecessor—it crashed every three days. Tower, then, was installing a time bomb. "These guys have already relied on us," he said, nearly shouting. "*We owe them.* We owe them a product that's not gonna crash. Because they've already spent the money on adopting our architecture that we sold to them. I mean, we sold them vaporware! And so they got vaporware and bad surprises! They just don't even know it yet. You've heard me harp on this a hundred times—no vaporware, no bad surprises. So this is really the essence of the problem: Tell me how we can solve these guys' problem, the problem that they don't even know they have. They're gonna have congestive heart failure in two days, and *die*."

This was particularly frightening in view of a test at Tower coming up in a few weeks. Microsoft, which had been feverishly working on Windows NT in the hopes of expanding into the web server market, competing head-to-head with expensive Unix systems developed by Sun Microsystems and SGI, wanted to set up an NT site at Tower and hold a splashy demonstration announcing NT's entrance into the market and showing the world how PC boxes running Windows NT could perform as well as competing products that cost ten times as much. Tower wanted to include BIG/ip in the demo, so as to ensure that the notoriously unreliable NT boxes would not crash under the heavy load of Tower's Internet traffic, and to pump up NT's performance. Hussey had just learned that Microsoft chairman Bill Gates would be flying down to Tower for the demonstration. The last thing in the world he wanted was for BIG/ip to crash while the whole world was watching.

The essential problem, of course, was that Hussey had oversold BIG/ip, telling potential customers that it was a finished product when in fact it was still being built and had yet to be tested. He was in this fix partly because of his overenthusiasm, anxiety, and inexperience, and partly because his company had no real process for communicating the status of its projects among its own people. There literally was no way at F5 for coherent information about BIG/ip to be disseminated. In the haphazard way the organization had come together, there now were some fifty-three different versions of BIG/ip code, each one replete with Band-Aids and indecipherable bugs, and no one really knew anymore which versions had which problems—or, for that matter, which version was best. This was partly due to lack of organization, partly due to Dave Olafson's refusal to show his code to Almquist, partly due to Almquist's inability to supervise Olafson, and partly due to Hussey's inability to understand software—or wetware—engineering.

Gradually, F5 took form as a company searching as desperately for a way to behave and function like a real company as it was trying to finish its core product. Hussey kept calling meetings in which the talk gravitated to process rather than product; Avi Bar-

Zeev would try to explain the way building, reporting, testing, and fixing was done at Disney; others would chime in about how often reports should be delivered, in what form, and to whom; Hussey would fulminate; and Almquist would repeatedly interject complaints that F5 was stuck in a way that he found embarrassing and inexplicable. "It's ridiculous to have meetings like this for a professional company," he said in a rare moment of seriousness. "If we're an amateur clubhouse write-off, which we're not, that's one thing. That's why we need design procedures, testing procedures . . . it's what takes us to the next level."

Most meetings ended with a frustrated Hussey shouting, his voice dripping with sarcasm. "Okay, so rather than you guys bore me with all these issues, I think that you just need to figure out all the issues and just solve them! We gotta get to work! Is it unreasonable for me to expect some kind of conclusive answer . . . ? You guys are going to be whining, two years from now, about how come you're not rich . . . ! After we fix this problem, then we settle the next thing, which is making sure that we never have another meeting like we're having today! Because I never want to have another meeting like this!"

Two or three days later, during yet another meeting like that, he would be shouting again, his audience looking more and more benumbed, frightened, and confused. "Maybe we should just call these customers up and say, 'Hey! We were only joking!' Does anyone here think that's the right thing to do?"

Finally, Almquist took Hussey aside and told him that his manner was upsetting Sommer and Olafson. "You're intimidating them" he said. In response, Hussey called a meeting and upbraided his workforce for being intimidated. "You've seen me in here with Taylor," he said, referring to his four-year-old son. "Do you think he finds me intimidating?"

Back in their L-shaped lair, the programmers pounded away day and night on BIG/ip, still not making progress toward solving its essential problem. Sommer found himself devoted to monitoring the Tower web site from afar, being sure to empty BIG/ip's memory before it overloaded and caused the machine to crash. His preventive maintenance kept the Tower system administrator from figuring out that BIG/ip was flawed, and for the moment, at least, Tower was happy, as its site was racking up huge customer-visit and sales numbers.

Bar-Zeev, Almquist, and Olafson, meanwhile, were getting more and more desperate about their lack of progress. Finally, late one night, deciding that their problem was essentially psychological, they exploded in a fit of exuberant high emotion. "Let's get *psyched*!" someone shouted. Suddenly all of them were tearing up boxes, ripping off long strips of duct tape, covering up windows, transoms, and doors with cardboard and paper. Then they scrawled warnings all over the outside of their sealed-off room: "Development in Progress! Do Not Disturb!" "Programmers only!" "Leave food at the door!" "Do NOT Enter!" The crowning glory was a piece of paper, affixed to the wall, on which was a photocopy of an adorable goat, seen in profile. The handwritten caption read, "So many goats. So little time."

Confronted by this spectacle the next morning, Hussey was uncharacteristically subdued and amused. "I'm just glad it doesn't say 'sheep,' " he muttered.

The days following this outbreak of exuberance were a long descent back into gloom and despair. Almquist, in particular, grew more and more frustrated with Olafson, all but giving up on him. He could feel tension and anger building up inside him to an intolerable level, but he seemed to lack a means of confronting Olafson and resolving their problems.

The whole programming team was hard at work one night when Almquist got a telephone call from Joey King. The call was inadvertently well timed—Almquist had been brooding about Olafson for hours, and needed to vent. He put King on hold, went into F5's conference room, closed the doors, picked up the telephone there, and commenced a typically colorful fulmination about how he felt he would have to throw out all of Olafson's work and start over, from scratch.

Suddenly there came a scrabbling noise from under the table, and Olafson's head emerged, face-to-face with Almquist. Olafson, exhausted, had crept into the conference room and crawled under the table for a nap, only to be awakened by Almquist's diatribe.

"Aaaaauuuggghhh!" They screamed, sounding like the hapless bank robbers in *Raising Arizona*. "Aaaaauuuggghhh!" "Aaaaauu-uggghhh!"

Olafson jumped to his feet and ran screaming from the room, running and shouting all through the office suite, slamming every door along his way. Almquist took off in pursuit, trying at first to placate him, then to kill him. The evening's festivities ended with Olafson fleeing the building and Bar-Zeev grabbing Almquist in a bear hug, restraining him until Olafson was safely out of range.

The month of August saw Tom Furness and the VRD team constantly trying both to decipher and handicap Microvision's IPO effort. Steve Willey's messages to the lab about exactly when and how the IPO would be launched grew increasingly cryptic. Day by day, Furness grew more and more troubled, as his heart and his head were pulling him in opposite directions. "The best thing that could happen," he said from time to time, "would be for Microvision to succeed, and get our technology off the ground." On the other hand, that would also be the worst thing that could happen, as it would vindicate Willey and Rutkowski, who had been acting counter to Furness's advice and interest for months.

Rich Johnston was more forthright. "This is just a slimeball IPO," he said whenever anyone asked. "They're way early in going after something like this. Normally, you don't see a company that's basically building a piece of hardware go public at such an early stage."

Johnston was not alone. Microvision's presentations to local investment groups and stock brokerages were roundly scorned, with one leading analyst describing Rutkowski's presentation as "the weirdest road show I've ever seen." M. Sharon Baker, writing in the *Puget Sound Business Journal*, detailed the company's precarious position and cast doubt on the viability of its technology, quoting figures from around the industry. Baker noted that Microvision "has not raised any money from venture capitalists and has no major corporate partners." Linden Rhoads was frequently cited in the article, telling Baker that Microvision had far more competitors, including Motorola and Reflection Technologies, than it was willing to admit, that its track record was horrible, its word no good, and the marketability of its technology years away. "A year ago, the company said it would have a full-color device for under one hundred dollars," she said. "But it is my understanding that they have a real *future* technology."

Yet Johnston was sure Microvision would succeed. "You have a public out there that is excited, sometimes panicked, they will jump on things and raise valuations way higher than I ever thought valuations would get raised," he said. "If I was going to put odds on it, I think it will go out, they will get it public." This was less because of market conditions, though, than because of conditions unique to Microvision. Its first investors, Johnston pointed out, were stockbrokers who were anxious to get something out of an investment that had proven worthless. The only way to recoup their losses was to take advantage of the market's hysteria over technology companies. Johnston suspected that these early investors were hoping that the company would succeed in going public and that they—the early, disillusioned investors—could sell off their holdings in the first, heady days after trading started, when valuation figured to be at its peak. "I think that these people will be buying at least small amounts more and encouraging their clients to buy more, to try to make what they've got liquid," Johnston predicted. "They figure they can buy a little bit more, and even if they sell that at a loss, they get to sell all the other stock they already have and might come out ahead."

Mike Tidwell, on the other hand, both expected and hoped that the IPO would fail, and David Melville—who at the moment, at least, had the biggest personal stake in Microvision's prospects—kept his own counsel. All three engineers spent the weeks before the launch so preoccupied with it that they seemed on some days incapable of doing any work on the VRD.

One thing in particular gave Johnston no end of confusion. He could not understand what was behind what he perceived to be a lack of due diligence on the part of investment houses and potential investors. As the IPO drew nearer—it was now August 15, and

Willey had let it be known that the IPO was scheduled for August 23—Johnston had yet to receive a single inquiry from a stockbroker or investment banker. Never, he said, had he heard of professional investors being so cavalier with their clients' money. Investors this time around seemed even more careless than the H Group had been back in 1993. "I've never met with a VC who didn't do more due diligence than this," he said. "It just doesn't make any sense that people wouldn't want to talk with the inventors of the technology, to see exactly what it was that the company had."

As it happened, the lab received only one inquiry from a stockbroker—a New Yorker who sent Furness an e-mail message declaring that he was "troubled" by the Rutkowski presentation he had attended. "I wondered why," asked the writer, "no one associated with the invention of the technology was present at the briefing, and why there was no mention, ever, of the lab where the technology was developed." He went on to ask if there was trouble between the lab and Microvision, and if that trouble was an indication of bad company management.

Furness agonized over what to do about the message. He could not bring himself to lie to the writer by assuring him that the company was in good hands and on the right track. But he feared telling the truth, as one disapproving word from him might kill whatever chances Microvision had at raising more money, and he still wanted the company to succeed. Ultimately, after consulting with an attorney who told him that an honest answer would surely result in a lawsuit, he decided not to answer the message at all.

Because relations between the lab and the company were so dismal, I was tempted to write off denigration of the company's chances to the anger and resentment that had built up in the lab over the years. But speculation outside the lab—in Seattle, at least—was no different. The financial community almost universally derided Paulson, the IPO's underwriter, as a "bucket shop"—an investment company, with no institutional clients, that sold exclusively to small, private, often uninformed investors—and suggested that Microvision had worked its way down from larger and better known underwriters who unanimously rejected Microvision's advances, in search of one willing to help take the company public. Had Paulson turned Microvision down, the start-up would have had to close its doors. "You look at a small-cap IPO like this," said the EnCompass Group's Richard Novotny, "and you can see that it's almost an act of desperation."

There was no question the company was desperate. In July, nearly out of money, Microvision borrowed $750,000 to pay its bills. The money was to be paid back immediately after the IPO, were it to go off successfully.

There was a great deal of confusion in the lab in the days before the IPO was scheduled to launch. Microvision itself seemed confused about exactly what was happening, and when. Calls to Willey and Rutkowski went unreturned. One day, the two were said to be on their way to Portland so they could be in their underwriter's office when the IPO was launched. The next day, they were still in their Seattle offices, trying to nail down final terms of the deal with the SEC. Now it was said that the first trade would take place in a few hours, then the next day. . . .

Finally, on August 27, Microvision went up on the NASDAQ board. Tidwell and Melville sat at Melville's computer, following the trading's progress through NASDAQ's web site.

The two were shocked by a number of things—not the least of which was Microvision's apparent, if improbable, ability to have actually pulled the whole thing off. More shocking was the opening price of the stock. Microvision's offering was not sold simply as shares but as $8 "units" consisting of one share and one warrant each. Each warrant—a certificate entitling the bearer to buy a share of stock in the future—cost $2, each share of stock $6. Since Melville had accepted his Microvision offer on the assumption that his option price would be $6.40 per share for stock valued at $9 per share on the market, he was surprised to see that the shares were worth $3 less than Willey had led him to believe they would be worth. Not only had Willey not told him that the unit price was less than $9—he also had not told Melville that the share price was only a portion of the unit price. Melville had thought that the unit price and the share price were one and the same thing.

Staring dumbfounded at his computer screen as the trading began, Melville asked Tidwell, "You mean two dollars of the price is in the warrant?"

"Can you believe they did that?" Tidwell shouted.

"Well, now," Melville said, his voice faltering, "I think it's just that they weren't very . . . thorough . . . when they were telling us what was going to happen."

"Dave! They lied to you! Give me a break!"

Melville watched in silence as his options grew less valuable by the minute. It turned out that Rutkowski and Willey had forgotten to file paperwork preventing Microvision's pre-IPO investors from dumping their stock as soon as it went up on the exchange, and everyone from the original H Group on down the line was selling off his stock as fast as possible. It was proof positive of the lack of faith in the company's management by the company's investors. By the end of the day, Microvision's stock, which had opened at $6 a share, had dropped to $5\frac{1}{8}$—more than $1 lower than Melville's option price. Microvision was to end its first day of public trading both $16 million richer and on NASDAQ's Ten Worst Performers list for the day.

Being what might euphemistically be termed "optimistic to a fault," Tom Furness never dreamed, when he started out on his Seattle adventure, that it would grow into such a complicated and multifarious monster. Just as he had expected his technological visions to be realized in relatively short order, so had he expected his vision of a little world of thriving VR businesses clustered around his laboratory to be realized in short order. He never commenced a research project without seeing at its end, just a few years off, a new, profitable business making products and advancing the art of the virtual-world interface into the mainstream of personal computing.

But now, in his bleakest moods—which began assailing him more and more frequently—Furness saw himself as someone who burned out researchers, disappointed industrial sponsors, hooked up with dubious characters who blackened his reputation, and birthed or midwifed failed business enterprises at a rate unequaled in the history of industry. This was as stark a contrast as he could imagine to the vision he had of himself seven years before, when he first set up the HIT lab as the charismatic leader at the center of a thriving array of businesses and laboratories run by his inspired disciples.

Furness felt like a spider at the center of a web that some sadist had charged with electricity. Every time some dire event transpired in the lab or in one of the companies related to it, however distantly or indirectly, there came a tug at the web that delivered a jolt to the poor spider. As he grew steadily weaker from this torture, Furness saw a steadily more desolate legacy taking shape around him.

He began to suffer distressing physical symptoms. He was troubled more and more often by pain in his side or in his stomach. His digestion began failing. Day by day, he grew more pale, until by September he looked ashen most of the time. Others in the HIT lab noticed that he was moving more slowly and that his fits of excitement and enthusiasm grew both more muted and less frequent. Where in the past he always had been able to summon up zest even under the most dire of circumstances, now his emotional well was dry.

Gradually, he sickened. Near the end of September, he started having mysterious attacks in which he would be immobilized by pain and begin hyperventilating. These attacks crested one Friday night when he was felled by unendurable stomach pain. He suffered through the weekend, with the pain growing ever worse, until finally on Monday his wife forced him to see a doctor. He arrived at the medical center in excruciating pain, barely managing to get himself through the office doors. He was immediately ushered into an examining room. When a nurse at last came into the room, she found Furness lying on the floor, curled up in a fetal position.

And the Earth
Shall Cast Out the Dead

———

FOR MARK LONG and Joanna Alexander, the contract offer from Disney had been as vital to the company's survival as it had been unexpected. The months leading up to their *Disney ex Machina* had been an exercise for Zombie's cofounders in desperation and disillusionment, as they came to terms with the unworkable business model guiding the flow of money through their industry. Every time I sat down with Long to discuss his company's fortunes, our conversation drifted toward the same two doleful pronouncements: "We're in the wrong business" and "Your book should be about the failed promise of the VR industry."

It was proving impossible for Long and Alexander to reconcile their ambitions with the two other forces they had to harness in order to finance and produce their projects. One was the force of technology, which was drawing more and more power and function to the personal computer and away from more expensive, single-function machines like the fax, calculator, television, stand-alone video game player, and reality engine. The other was cash flow, which was controlled by entertainment-industry executives who were trying to mold the emerging VR market into something along the lines of the popular music market.

In mid-1996, the technology underlying CD-ROM-based games was too new and too protean to allow game publishers to predict the future of their market. It also was evolving both too quickly on the technical side and too slowly in marketing departments to allow a company to target a mass-market purchasing audience with reasonable accuracy. Because personal-computer technology was constantly improving, and because nearly all game purchasers were computer freaks interested solely in new technical tricks, a game developer like Zombie—in other words, one with artistic aspirations—was constantly frustrated by the mandate on the part of game consumers to concentrate on technological advance at the expense of artistic expression. The PC game-playing world was made up almost exclusively of hard-core computer enthusiasts whose interest in new games was limited to their new technological advances (stereo sound, three-dimensional environments, faster video frame rates, motion capture . . .). Game buyers cared nothing for such aesthetic refinements as narrative, plot, theme, or graphic art—the very elements games needed if they were going to attract new players and buyers.

Non–game buyers, conversely, remained disinterested in the PC because it persisted in being—the best efforts of Microsoft and other software companies notwithstanding—both too expensive and too difficult a machine to learn to use. Compared with the television and the VCR, the computer was an exotic, pricey, and complicated machine that most consumers regarded as more a tool for experts than a mass-market entertainment medium.

Thus attempts by Zombie simultaneously to appeal to traditional computer-game enthusiasts and to attract new buyers and players by concentrating on the artistic side of game production failed on both fronts. Aesthetic advances not only left the core audience cold but also went ignored by nonplayers, who could not be made to think of games as anything other than toys for computerphiles.

This proved painfully true of ZPC, the company's latest and best title, and one on which Long and Alexander had placed heavy bets. ZPC entered the game market on Thanksgiving weekend 1996, was rated by *Parade* magazine as one of its Top Ten Best Buys

of the year, and promptly bombed. It proved to be a classic example of the bind in which artistically ambitious game developers
were caught: The efforts to develop a narrative and compelling
graphic environment went unnoticed by everyone. Consumers of
fiction never encountered the game; and consumers of games ignored ZPC because it contained no new technological wrinkles.
"We used an existing game engine," a disappointed Long said just
after Christmas 1996, when it was clear the game would never
take off. "That was a big mistake—players ignored it because it
didn't have anything technologically new in it."

In trying to sell ZPC as narrative art, then, Zombie was in some
respects repeating the mistake it had made when it developed
Locus, the game designed to exploit head-tracking technology. Just
as game players then did not own headsets with head trackers, so
now did they not own, or care to acquire, the aesthetic sense of a
reader of books or a connoisseur of film. In the case of both games,
Zombie had targeted markets that did not yet exist.

This did not sit well with the publishers who financed Zombie's
development efforts. Game publishers wanted hits, and after
putting three games on the market, Zombie had failed to deliver
one. GT Interactive, publisher of Zombie's first three games, declined to underwrite a fourth, and Long and Alexander signed on
with BMG Interactive, a German music company with corporate
headquarters in London and game headquarters in San Francisco.
The two found that their new publishers wanted to exert more
creative control over their work, holding them to strenuous milestone schedules and doling out money grudgingly, forcing Zombie
to lead an increasingly uncertain, hand-to-mouth existence. BMG's
advance payments, given in installments at project milestones,
tended to be just in time, and barely enough, for Long and Alexander to meet their payroll—a pattern, common in the industry, that
kept them in a constant state of precariousness and suspense. All of
this, of course, served only to make the two feel that their publishers were continually looking for an excuse to abandon them.

Disney, by contrast, seemed thrilled with Zombie. "Disney is
great to work with," Long said. "They know exactly what they
want, they understand how much it costs, they understand we

need lots of expensive equipment, and they let us build profit into all of our bids." There would be none of the desperation on the Disney project that characterized Zombie's other work. Money from Disney came in large amounts and on time, and the company eagerly acquiesced whenever Zombie ran into unexpectedly high costs. Disney immediately ponied up more cash whenever changes in DisneyQuest's design required Zombie to spend more than had been budgeted.

The end of 1996, then, saw Zombie renting separate office space for the DisneyQuest project, stocking it with expensive Silicon Graphics reality engines, and madly hiring and contracting with new staff.

Long and Alexander envisioned the product of Zombie's labors—it was to be one of several "rides" in the new Disney arcades—as a "design your own roller-coaster" attraction. A user would step into a booth, sit facing a computer screen, don a pair of Crystal Eyes glasses, pick up a wand, and draw the roller-coaster's track. Crystal Eyes are glasses with high-speed LCD panels that act as shutters, their action making images on the computer screen appear to be three-dimensional objects floating in space between the user and the screen. Using the wand, the guest appears to be drawing three-dimensional images in midair.

After the design was complete, the guest would store it on a "smart card," then step out of the booth and take the card into a "motion pod." The guest would sit strapped into this pod, again facing a screen and wearing Crystal Eyes, stick his or her card in a slot, and take off on the ride that had just been designed. This pod would move in concert with the view on the screen, around both the X and Y axes, according to the user's designs.

Alexander saw the project's biggest challenge as "the integration" of its various hardware and software systems. It was one thing to compose images and sounds that could be played at high speed on a screen; it was another to integrate sound, images, and motion at roller-coaster speeds, and give the illusion of a fully immersive real world. "It has to be very highly immersive, with split-second timing," Long added. "Everything has to happen at the right time and in the right order. The music and the sound effects have to come exactly at the right moment—you know, you're veering off to the side or something, screaming, lurching—or you won't have the sensation that you really are in this 3D world. I don't think that individually the components are that challenging to construct, but I think system integration will be."

As the project got under way, Long was particularly worried about the behavior of the motion pod. "Disney is really underestimating the difficulties we're going to have with that thing—particularly integrating the video with the motion," he said. "The military pods are in these huge cubes . . . Disney wants to make it move in ways that even the military doesn't try." He also was worried about the same thing that had driven F5's Avi Bar-Zeev out of Disney: the fabled corporate buy-off process. Marvelous as they had been about money, and as understanding as they had appeared before the project began, now that it was under way Disney was showing classic corporate signs of uncertainty and hesitation. "Already, it looks like there is some confusion at Disney. They will okay one of our milestones, say go ahead, then a week or so later start changing their minds, asking lots of questions. You can tell they're kicking everything upstairs."

One of the first things Disney changed its mind about was the Crystal Eyes glasses. I had seen Disney executives tour the HIT lab, paying particular attention to the VRD and to head-mounted displays in general, and they invariably worried out loud about durability and sanitation. How willing, they would ask Furness, are people going to be to put on a headset someone else has just taken off? How can we clean them? Can they stand up to repeated rough use? Zombie had barely gotten started on its DisneyQuest project, then, when Disney scaled back Long and Alexander's plan, removing the Crystal Eyes and wand and having the user design everything on a flat screen.

At first Long was wildly enthusiastic about DisneyQuest—it was, after all, as close to being legitimate virtual reality as anything Zombie had ever done. "You know, the game stuff is great and interesting, extremely challenging, but you don't get to integrate, it's not, you know, super high-end VR; you don't get to get in a pod and move people around," he said. "That's pretty cool right there."

Yet the project never really seemed to excite him the way Zombie's game projects did. Whether his relative disinterest was occasioned by the Crystal Eyes decision, the gradual scaling back of refinements in the project until DisneyQuest struck him as having been withdrawn from the cutting edge, or the indecipherable strategy behind opening new video arcades when national arcade attendance had dropped by 20 percent or more, with PCs and home game machines gobbling up market share, it was hard to tell. But there was no question that Long was far more interested in his two newest game projects—SpecOps and Spearhead—than he was in DisneyQuest.

SpecOps in particular was a classic Zombie project, born of a sensational collision of various forces inside Long's head. The game was a mix of his army experience, fascination with action films, esteem for art and production values, entrepreneurial instincts, and a drive to turn games into interactive fictions. Long hired artist Sandra Smith away from her position as assistant director of Seattle's Center on Contemporary Art, a struggling nonprofit arts organization, to manage the SpecOps project. He steeped Smith and her young charges in military lore, deluging them with war stories and reference books on weaponry, uniforms, military tactics, and history—not only about America, but about Korea, the Middle East, South America, the former Soviet Union, and any other regions that might be involved in the game—and he arranged for Smith and her team to attend live fire exercises at nearby Fort Lewis, Washington, where they could study military tactics and record live weapons fire for use in their game.

I often wondered who was the more amazed by the SpecOps production spectacle: me or the kids recruited by Long to build this game. I would sit in on meetings where Long, dressed like action hero Jackie Chan in a tight black T-shirt and black jeans, with his tattooed wreath of thorns peering out from under the sleeve of his shirt, would be lecturing a group of Gen-X slackers whose only previous exposure to military tactics and weaponry was a single late-night TV viewing of Bill Murray in *Stripes*. Sandra Smith, a winsome, arty young woman with delicate features, wide blue eyes, and a thin silver ring through one nostril, threw herself into her research with a mixture of high energy and bewilderment. She covered the ceiling over her workstation with camouflage netting, spent countless hours poring over military reference books, and constantly found herself asking, "What am I doing here?"

This question seemed particularly pertinent one afternoon when she and her teammates, resplendent in helmets and huge Kevlar vests, were standing in the middle of a desolate field on the U.S. Army's Fort Lewis firing range watching soldiers run and crawl around them while the air was filled with the deafening noise of artillery shell explosions and high-powered weapons fire. "They put us in a Humvee and took us out farther into the field," she said later, "and I'm thinking, 'This is pretty cool.' This guy runs by me with his rifle, I'm right next to him taking a picture." Later, relieved to have been moved to high ground when the soldiers started using live ammunition, she found herself asking a question that was to haunt her for months: "I have a degree in fine arts . . . why on earth am I doing a military simulation game?"

Long's rather ambitious vision for SpecOps was driven in large part by the tremendous advances in computing hardware and software that had attended the release and massive acceptance of Microsoft's Windows 95 operating system, which computer game designers had been eagerly awaiting for years. Now that the operating system was the industry standard, new graphics accelerator cards and chip sets had come on the market that made it possible to display and move through extremely detailed and realistic environments. The lavish textures artists could create on computer screens had Long thinking more and more in terms of movies. Hence his adoption of motion-capture technology, texture mapping, rich and realistic sound effects, real-world military tactics, situations, uniforms, weapons, and decorations, and his insistence that SpecOps artists spare no expense in detailing the game's environments. It all was born of his desire for a photorealism rivaling that of a serious movie director.

Long's obsessive insistence on accuracy wore on his young charges. He had Smith going back again and again to libraries and military surplus stores looking for real medals, patches, goggles, canteens, and even bootlaces. "He might be insane," I heard Smith say one day as she listlessly leafed through a library book on Iraqi Army equipment.

Long came to seem more and more like an auteur, insisting on a kind of "High Art" from his design team. He drove his technical team just as hard, directing them toward production of an entirely new game engine that introduced an array of new technologies, including rapid rendering of three-dimensional environments, a game system that departed from the traditional model of making each distinct level in a game more difficult than the previous level, and an artificial-intelligence system that made game play both more random and more complex. Among the complexities was a function enabling a player's fellow soldiers, or "Ranger buddies," to collaborate with the player by firing weapons, moving in concert with him or her, and warning the player of approaching enemy soldiers. The game also was complex enough to react differently each time a player attacked. "We're using some pretty sophisticated AI techniques," Long explained, "something called potential fields or strange attractors, which allow for pretty complex behavior from the nonplayer characters. You have six Rangers in the game who flock and move appropriately with you."

Hardware had finally advanced to the point at which Long could have it all: While previous Zombie games had been forced into painful trade-offs between production values and engine power, this game could go nearly full bore on both fronts.

By mid-December 1996, there was enough SpecOps art and engine completed to get a look at how it would perform on the PC. You could watch a Ranger figure, manipulated by the player, pick up a weapon and make his way through jungle toward the wreckage of a spy plane. Moving slowly, looking constantly to the left and right, he would creep down to the wreckage, through a massive hole in the side of the plane, into the cockpit where pilot and co-pilot sat slumped, dead, over their control panels . . . then right through the wall of the cockpit as if it weren't there. "We've got to work on our collision detection," Long said with a laugh.

While far more serious and less outwardly energetic than Long, Joanna Alexander was no less driven to make Zombie's games into groundbreaking technical and artistic achievements. Still, she often found herself looking bemused at Long while the two worked at their desks at one end of their long, narrow room at Zombie. The two desks were side by side, set at slight angles, in the embrace of a huge window that looked down on Seattle's First Avenue. Long faced the window, Alexander faced into the room. Alexander sat silent for hours at a time, constantly reading both paper and screen documents, while Long read, wrote longhand notes, typed, talked on the telephone, and cruised restlessly around the World Wide Web. Along the way, he would call out proclamations, dreams, wishes, and plans at Alexander.

He hung up the telephone one day near the end of December, glanced at his screen, then looked over at his partner and said, "I think we should go to Sundance." He was referring to the annual festival of independent filmmakers founded by Robert Redford. Alexander stared back at him, in silence and with aggressive lack of affect, as she often did during his sudden enthusiasms. Long picked up the telephone again and began a frantic round of calls to other game developers. "We need to have a gaming presence at that thing," he said at one point, between calls.

By the end of the day, he had lined up commitments from two other developers to tag along and was working the phone in search of lodging and exhibition space. He also was trying, with considerably less success, to find companions for a hunting expedition he wanted to undertake while at Sundance. "You hunt rabbits at night with combat rifles," he explained. "It's really a lot of fun!"

However detached from reality Mark Long might have seemed, he was the soul of sanity when compared with Linden Rhoads. After a months-long series of broken appointments, I met with Rhoads near the end of the year as Virtual i/O's board, led by TCI, was closing in for the kill. The e-mail-mediated voice of Deep Bile, its members gathered around the company now in a figurative circle of lugubrious and gleeful expectation, rumbled news in my ear of Rhoads's coming demise as I sat down in her office to hear her discourse on Virtual i/O's continued success and good fortune.

"I'll be very honest with you," she began, referring to Microvision's recent IPO. "You look at Microvision getting the kind of valuation they did, they got a sixteen-million-dollar company valuation with eight people and no product. Sixteen million is a pretty high valuation for that, and you go, 'Huh! We have a better story than that!' And so, as you can imagine, I've been fielding more than my fair share of underwriter calls this week!"

A few months before, however, Sony had come out on the Japanese market with a dire twist to the Virtual i/O story. It was the commercial fruit of the laboratory research Joey King had first seen back in 1994. Called the "Glasstron," it was a head-mounted display packaged with earphones and a video CD player (months later, the CD player would be replaced by new technology, the Digital Video Disc [DVD] player) that ran on batteries and played full-length movies stored on a CD. Essentially a movie Discman, it used a red laser diode and new compression technology from Hughes Research. There was no word yet on when Sony planned to enter the American market, but it was clear that the company intended the Glasstron to serve as a vehicle for DVD sales of Sony software—the vast libraries of feature films the company owned because of its purchases of American film studios. The Glasstron, like Nintendo's game machines and Sony's own portable CD players, was destined to be an inexpensive piece of hardware designed to spur sales of the manufacturer's high-margin software products.

Virtual i/O, it seemed to me, was doomed. The company's i-Glasses!, sold without a disc player, would eventually be competing against a combination player-display package that likely would cost less than Virtual i/O's headset alone. Moreover, Virtual i/O would have to compete for retailers against a company with immeasurably greater market clout. Faced with a choice between Virtual i/O's headset and Sony's entire line of products, retailers would have no choice but to stock the Glasstron on Sony's terms and show Virtual i/O the door.

"Actually," Rhoads said when I voiced my concerns about the Glasstron to her, "I think this has really helped us a lot, because their confidence in the category has really given us *huge* credibility as a category. All the big companies that we work with are now very, very excited about the category, because Sony too is working on it. It helps you get better meetings. And once you get better meetings, then of course you have to have the technology to impress them, and of course we have it. I think their entry into the market has really just helped us to no end."

It took considerable effort to get Rhoads off her happy track, but I did eventually manage to ask some questions inspired by things I had read and heard in messages from Deep Bile. When I asked Rhoads about layoffs or firings at Virtual i/O, she denied that there had been any, then set off on a long, sober, frenetic monologue: "We had some employees who were dearly, *dearly* beloved people. In fact, one of the great ironies is that those who work less hard socialize the most. You're here working until two A.M., and they're at the pool hall every night; you never take a lunch—I rarely do—and they lunch every day; and they get on their social soapbox more often, and so we let go some people who were *dearly loved*, because they weren't getting their jobs done, or they were very unsupportive of the company and its efforts, or Greg. And employees were really angry about it, and we had some fallout from one of these firings for about six months. And I had a really difficult situation in which I had to go around to every department, one on one, and I had to sit down with each department and say, 'I think everyone expected a big apology,' and I just said, 'Look, no apologies, I'm holding every job in this company in my hands, and on an ongoing basis if the people who don't perform stay here on their jobs not to get the work done, or not supporting our efforts to make decisions and get things done, if I do that for a long enough time, *everyone* will lose their job. So I've got to make the few hard decisions and do it right, and I believe what I did was right, and if there's anyone here who feels there is a way to be supportive of the company without doing what you are requested to do in your job, or being supportive of my vision or Greg's vision or your department head's vision, at this point, while your talents are needed here and are valued, and your camaraderie, it is most likely that I will ask you to leave and make it easier for me now sooner than later.' I did that throughout the company, and we definitely had company culture, you know, chasms that we had to cross, as you are a growing, struggling company. . . ."

Eventually, I was able to make my escape and ask Deep Bile

about Rhoads's pronouncement. The characteristically angry answer came in e-mail:

> The pool player she's talking about was one of
> the original first hires and the hardest working
> man in the company. He literally hand built many
> if not all of the units for the first year. He
> was a very outgoing and enthusiastic man who
> worked far too many hours, was very sociable and
> did like to play pool and ski. And he put those
> and many other things on hold for a full year.
> He was also more or less the sys admin (so he
> was way overworked) and all he wanted was to be
> guaranteed that he could have EVERY OTHER
> WEEKEND OFF. Yes, that is right, he would be
> willing to work 18 hours a day MTWTFSSMTWTF (12
> days on, 2 days off). Another poor bastard
> wanted the same deal, so he would cover the
> other weekend while this guy was off and vice
> versa. This would assure that there was always
> someone to be at Greg's beck and call for his
> weird last minute trips to God knows where in
> the middle of the night. (They called me more
> than once at 2:00 am trying to get me to drive
> to the airport right then and there to catch a
> 4:00 am flight, so I eventually got an unlisted
> number.)
>   And this was just too much for Linden, so she
> fired him.
>   And contrary to what she is saying, she NEVER
> fired anyone because they weren't doing their
> job. Being incompetent usually meant you were
> guaranteed a job. Everyone she fired, she fired
> because they stood up to her or Greg.

It was becoming psychologically more difficult for me by the moment to hear the soaring good cheer from Rhoads in one ear, and the escalating rage from Deep Bile in the other. The blithe bluster with which Rhoads dismissed any hint of error, failure, or wrongdoing on the part of her or Amadon, combined with the ineradicable and deepening bitterness in the collective heart of Deep Bile, soon set me to brooding on the pattern I saw forming in nearly all of these endeavors: Everywhere I looked I saw engineers and inventors with whom I couldn't help but sympathize being—at least in my emerging view—manhandled by businesspeople (all of whom struck me as either evil or inept, or both) with whom they were forced by necessity to ally themselves. At the HIT lab, Tom Furness, inventor of the VRD, was watching wheelers and dealers wrest control of his invention away from him and destroy his dreams in the process; at F5 Labs, the widening chasm between inventor Mike Almquist and businessman Jeff Hussey looked to me to be destined to resolve itself in Hussey's favor, if only because Almquist seemed clueless when it came to corporate maneuvering; at Microvision, David Melville, inventor of the VRD's scanner, was starting his new job having been deceived about his stock options in a way that made him feel that his new employers had no regard for his talents; at Zombie, Long and Alexander were being squeezed by their publishers to the point where they were on the verge of giving up on their vision; and at Virtual i/O, virtually every clever engineer from cofounder Wolfgang Mack on had been thrown out the door and left to nurse hideous psychological wounds while Rhoads and Amadon kept happily churning up the company, its technology, and its people.

This last example, though, did not look as if it would prevail for much longer. While Rhoads was saying in one ear, "I think, you know, before the year is out, one of the best things we'll do is we'll be allowed to announce all these OEM deals that we're very close to signing, with really large companies, to provide them with HMDs . . . that's really very exciting," my other ear was hearing, "At the risk of ruining my so far flawless predictive record, I'm going on the record that G and L will either be gone completely or at the very least there will be a new CEO and president in the next two to four weeks. There will probably be one combo CEO/president position since I don't know how they could afford both a CEO and president. May God strike somebody else dead if I am wrong."

Once they had scraped Tom Furness up off their examining-room floor, it did not take his doctors and nurses long to discover that he had a gangrenous gall bladder, the cocktail of its causes including a hefty dose of stress. He was transferred immediately to an adjacent hospital, operated upon, and sent home two days later.

He did not, however, bounce back. On his first forays back to the HIT lab some two weeks after his surgery, he looked gray and spectral, walking and talking with shocking zestlessness. His eyes were dull, his voice barely audible, and his interest and attention fleeting. For nearly a month, he would either come into the lab for only a few hours or call in sick in the morning and then stay home for the next few days. Finally, he left town on vacation.

Some in the lab speculated that the surgery, coming on top of years of overwork and high stress, had worn him out. Others suspected that his brush with mortality had unduly depressed him. The only person in the lab who seemed unworried about Furness was Joey King, who had been at the hospital when Furness was wheeled out of the operating room and who spent hours at Furness's home in the ensuing days talking about the future of the lab. "Tom's just trying to avoid the lab," he said, recounting his conversations with Furness, "because he doesn't want to face up to the reality there. When he comes back, he's going to have some hard decisions to make, and he doesn't want to have to do that." With the lab's two biggest contracts—one with Microvision, the other with the AFOSR—coming to an end, Furness would be forced either to terminate some of his researchers or ask them to work for no pay while others, whose projects were funded, would be collecting relatively high salaries. "Now," said King, "you're going to have people who are rich, and people who have nothing. Which doesn't bother me, because that's the way it should be in a soft-money situation. But it's going to kill Tom."

King felt that Furness's tendency to depend on miracles had finally caught up with him. "Tom thinks that there's some *thing*, this *thing* that we're going to be able to do that's going to solve all of our problems. But it just isn't going to happen!"

Thus King was about to embark on a long trip to California, Texas, and Japan in search of money for the lab. He had lined up visits with Hughes Training, Inc., Texas Instruments, Sony, Sharp, and Fujitsu. "I'm going to be beating the drums for the lab. I'll show them cool stuff they can do and where they should take corporate research, and make my pitch. I'll try to get a cash gift out of them . . . it's happened before!"

King had always been perplexed by the yawning gap between the reality of Furness's enterprise and its image. People outside the lab, from the general public to the lab's consortium members, generally had the impression that the HIT lab was prospering. "The lab is always going through these *huge* [pronounced, in King's grandiose Texas twang, "hee-YOUdge"] financial troubles and nobody knows it," King said. "A lot of books I've read about start-up companies, we're sort of the *same thing*. The general perception is, 'We're just slugging it out! It's great! Beautiful!' And the next week it's, 'Okay, we're dying, we're dead, we don't have enough money, we have no future.' "

The more he thought about his experiences at the lab, at more established labs, and at F5, the more he realized that the HIT lab was the academic equivalent of a start-up. Just as a start-up business is essentially proselytizing to the marketplace for a new technology, so is the academic start-up proselytizing to researchers and corporate sponsors for new technologies and new approaches to old problems. "I mean, the HIT lab is a start-up!" King exclaimed. "It is a start-up that never has a chance to really go over the top. Because it's in a 'business segment' that hasn't got any growth potential." He laughed mordantly. "So actually, I've gotten really great training at the lab for being in a start-up company. Because I haven't had a chance to actually succeed! And I think Squish has actually gone through the same thing. I mean, he was in this company, he was always on the edge, and he was always pushing as hard as he could, but there's no success! Even success wasn't success."

Reaching for a metaphor, King found himself looking, in grand American business tradition, to football. Corporations forever have turned to football for inspiration, drawing on the sport for symbols of success and determination. It was an indication of the difference between the start-up and the established corporation, however, that King's sporting image was one of exhaustion and futility rather than teamwork and triumph: "I remember they used to train football players by putting them in these rubber harnesses and basically staking them to the ground and telling them to run."

Meanwhile, as Furness was convalescing, his nemeses at Microvision were preparing yet another unpleasant surprise for him. Ever since the company's IPO, the lab's VRD researchers had been eagerly awaiting delivery on a Microvision promise of stock options for the entire research team. Even the researchers who would not be moving over to full employment by Microvision had been promised options, and Rich Johnston and Mike Tidwell in particular were eager to see what the company would give them. The two had had occasional conversations with Steve Willey, in which Willey outlined in general terms the sort of package he had in mind. Tidwell and Johnston expected that their packages would include options at a below-market price, exercisable in four or five years. If the company somehow pulled off a miracle and amounted to something down the road, the packages could well be worth several thousand dollars each.

Near the end of fall, during Willey's weekly visits to the lab, Johnston would ask where his and Tidwell's offer letters were, and Willey would slap himself in the forehead every time and exclaim, "I can't believe I forgot them again. . . . I've been meaning to bring them up. . . . I'll bring them up next time. . . ." Willey's evasions had become yet another running joke for Johnston and Tidwell.

Finally, just before leaving the country on another sales tour, Willey came up to the lab late one afternoon and handed Johnston his offer letter. Quickly perusing it, Johnston noticed a devious provision: Members of the HIT lab's VRD research team had six months from the end of the VRD project to exercise their options, at $6 a share—more than the current market price of Microvision stock. Failure to exercise resulted in forfeiture of the stock.

The options, then, were worthless. They were designed not to reward Johnston and Tidwell for their work, but to bring more immediate cash to Microvision. Worse, they made it look as if Willey himself did not expect Microvision to be around years from now, and was trying to get as much cash out of Furness's invention as quickly as he could.

"We never talked about anything like this," a stunned Johnston said.

"Well," said Willey, already on his way out the door, "we just decided to do it that way."

Minutes later, Johnston and Tidwell walked into Furness's office, where the director was languidly trying to get his bearings. They told Furness about the offer letter, then told him they were resigning from the lab.

"Steve brought that stupid letter down and made all these negative comments," Tidwell said later. " 'We don't think you're proven enough to justify paying you more. . . .' I've invented the thing, I've worked on this for three and a half years. . . . I'm a fuckin' retinal-scanning optical engineer—what's the pay scale for that? Those guys are just fuckin' criminals, man . . . they can kiss my ass!"

Within days, he was working at Virtual i/O, and Johnston was working at Information Optics, a start-up developing laser data storage systems that promised one day to replace CD-ROM drives.

Tidwell's break with the lab brought him little in the way of satisfaction—a point that was hammered home to him late one Friday, when he, Johnston, and Melville met in the VRD lab to go over their files. Afterward, standing out in the hall, Johnston said, "Dave, I think you should know that I'm leaving the lab."

"Are you still going to consult with us?"

Johnston set his jaw, his eyes flashing. "No."

Melville turned to Tidwell. "And what about you?"

"I'm going to Virtual i/O," Tidwell snapped.

Melville knew there was no chance that his new bosses would allow Tidwell, now working for a competitor, to work with him. And with that, the VRD team was officially dissolved.

"That's the thing that makes me sick," Tidwell said later. "I don't know . . . it was sad, after all we'd done and been through together, and now it was just scattering."

Furness, yet again, was utterly bereft. With no real warning, he suddenly found himself with no research team for his "life's work," and since the project had less than a year to run, he knew he would find it impossible to hire new, qualified scientists. No one would leave a secure job for the sake of one that had only a few months of funding.

He also was losing his most talented, successful research team all at once. "Man, this is about as low as I've ever felt," he said dispiritedly to me. "To lose good people like that . . . and for no good reason. If these Microvision guys would only . . ." Here, his voice trailed off, and he stared into space. "I'll tell you this," he said at last. "If it weren't for my religion, I couldn't find a way to be at peace with this."

He may or may not have found a measure of peace in what happened a few days later. The University of Washington conferred regularly with a board of financial advisers who examined the school's stock portfolio and made buy and sell recommendations on stocks. After looking over Microvision's management and prospects, the board recommended that the University of Washington sell all of its Microvision stock as soon as possible. It was an unprecedented piece of advice, a declaration that the school had lost all faith in its own corporate partners. Willey and Rutkowski, getting wind of the recommendation, realized immediately that the sale could be a public-relations disaster for the company, making the price of their stock plummet. They contacted the university and begged it not to sell until they could make a presentation.

The board agreed, and the two came out to the school. A few minutes into their presentation, they started arguing with each other over how many employees Microvision had. After they were finished, they were no sooner out of the room than the advisers upgraded their recommendation from "sell" to "sell immediately!"

Within days, the university had divested itself of nearly all its Microvision stock.

After his inadvertent confrontation with Mike Almquist in the F5 conference room, Dave Olafson quietly lined up a new job for himself and waited patiently for CEO Jeff Hussey to get around to firing him. "I don't want to stay in a place where people don't respect my work," he said to me one night. "I told Jeff that I didn't think I could stay with this company much longer no matter what they decide." He felt it was impossible to get the company CEO to listen to his side of the argument. "Jeff trusts Squish too much, and because of that, he doesn't trust me. No matter what kind of Band-Aid we put on our problems, we still have to play Squish's way."

As it happened, Almquist and Hussey were so preoccupied with another problem that they didn't have time to consider what to do about Olafson. *PC Magazine*, the nation's leading mass-market magazine reporting exclusively on the computer industry, had heard about F5 and wanted to test and review BIG/ip for a cover story the magazine was writing on Internet products. It was a significant coup for F5, and an opportunity that wildly excited Hussey and Almquist. Since *PC Magazine* was one of the most influential publications in the industry, the exposure F5 would get just as its first product was nearing release would be invaluable.

The timing of the *PC Magazine* test and article, though, which initially had seemed perfect, now was a disaster. With the discovery that BIG/ip didn't work properly and the understanding that it would take months to fix it came the realization that the opportunity could be fatal. If Almquist were to take a BIG/ip down to the magazine only to have its testers uncover its hideous flaws— a high likelihood—the company would be ruined. Not to be part of the story at all, however, would be almost as bad: More visible and established competitors would be showcased, the world of web site owners and operators wouldn't even know F5 existed, and service providers all over the world would be making their one and only load-balancing investment in someone else's products, effectively freezing F5 out of the market before BIG/ip was finished. Internet technology was changing at a breakneck pace, and F5's exclusion from the *PC Magazine* article threatened to slam shut the company's already narrow window of opportunity.

Hussey and his employees held meeting after meeting at which they agonized over which would be worse: to be slammed in a review or be ignored. Hussey kept peppering Almquist with the same question: Can we survive a rigorous test and review of this product? Every time he asked, he got the same answer: We don't know, but we're pretty sure we can't.

Finally, Almquist and Hussey decided they had no choice but to hack together a BIG/ip and hope for the best. Almquist, Olafson, and sales VP Lynn Luukinen flew down to California one morning to make a presentation to *PC Magazine* and give them a machine for testing.

It came as something of a relief to Almquist to see that his examiners at the magazine were relatively unfamiliar with Internet issues, and he performed what might be called a "Full Godzilla," staging an elaborate, entertaining, and energetic presentation for which he pulled out all the stops on his considerable—if eccentric—charm. Almquist regaled his audience with his vision of the Internet's future, the infrastructure weaknesses contributing to its present problems in handling traffic, and his invention of a real-time load-balancing switch that dramatically upped the power of a web site.

Finally it came time to set up for the test, and Almquist watched, terrified, as Olafson tried to configure the BIG/ip they had brought down for review. "I was torn," he said later, "because I wanted to take Dave to show him what kind of a fucked-up situation we're in. He doesn't get it. He doesn't understand it. But part of me didn't want to take Dave, because I knew he'd come off as a buffoon, and he'd damage the company." Now, the buffoon in Dave emerged, as he started muttering exclamations within hearing range of the magazine reviewers: "This isn't working! What the . . . Now *this* isn't working . . . !" Almquist, who had been frantically trying to distract the reviewers, finally took over at the controls and got the machine properly configured. His satisfaction turned immediately to dismay, however, when Olafson began exclaiming his relief—"Oh my God! It's working! I don't believe it! It's working!"—as if a functioning BiG/ip were the last thing in the world he expected to see.

Somehow, Almquist managed to keep the reviewers from tuning in on Olafson's revealing performance, and the writers asked the two to wait outside the room while they set up their test. Then they all went off to have lunch together while the test program put BIG/ip through its paces.

When they returned an hour later, they walked back into the room with a panicked Almquist putting all his energy into maintaining a calm exterior. *PC Magazine*'s testers had hooked BIG/ip up to sixty computers that hammered the box constantly with connection requests; this made for a rigorous test that Almquist had severe doubts about BIG/ip's ability to withstand.

No sooner did the group walk into the magazine offices than one of the testers came out and said to Almquist, "Um . . . could you come in here for a second?"

With visions of his company going down in flames, Almquist walked into the testing room and looked at the big bank of monitors hooked up to BIG/ip. Each monitor was supposed to be displaying either a large "R," for "Running," or a large "D," for "Done." Instead, every screen in the room was displaying a large "X."

"What happened?" asked Almquist.

"For some reason, our test program stopped functioning," came the answer.

"Look at BIG/ip!" Olafson said, elated. "*It's* still running! Something must be wrong with your test suite!" Thrilled, he started looking up numbers on BIG/ip and saw that it had handled monstrous loads of traffic without crashing. "Look at all the traffic it did! This is great!"

A cursory glance at BIG/ip's log showed Almquist that instead of handling the traffic requests as they came pouring in, an overloaded BIG/ip had instead "hung" all sixty test computers, putting them on a kind of indefinite hold until the test program grew hopelessly confused and crashed itself. "Shit," Almquist said to himself, "BIG/ip hung all their tester boxes. It's *so cool* that it crashed their test system." A Band-Aid Olafson had patched into the code, designed to keep it from crashing, now hung connections whenever it grew too stressed. "Dammit, Dave," he hissed, trying to calm down the excited Olafson. "You don't get it . . . the only reason BIG/ip stayed up and running is because it took all their test boxes down."

Almquist looked around the room and saw that the magazine's

testers were going over the source code in their program, looking for the error that had caused the test to fail. Suddenly he realized that they thought the problem lay in their code rather than in BIG/ip's. Hurriedly offering regrets, he told his hosts that he and his companions had a plane to catch, then packed up his BIG/ip and ran out the door.

"Let's get the hell out of here," he said to Olafson and Luukinen when they were safely out in the car, and the three sped away like criminals fleeing a bank job.

Back in Seattle, Almquist explained to a transfixed Hussey what had happened, and offered him a ray of hope. "Now, if they're smart guys," he said, "they'll be able to figure it out. They were only going to spend a day on each box they tested. I think that *incredibly* smart guys would be able to figure it out. *Regular* smart guys would need more than one day to figure it out. *Really stupid idiots* are going to need like a few weeks or something to figure it out. So I don't think they're ever going to figure it out, because they're spending one day on each product, and actually today they're writing the article. Today they're supposed to have all the testing done, of all four products, and they're going to write the article."

They had to wait a month to find the answer. "True to its name, the BIG/ip, from F5 Labs, is up there with the other big boys in our load-balancing roundup," the review began. Then, after describing BIG/ip and comparing it favorably with its more expensive competition, the review went on to note that BIG/ip "was in beta at the time of testing, but it should be shipping by the time you read this."

For once, Almquist and his company had caught a break.

Almquist came back from the testing fiasco determined to get rid of Olafson, and the atmosphere at F5 turned into that of an unacknowledged death watch. Olafson printed out all of the code he had written, and he, Almquist, and Avi Bar-Zeev, pretending that they were conducting business as usual, spent long hours going over it line by line, analyzing its structure and looking for the bug that kept making BIG/ip crash every three days. Outside of the conference room, Almquist would refuse to speak to Olafson, and I heard increasingly angry exchanges in which Bar-Zeev would ask

Olafson a pointed question about a line of code and a defensive Olafson would snap, "Keep in mind that that was written under enormous time pressure!"

Finally, one morning, Hussey took Olafson out for breakfast and told him he was fired. After Olafson had gone, Hussey sat alone in the conference room, clearly shaken. "You just have to turn all your nerve endings off and force yourself to do that kind of thing," he said.

It is interesting to note that Olafson was happier than any of the people he left behind at F5. "I thought the firing was done in a professional, respectable manner," he told me that night. He had decided that Hussey had fired him not because of dissatisfaction with his work but because he could not fire Almquist, a company founder and holder of one-third of F5's stock. "Everyone understood that it was a personality conflict," he said. "I would have loved to have stayed if we could have resolved the personality issues, but there was no way." Hussey had given him a severance check that Olafson regarded as generous, and he was to start a new job in two weeks for a larger salary, more vacation, and the guarantee that he could go home at night.

Hussey, meanwhile, sat in the conference room and eagerly fed his growing anger toward Almquist, whom he blamed for having let Olafson lead the company down a path that led to an indefinite—but definitely long—delay in shipping a reliable version of BIG/ip. "I have a job," he shouted at me one morning. "Predict the future. *Be right.* Squish doesn't know what the fuck he's doing, managerially speaking." Another time, furious and frustrated, he screamed—referring to what he regarded as his success in the first round of fund-raising—"*I* shipped F5! Now it's up to these guys to ship BIG/ip! *I've* done it! *I've* performed! *I've* delivered! These guys haven't done shit!"

He felt Almquist bore nearly all the responsibility for F5's predicament. "I'm putting the screws to Squish! He's deceived himself into thinking that he can supervise himself." Oddly, he seemed particularly furious at Almquist for working late into the night—sometimes all night—and hated the fact that Almquist was always at his desk when he, Hussey, left the office at the end of the day. "I'm tired of these *heroics* . . . staying here late. . . . I'm not impressed!"

Much of Hussey's resentment seemed occasioned less by Almquist's failure to deliver than by Hussey's inability to understand computer programming—a common problem for financiers who involve themselves in high-tech start-ups. Since he had no background in software, he had no way of evaluating the information and predictions given to him by his developers—a circumstance that made him less and less confident, and more and more frustrated, as he tried to chart a course for his company. He would often mutter furiously to me about "developers having me by the short hairs," and would greet good news from Almquist with a shout: "Don't blow sunshine up my ass!"

As time wore on, his frustration came to seem more and more like jealousy. In meetings with prospective partners, where it was necessary to explain the technology behind BIG/ip in some detail, Hussey would try to keep Almquist quiet while he shouted such oddities as "Voice is data! Voice is data!" Almquist spent more of his scarce speaking time correcting Hussey's errors than he did explaining the nuts and bolts of BIG/ip, and often I would catch him making manic, mocking faces behind Hussey's back while the CEO perorated. Almquist fell into the habit, when Hussey was out of the room, of chuckling indulgently and saying, "It just kills me the way Jeff thinks he invented BIG/ip," his tone that of the affectionate parent of an involuntarily cute child. Hussey, for his part, would tell me at great length about his self-imposed reading regimen—one that he expected would soon make Almquist irrelevant. "I've got a foot-thick stack of books on programming at home," he said. "I'm reading this stuff every night." His newfound knowledge "means I don't need Squish anymore! *I* can do BIG/ip! All I need is four programmers!"

As news of BIG/ip and its inventor began to filter out into the industry, F5 began getting inquiries from magazines and newspapers. Occasionally, publications would send photographers to the company to take pictures of Almquist or Bar-Zeev. These episodes sent Hussey into a frenzy of complaints about employee time wasted being photographed and interviewed, and about the risk of press attention making Almquist and Bar-Zeev complacent. "The history books are filled with stories of companies with fabulous technology but lacking business acumen," he wrote in e-mail to me. "And history is what they become. I don't want that to happen to F5. If Mike and Avi continue to think they are the 'story' when in fact they are the reason our story sucks, we will be history too. . . . I will require them to pay homage to the individual and group which makes their adulation possible . . . me and the rest of us."

November and December saw Hussey grow increasingly given to fits of rage as it became ever clearer that BIG/ip, originally projected as a quick six-month project, was turning into a complex and indefinite endeavor. Every day, it seemed, Almquist would deliver the news that some new discovery meant the latest deadline for BIG/ip had to be moved back yet again. He would turn aside Hussey's outrage and dismay with a joke: "I thought it could be done by November because . . . I was smoking crack!" This sort of answer, of course, would leave Hussey shaking and sputtering until either he or Almquist left the room.

For all his righteousness, Hussey himself was often finding ways to impede progress on BIG/ip. Every time he talked to a potential customer, he would come back and insist that a new function be added to BIG/ip, thereby pushing back its time to completion even further. He spent hours each day trading stocks at work—an endeavor that required him to have a dedicated stock-feed computer, displaying instantaneous news of all stock trading, installed in his office. During one of his meetings with F5 employees in which he ranted about their inability to move forward, he was finally interrupted by Matt Sommer, F5's system administrator, who asked him which of the five tasks on his list Hussey wanted him to finish first. "My *stock feed*," Hussey hissed, putting the four BIG/ip-related tasks on the back burner.

The dedication of time and resources to Hussey's hobby was a sore point with Almquist, as was Hussey's apparent disinterest in hiring new developers to help ease Almquist's burden. Ever since the two had raised their first round of money, Almquist had been begging Hussey to hire more developers. After nearly a year,

Hussey had found none, and his sporadic placement of employment ads generally failed to draw any applications from what he deemed qualified people. Under the pretext that Almquist should not be distracted from his programming, Hussey wrote the ads with little or no input from him and seldom arranged for him to interview potential new hires—a baffling policy, to say the least, and one that made it all but impossible to find good engineers.

Now, with Olafson gone and the company getting too low on money to hire anyone new, nearly all of the burden of finishing BIG/ip rested on Almquist's shoulders alone.

The departure of Olafson made it irrefutably clear that Hussey would have to secure a second round of funding from new investors, since BIG/ip would not be bringing in money before the company coffers ran dry. The prospect depressed him, not only because he hated writing placement documents—complex combinations of history, prognostication, and technical description—but because he hated running the risk of making his developers complacent. "I'm not getting more money so I can buy these guys more time," he insisted. "I'm getting more money so I can get more bodies in here. I want these guys to know that they're not indispensable! I want to be able to get rid of people!"

Although he seemed blisslessly unaware of it, Hussey was caught in a complicated paradox. In order to attract new investors, he needed to hire more developers, making it look as if the company was a growing concern. But now he could not hire new employees until he raised more money, for F5 was nearly broke. It was almost the end of November 1996, and F5 would have to hoard its money carefully to make it stretch through January.

Once a start-up is launched, it has to meet certain performance criteria in order to attract more investors. Venture capitalists look for signs that the company asking them for money is increasing in value, even if it has not yet shipped a product. The two prime indicators of a company's prospects are how well it is adhering to its own schedule and how effectively and quickly it is adding skilled people. Since raising its first $1.2 million, F5's workforce was unchanged in terms of numbers, having shed two programmers—Adam Feuer and now Dave Olafson—and its VP of sales, Ross

Morris, and hired programmer Avi Bar-Zeev and sales VP Lynn Luukinen. Hussey was supposed to somehow persuade investors that the company was on track even though its product, behind schedule, was essentially being written by two people, one of whom was a company founder and had been designated to supervise development rather than actually undertake it. Hussey had to go out and make the argument that F5 was growing more valuable even as it was failing to grow and failing to meet the schedule it had promoted in its previous round of fund-raising.

In the face of all this, Hussey was all bluster and optimism about his chances of raising more money, while his board was skeptical. "He's going to have a lot of trouble," predicted board member Richard Novotny, who represented the EnCompass Group, F5's largest investor. And fund-raising was only one of Hussey's troubles. Already, Novotny was talking with other board members about finding a COO for F5, taking away Hussey's management responsibilities and having him concentrate on strategic alliances and sales. "We've been patient with Jeff because he's young and he's inexperienced," said Novotny. "But it's clear that he's in way over his head."

Matters were not helped by the atmosphere of paralysis that settled over F5 in the days after Olafson's firing. Employee initiative ground to a halt. Hussey would call meetings at which he alternately exhorted and upbraided his charges, then laid out a list of tasks to be accomplished and asked for volunteers to take them on. Then he would sit, growing gradually more angry, as his employees artfully dodged him. "They're afraid to volunteer for anything," Almquist said after one such meeting, "because they figure it's just a setup for getting fired."

The atmosphere finally grew too chaotic and depressing for Avi Bar-Zeev, who commenced a campaign that looked at first like an attempt to improve F5's chances of success, then like an attempt to undermine Almquist and take over control of the BIG/ip project, then like an attempt to destroy his friendship with Almquist.

Bar-Zeev had agreed, he said, to come to F5 from Disney because he believed he would have to work on its network product for only a few months before moving on to his passion—building tools and systems for VR applications. He had expected, as had Almquist, that BIG/ip would be a minor, obligatory, boring inconvenience on the way to working on their dream project. But with the collapse of the first try at writing BIG/ip, it now was obvious that the few months would be stretching into a full year or more. Worse, Bar-Zeev felt, Almquist's lack of discipline was threatening to make his wait indefinite. "I came here to do VR," he told me. "Now I don't see them doing that for at least a year. This just goes on and on and on. It'll never end! Squish just keeps adding features and functions. He doesn't understand that you can't work that way. I just can't take this anymore."

He professed to have lost all faith in Almquist. "He's just hopelessly scattered. It's okay to have a CTO who's scattered if you have a CEO who's in control. But Jeff isn't in control. He doesn't really understand the technical issues, and he doesn't understand the people issues."

Bar-Zeev began complaining that Squish had betrayed him. "My deal was that I'll come up after the company has shipped something and is stable. Now, it hasn't shipped anything and it isn't stable. It'll take till mid- or late February to finish all the stuff he wants to do on 1.2 or 3 or whatever it is. [Almquist used decimals partly to denote improved and debugged versions of BIG/ip, and partly to parody the industry practice of designation-by-decimal of product improvements.] I think eventually they'll do fine, but I don't want to go through any more of this. You talk to Jeff, he says it's Squish. You talk to Squish, he says it's Jeff." He felt that the road to success lay along a route only he could define. "We need to freeze this product and start work immediately on 2.0 [a new version he had begun designing himself, with a radically different internal code structure]. I can understand their thinking, because the company has to survive, but you just can't develop products this way. Squish keeps adding functions, new things. He doesn't understand that you introduce problems when you do that. You need to make a clean break and start over."

He wanted to abandon the current BIG/ip and start from scratch with a new version built according to his own design, and he began meeting with Hussey when Almquist was out of the office to argue for his approach. In F5 meetings, he would interrupt Almquist constantly, objecting to any plan that involved improving the existing version of BIG/ip. Almquist and Joey King were consistently dismissive and scornful of Bar-Zeev, as both were convinced his ploy was a grab for power rather than a sincere attempt to make F5's product better. "His version 2.0 thing," Almquist said, "is just Avi saying, 'Jeff, look at me! Look at me! I'm indispensable! You need me! You need me!' " "Avi is Hitler," King liked to say. "Give him Czechoslovakia, and he'll march right through it and into Poland."

Indeed, it did look like Bar-Zeev was trying to insinuate himself, to his own advantage, between Hussey and Almquist. He argued ever more strenuously to Hussey that the company should adopt his plan to drop everything and work exclusively on BIG/ip 2.0, and give Bar-Zeev more responsibility for the project while reducing Almquist's. He kept enumerating Almquist's flaws and feeding Hussey's growing conviction that Almquist would never finish BIG/ip. "He *wants* to fail," Bar-Zeev insisted. "He's afraid to finish."

He also began angling with Hussey for a better deal. Bar-Zeev's contract with F5 gave him options on only 3 percent of the company's stock, and he had no formal compensation agreement with Hussey and Almquist for his employment by their new VR company. While presenting his grand plan for BIG/ip 2.0 to Hussey, he also tried negotiating for F5 stock options. When Hussey made it clear that that was out of the question, Bar-Zeev asked what percentage of stock in Hussey and Almquist's new VR company—the planned successor to F5 Labs—he might expect to own, and Hussey said, "None."

"But Squish promised me stock," Bar-Zeev said.

Hussey answered in a way that struck me as eerily ominous at the time, although I didn't quite know why: *"It wasn't his to give."*

When Hussey refused Bar-Zeev's request for stock, the developer went on an unofficial strike. Upon arrival for work in the morning, he would lie down on a black leather couch in the office he shared with Almquist, and stay there all day long, leaving once in a while for food or coffee. Almquist, relieved to have Bar-Zeev finally cease his relentless campaigning against him, was amused;

Hussey was apoplectic in private and manfully tried to ignore Bar-Zeev whenever he had to go back to Almquist's office.

This more or less bizarre state of affairs went on for nearly a month. Almquist worked, Bar-Zeev lay on the couch, King made Hitler jokes, and Hussey shut himself up in the conference room and raged. Occasionally, Bar-Zeev would get up off the couch, fiddle with his computer, and make telephone calls. He generally made calls only when Almquist was wearing his oversized headphones, on the theory that his erstwhile friend could not hear his conversations over the roar of music in his ears. He did not know that Almquist often wore the headphones with the sound turned off, so he could learn—as he soon did—that Bar-Zeev was looking for another job.

"Avi's negotiating with Zombie," Almquist told King one day. "I'm finding this to be incredibly humorous . . . one of the most fun things on Earth. . . ." He found himself invoking Godzilla with greater frequency, referring to himself in the third person, and conjuring up his favorite image of enraged futility: "Squish is very good at being Godzilla! With his bright and shiny teeth! Clawing at the sky!"

Bar-Zeev was indeed considering a move to Zombie, where Mark Long was offering him a job as member of the Spearhead team. The only factor holding Bar-Zeev back was that the offer was for a subordinate rather than lead position. "It really wouldn't be appropriate for me not to be the lead," Bar-Zeev said to me. He felt that wherever he turned, he faced either the frustrations of the corporate world or an array of shortcomings among entrepreneurs in the start-up world. No one seemed to share either his vision for the VR industry or his vision of Avi Bar-Zeev. "Ultimately, I think I'm just going to have to go start my own company," he said.

Hussey, who had been listening closely to Bar-Zeev and gradually allying with him and against Almquist, did an abrupt about-face when Bar-Zeev asked for more stock and money. Now he regarded Bar-Zeev as an evil egomaniac who was threatening to destroy F5, and as Bar-Zeev's informal strike lengthened, Hussey's fury grew. "He just lies there on the *couch*; he never does any *work*." Referring to a recent photo shoot for a *Fast Company* article on high-tech Seattle start-ups that had included Almquist and Bar-Zeev but not Hussey, he added: "He's always going off to be photographed for *magazines*. . . ."

I followed Almquist across downtown Seattle one day when he fled the "madness and badness" in his office and walked over to the office suite containing F5's web machinery. Almquist wanted to update the version of BIG/ip that was servicing the frantic requests of F5's pornography server. He also wanted a little surcease.

Since Almquist routinely dealt with the fulminations of Hussey, the machinations of Bar-Zeev, and the constant series of disappointments and disasters that attended his work with a series of exclamations—"Incredibly humorous!" "Amusing!" "Madness!" "Quite hilarious!"—manic facial expressions, pirate speak, jokes about Matt Sommer's goat fetish, and long stretches of "coding like the wind" with his headphones on and his back turned to his tormenters, I had not really noticed, until we were safely locked inside the secluded room full of web servers, how frantic, depressed, and exhausted he had become. But we no sooner settled down in the room there than he started tinkering with his machinery and screaming out his frustration and anger. "The whole situation has become so incredibly ludicrous that it's difficult for me to get really upset about it," he began, clearly upset. "Yesterday I was incredibly *pissed*, incredibly mad, which is weird, because that now makes the tenth time in my life I've ever been really mad. There are so many people milling around, fighting, screaming, backbiting, and milling about because they don't have a clear vision or clear focus. So I went home really pissed, really burned out, and this morning I woke up and said, 'It's obvious! Fire everybody!' This is not, like, 'Things are broken.' This is my last recourse. This is, like, a moment of *absolute calm*. A moment of absolute clarity."

F5 at that moment had ten employees: Almquist, Bar-Zeev, Joey King, Hussey, Sommer, Andre Helmstetter—hired out of Evergreen State College to do product testing and put together BIG/ip boxes for shipment to customers—a CFO, a VP of sales, a marketing manager, and a receptionist. Nearly all had been hired because Almquist and Hussey felt they needed to ramp up to handle testing, shipping, and sales of BIG/ip 1.0. Now that there was no product and likely not to be one for months, there was no need to spend what little money F5 had left paying salaries for people with nothing to do. Almquist, though, didn't want to stop with laying off the obviously unnecessary people. He also wanted to unload the disloyal, incompetent, and superfluous, leaving no one in the office save himself and King. "And so my feelings are, Let's fire people, lay 'em off, get focused. . . ." Hussey, in particular, so galled him that he put him at the top of the list of people to be fired. "I'm also pissed off because now he's got his stock feed, and now he's trading stocks, and now he's making money. It's like, 'What the hell is that doing for *me?*' "

He looked back over the company's history as one long disaster. He had hooked up with Hussey largely because the banker had connections in the financial community and Almquist had had no idea how easy it would be to raise money. He and Hussey had hired everyone else either because they had asked or because a friend or acquaintance had recommended them. Relying entirely on instinct, they had more or less given a job to anyone who showed up at F5. Now, his company was on the verge of collapse. "Now, is this a crater in the making?" he asked rhetorically. "We got, like, two or three more months. Two or three more months from now, we'll find out. But we can't continue on the course that we're continuing."

He kept telling himself that he had been through worse and that this time around he was better equipped to deal with his adversity. "You know, I could be like freaking out, screaming, crying, running in front of traffic, but this still is not a big deal. This is no way, shape, or form a bad situation for me. It stinks, it sucks, but I've been in worse. Living in a basement, eating my industrial-size Tater Tots from Costco, washing in a sink, wishing I had money and focus and direction and vision and hope."

Yet when compared with his previous failures, this one was monumental because the potential payoff was so much larger, and Almquist felt he had been so much smarter at F5 than in his previous ventures. He had carefully researched the state of technology and the state and direction of the Internet marketplace, and come up with a can't-miss mother lode of an idea. Now it looked as if all he was going to take away from his F5 adventure was yet another lesson: The greater the potential success, the more devastating the failure. *"I nailed BIG/ip and the BIG line squarely on the head.* People are begging for this and all the other products. Now sometimes we talk about the half full kind of thing. You know, we've got a prototype, it works, got a proof of concept, we've got a market, we still have half of our money, we still have some time. . . . But my gut tells me that if we can't get BIG/ip done, fixed, and out there in the field within six months, we're toast."

In his anger and confusion, he had so lost his bearings that he no longer knew whether he could even rely on his own judgment, let alone the judgment and ability of others. "I know myself pretty well in that I always build up my own fantasies, I'm a reality warper. But I do that in a tongue-in-cheek manner to humor myself and humor others. I know we're in an incredibly bad situation, but it solves absolutely nothing thrashing, crying, moaning, or doing any of that. So I don't know if that makes me an incredibly functional dysfunctional individual or a dysfunctionally functional individual."

It was small consolation to Almquist that he was learning yet another set of lessons about his own shortcomings. "You know, I keep thinking, 'Wow! I've learned *so much* doing this! Wow! You know, I'm going to make like an *incredibly great* person! I'm incredibly experienced, incredibly *wise*, I've condensed the learning of like a lifetime, or job experience, which may be like five years of being at a job, into like *two weeks!*' It's like, AAAAUUU-UGGGGHHH!"

He began to see the impending failure of F5 as yet another manifestation of a recurring theme in his life, almost a manifestation of his soul. "You know, it's kind of been like my life, like at the HIT lab, you know. . . . It's just like how *I've always been.*"

With Almquist's invocation of the HIT lab, I realized that I had been witnessing in his travails an engineerish reenactment of the poetic torment described in Harold Bloom's *The Anxiety of Influence*. In order to realize his or her potential as a great poet, Bloom argues in that book, the young poet must find a way to break free of the bonds of influence exerted by the great poets of the previous generation. Only by both learning from and rejecting—often by misunderstanding—his or her predecessor can the younger poet move on to create great art.

Almquist, who spent a lot of his time complaining about Furness and obsessively pointing out what he saw as the older man's failings, nevertheless had inherited far more of Furness than he could force himself to admit. Like Furness, he had a terrible inability to judge the strengths and weaknesses and intentions of businesspeople. He was far more at home doing pure engineering than dealing with business issues or employees. He could not manage to mold an organization that did not turn into an extension of his personality. In trying to start business enterprises rather than contenting himself with lab research, he was taking his quest one step farther than Furness did—"We [Americans]," Bloom writes, "tend to see our fathers as not having dared enough"—but he could not manage to succeed at business the way Furness had succeeded at invention. Instead, he was managing to fail as a business manager in many of the same ways Furness failed at being a laboratory manager. "Be me but not me," Bloom writes, characterizing the paradoxical mission of the younger poet. Almquist still had not figured out how to separate the engineering truths he had learned from Furness from the psychological chains he had inherited along with them. Now, as darkness settled into the room, I saw him as a pitiful figure wrestling against the influence of his mentor, Furness, who had become what Bloom would call Almquist's "Covering Cherub," the "demon of continuity; his baleful charm imprisons the present in the past. . . ." Until Almquist could break free of the psychological legacy of Furness, he would be trapped in the visionary's classic cycle of dream and loss. He was young Shakespeare to Furness's Marlowe, Stevens to Furness's Whitman. . . .

Or maybe I was just coming unhinged from an excess of sympathy.

My flight of fancy was interrupted by the telephone. "Drat!" Almquist said. "That'll be Jeff checking up on me, asking where the hell I am." He picked up the receiver and listened for five minutes or so in silence, his face growing gradually angrier. Suddenly an eerie calm settled over his features, steam came out of his nostrils,

little bolts of lightning shot out of his eyes, and he said with surprising gentleness, "You're fucking with my dream, pal. And if you
had any fucking brains at all, you'd realize you were fucking with
your dream, too." Then he hung up the phone, turned to the terminal on the rack in front of him, and started maniacally typing.

Behold, 1 Am in My Anger

AT THE END of January 1997, when Virtual i/O's board finally jet-
tisoned Greg Amadon and Linden Rhoads, the move was greeted
throughout the Deep Bile network with the kind of unbridled joy
not seen on Earth since the fall of the Berlin Wall. Within a day of
their departure, everyone in the network had been alerted, the glee
building e-mail message by e-mail message:

```
Subject: Will the last one left please turn the
lights out?

I ran into [ . . .] (!) over here in Redmond,
and he told me that Greg resigned last night
(!!!).

Can anyone confirm or deny or at least offer up
some scintillating information?
                              .
Yippie kayea @#$@#$@# I never thought I'd live
to see the day. So what exactly does his "golden
parachute" clause say?
```

.

Ding dong the witch is dead!

.

Touché
I think we'd all like to see "Fatty & Co." do
the great disappearing act . . . . but
then we'd have nothing to talk about anymore.
<grin>

.

And on another note . . . . Have any of you got
your W-2 forms from VIO?????

I hear it is really difficult to get them after
a company goes tits up.

.

I got my W2 from my stock purchase. BTW and for
the record I did buy some of my stock and YES I
did sell it for a profit. And YES Linden is
pissed because as [. . .] said "Linden did not
give me her permission first." Oh well Shit
Happens and I hope soon to "Fatty & Co."

Rhoads herself had no sooner announced her resignation to the remaining staff at Virtual i/O than her written announcement was circulated through the network of her enemies. Amadon's resignation followed a day later, and the board announced that a "turnaround CEO," as one piece of e-mail described him, would take over within the next two or three days.

The departure of Rhoads and Amadon was celebrated at Seattle's Elysian brewpub—one of a wealth of microbrew bars in the city—far into the night on Saturday, January 25, the day after Amadon's resignation. Some thirty-five former Virtual i/O employees showed up to "dance on their grave, gloat, and make further predictions."

The predictions, of course, related to the future of the company. Some in the Deep Bile network expected bankruptcy proceedings to begin immediately, and the company to be shut down. Others expected TCI to pour more money into Virtual i/O and revive it because its products, they believed, could still win in the marketplace with proper company management.

The issue seemed settled on Monday, when the new CEO, Stanford Springel, was introduced to the company (and, without his knowledge, to Deep Bile). Judging from Springel's track record, Virtual i/O would be shut down within weeks. A member of the Diablo Management Group—a firm that specialized in taking over management of troubled companies—Springel's last two projects had been the orchestration of Chapter 11 bankruptcy proceedings and the closing of company doors.

Even so, many of those still at Virtual i/O were determined to believe that the company would somehow stay in business. Springel introduced himself by explaining that Virtual i/O's board would commence a long evaluation of the company and its technology and that its ultimate fate had yet to be decided. He asked Virtual i/O's engineering and marketing departments to present detailed plans for the future regarding new products and sales strategies, and said that any marketing strategy would necessarily involve asking the board for more money. He pleaded for patience and trust, then disappeared into his office.

Mike Tidwell, who walked off the HIT lab's VRD project after reading Microvision's unpleasant surprise of a stock options letter and had been at Virtual i/O for scarcely two months, watched the proceedings with gloom and foreboding. He was beginning to regret the pique and principle that had led him to walk away from his HIT lab job, where he at least had had a full year's salary guaranteed. Now he no sooner had moved to a new job than it looked as if the job would disappear. He had looked up Springel's résumé on the Internet and been discouraged by what he found, and meeting Springel face-to-face was hardly reassuring. The new CEO had never seen a headset before and knew nothing about the head-mounted-display market. Springel, in fact, had asked Tidwell to bring him a headset, show him how it worked, and explain the variety of ways it might be used.

Moreover, as Tidwell noted in an e-mail message to me, mysterious events were unfolding:

I talked to Richard [Hockenbrock, head of
engineering at Virtual i/O] on Friday and he is
of the mind set that the new guy is probably a
hatchet man. I think he was in fear of Greg
firing him for a few months now. There is the
definite possibility that even if the new guy
was hired to turn around the company, the new
guy may finish cleaning house. It looked like
the Diablo Mgt. Group does specialize in "turn
arounds". You know that web page I sent you
about Springel (which you probably already saw)
said that it was the intention of the mgt. to
continue the company and take it public after
the creditors were paid.

They did do a funny thing yesterday. Did I tell
you? They told us definitely to NOT come into
work this weekend. Protecting the goods for a
fire sale? Preventing maliciousness in the event
that employees SUSPECT a fire sale is coming?
Preventing a maliciousness from former
executives?

The water is murky Fred and I can't see a damn
thing. Right now I'm 60/40 toward the hatchet
job. I did, however, hear a rumor indirectly
from someone who knows someone at Planar
(observation seat on the board) that "Virtual
i-O will survive".

Springel's arrival was publicly announced in a press release—
the last, as it turned out, to be issued by Elgin Syferd Public Relations on Virtual i/O's behalf:

VIRTUAL I-O ANNOUNCES NEW CEO

SEATTLE-Seattle-based Virtual i-O, the world
leader in design and manufacture of virtual
reality headsets, has named Stan Springel its
new president and chief executive officer. As
president and CEO, Springel is responsible for
the company's strategic direction. Springel
brings more than 25 years of management
experience to Virtual i-O, including 17 years at
General Electric.

The change marks an effort by Virtual i-O to
transition the company from a development stage
to that of an operating company. Springel
replaces company founders Greg Amadon and Linden
Rhoads, who served respectively as CEO and
president during the company's first three years.
Both Rhoads and Amadon remain with the company
as board members.

Virtual i-O was founded in May 1993 and is
funded by private investors. The company's
Virtual i-glasses product line is distributed in
the US, Canada, Europe, and Japan, and available
domestically at major PC and consumer electronics
retailers.

The "strategic direction" Springel took was to cut back as far as
possible on Virtual i/O's costs while looking for new financial
backing. He would be asking a lot of his new investors: Springel
discovered that Virtual i/O had, by his reckoning, some $9.7 mil-
lion in assets, and owed upward of $21 million—the bulk of that
owed to TCI, which had been keeping the company alive with
bridge loans toward an IPO that never came.

During his search for an answer, Springel brought in Joey King for consultation. King had just returned from another of his trips to Japan, and Springel wanted to get some sense of the future competitive landscape and whether there were any big opportunities for Virtual i/O on the horizon.

For the better part of an afternoon, King looked over Virtual i/O's present and future products, then delivered a devastating report. King had seen inexpensive headsets, usually bundled with video players, from four different manufacturers in the Tokyo electronics markets. Particularly noteworthy was Sony's Glasstron, which was selling well in Japan and which King expected to be entering the U.S. market within a year. King also had seen intriguing work in Sharp's laboratories, where researchers were developing a display device that looked something like a miniature version of the old stereopticon. This device was mounted on a delicate boom and could be brought up to the user's eyes. When you peered into it, you saw what looked like the interior of a theater; you looked over the backs of successive rows of chairs down to a movie screen. Sharp planned to market the device for use on airplanes, with passengers swinging the boom out from the armrest on their seat, fitting the viewer over their eyes, and watching movies in private.

Between Sharp and Sony, then, Virtual i/O was for all practical purposes shut out of the marketplace. "You have really impressive technology here," King said, "but there is no way you are going to be able to compete against these companies"—particularly Sharp, which manufactured nearly all of the world's LCD panels (the flat liquid-crystal displays found in everything from laptops to the viewfinders in video camcorders) and figured to leverage that advantage in any market competition with Virtual i/O.

Springel was crestfallen. Not long after King's visit—on February 26, to be exact, almost one month to the day after Springel had taken over leadership of Virtual i/O—the company filed for Chapter 11 bankruptcy protection. TCI loaned the company another $700,000 and directed Springel to put Virtual i/O up for sale. TCI's plan, according to people still working at the company, was to make a "credit bid"—offering to forgive some of its debt in return for taking over the company free and clear of obligations to all of Virtual i/O's other creditors. TCI, in other words, would pay next to nothing for Virtual i/O and would owe the company's other creditors nothing. In the likely event that no one would bid more than TCI's "virtual bid," it would be a relatively simple matter to take Virtual i/O over, restructure it, and start over with a clean financial slate.

The court papers proved a source of entertainment and nostalgia for former Virtual i/O employees, who circulated them and cited them as proof of Amadon's and Rhoads's ineptitude. The documents showed that Virtual i/O owed $395,176.27 to Bogle & Gates, the law firm that had represented the company in its lawsuit against Forte Technologies; $166,322.74 to Elgin Syferd, its public-relations firm; $5.3 million to parts suppliers; $81,450 to *Rolling Stone* magazine; and hundreds of thousands more to focus-group research firms, advertisers, putative partners, furniture and light-fixture stores, copy centers, the Seattle Bagel Factory. . . .

Springel proved an indefatigable CEO, traveling up and down the West Coast and working the telephone in search of a buyer for Virtual i/O. According to court papers, he contacted a hundred possible buyers, of whom fifteen signed nondisclosure forms—the first step in the due diligence process of examining a company for possible purchase. In the end, though, none of the companies and people Springel approached even went so far as to visit the company to hear its sales pitch.

When finally it came time to submit offers to take over the company, TCI was the lone bidder, putting up a credit bid of $4 million—a small portion of its $17 million debt. A committee representing Virtual i/O's other investors and creditors, though, strenuously objected to a takeover that would recoup none of their money while TCI would be given a second chance. Arguing that TCI's "debt" was not a debt but an "investment," the creditors' committee argued against the plan in bankruptcy court, and the judge there gave the disputants two weeks to reach some kind of agreement.

Springel, thinking the issues could be resolved, was surprised when TCI said on Thursday, April 24, that they would not underwrite Virtual i/O's operations on their own for the two weeks the negotiations were expected to take. Find investors to keep the company operating during this interim, they said, or we will shut everything down and auction off the company assets. Three Virtual i/O representatives left immediately for Silicon Valley, confident that TCI's apparent willingness to be part of a group continuing to invest in Virtual i/O's second chance would help raise money from other investors. Springel himself was hopeful enough to tell his troops that it looked as if the company could be saved, and everyone went home that weekend excited at the possibility that they might be able to keep their jobs.

But the trip south was fruitless. On Monday afternoon, April 28, a chagrined Springel returned and immediately called a company meeting. Most of his employees thought that he was about to announce that the company had been saved. Instead, they listened, disbelieving, as he said, "You've been a pleasure to work with, a real class act. But we could find no buyer for the company, and we have to close our doors."

The HIT lab staff and students, who met one Monday every month, were somewhat relieved when Furness started off the April meeting with the kind of Furnessism no one had heard him utter for months. "What's most important here," he said during an accounting of the lab's funding crisis and search for new money and projects, "is direction and diligence of the lab rather than speed. It's the tortoise and the hare thing. We need to maintain a direction and keep going, and work on problems that *burn within us*. Pervasive problems: low vision, aids for handicapped people, pain alleviation, environmental issues . . . all those kinds of things are real problems, where a university laboratory ought to be working."

It looked as if the director was finally emerging from his months of depression and physical illness, and was ready to resume his quest with something like his old zest and inveterate optimism. Having suffered a bitter blow in the form of Johnston's and Tidwell's resignations, he now looked back over the experience and was able to see that it was good. Over the ensuing months, he had talked himself into the notion that the lab was designed as much to send people on as to draw people in. "I was as low as I've ever been when Rich and Mike followed Dave out the door," he said to me. "But then I realized, you know, that one of our functions and one of the things that does bring me a lot of personal satisfaction is that people do come, and then they go from here. It's really a launching pad. And so we are performing our educational function not only with undergrads and graduate students but with staff as well. This is really part of our function. And these moves for both Rich and Mike are good moves." They were good for the lab in large part because they forced Furness to reinvent his enterprise, keeping it agile and fresh and creative. "When these kinds of changes happen, in a way it's good to stir the pot every once in a while. Because it makes us rethink: 'What are we really after?' And I keep thinking that a thousand years from now it's not going to matter really what we did in the lab. What's going to matter are the relationships we had, the process, the good feelings we had in working in that environment."

This sort of unreasonable happiness invariably had Joey King rolling his eyes, as King believed that Furness's ability to find the good in the bad bordered on madness. "There's an example," he said after Furness's talk to the staff, "of the pathology that is Tom!" King was appalled by Furness's happiness largely because the lab's financial problems were too big and too real to be wished away by vision and hope. He felt that Furness tended too much to believe in miracles, and to come up with wishful schemes that stood no chance of succeeding.

It did seem that Furness was growing ever more unrealistic in his plans for getting the HIT lab on stable financial footing, and I began seeing his dreaminess as a sign of increasing desperation. The mass departure of his VRD team, for example, he now viewed as an opportunity to "play the role I was playing before Rich was hired, doing the things that he was doing—at the bench level"—as if there was any realistic chance at all of his having time to start doing hands-on lab work again. He began sketching impossible financial visions during our conversations, saying that he was considering raising Virtual Worlds Consortium membership fees from $50,000 to $250,000 per year, and creating a "HIT lab venture fund" that would add up to a "perpetual million-dollar-a-year discretionary fund that we could go off and seed new ideas with." He talked of generating this fund with "a single simple ten-million-dollar grant . . . ten mil, invested, would give us a million a year in perpetuity, it would give us the seed funding we need."

King was furious at these dreams because he knew firsthand how hard it was to get corporations to give money to research labs. His "save the lab" trip at the end of 1996 had come up empty, as two out of his three presumed benefactors more or less went out of business. Texas Instruments had sold off its computer division and King's contacts there vanished, and the Electronics Technology Office in DARPA had decided not to fund human-system interaction proposals during the next two-year funding cycle. "So it was not one of the more successful trips," King said glumly.

Now the lab—Furness's renewed optimism to the contrary—was on the verge of losing more than half of its annual budget. Furness had been spending approximately $4 million per year for the past four years, with $1.3 million coming from the VRD project, $600,000 from the lab's AFOSR grant, and $250,000 from the Washington Technology Center, in the form of its no-strings-attached "seed money" for Furness's most far-reaching visions. Now, the AFOSR project was to end in June, the VRD project in November, and the WTC wanted to eliminate its annual seed-funding grant. Looking ahead a year, Joey King saw the very real possibility of the HIT lab closing its doors.

King was not the only one who knew Furness well and considered his inability to give in to gloom rather peculiar. Mike Almquist, who kept a close eye on Furness from his new home at F5 Labs, often punctuated King's reports with exclamations like, "He's a madman, Joey!" And Furness's supervisors on the Washington Technology Center board sometimes reeled in disbelief at the jarring contrast between the substance of his status reports and his demeanor.

"Tom, wouldn't you call this present difficulty you're having a . . . crisis?"

"No."

Even so, Furness spent a lot of time in his office with his head in his hands. He was distressed not only by the lab's overall financial picture, but by what he saw as a betrayal by the Washington

Technology Center, which, he said constantly, had broken its promise to him and compromised his highest ideals. "Of all the things that are frustrating in terms of our financial problems, that's the most frustrating," he said of the WTC's seed-funding decision. "Our own state support is essential for us to have, to maintain this model of an entrepreneurial type of operation. Without that, we become a warm-body operation. That means we sell our time, and that's what I did not want. I did not want in the laboratory setting to end up just going around hustling contracts. I wanted to create new stuff, then have a chance to make mistakes, screw up every now and then, but maybe have thirty percent of the stuff really amount to something." He stood no chance of doing creative science if his lab was confined to doing directed work for hire. "I mean, with enough effort, we could go out and get lots of contracts, but that's not really what a laboratory like us should be doing. We should be working on our own agenda, what we feel most needs to be done in this field. If we're just doing contract work for people, we're just following other people's ideas."

Finally, Furness's desperation reached the point where he decided to effect a reorganization in the lab that he had been resisting for years. From the time he had established it, the HIT lab had operated very much as a paternalistic enterprise, with all lab money flowing to Furness, who then dispensed it to his staff and students as he saw fit. It was an arrangement under which even his longest-serving and most loyal researchers chafed, and that kept many well-connected scientists from moving to the HIT lab and setting up shop. Now Furness decided to open up his doors to scientists whose stature and connections in the grants communities were equal to his own, allowing them to be part of the lab without having to answer to him the way his current staff did. Rather than find a way to work under Furness, who would scrounge up money and pay them, researchers would be responsible for bringing in their own grant money, directing their own research, and paying their own students and staff. And rather than serve as their boss, Furness would be a collaborator sharing his laboratory space with them.

The new arrangement conformed to traditional research laboratory organizational models. "This is amazing!" Joey King said when it was clear the reorganization really would be enacted. "I never thought he'd actually do this. This probably will bring about a big reduction in Tom's power. Now we're going to get more people in here who can bring in *money*. . . ."

Once he had gotten himself over that psychological hurdle and reconfigured his lab, Furness seemed greatly relieved. He would no longer be principal investigator on all the lab's projects, doling out every dollar that came into the HIT lab. Now, he would serve primarily as a manager, facilitator, and visionary, bringing talented researchers into the lab and leaving them to direct their own projects and raise their own money.

I ran into him a few days after the meeting where he officially unveiled the lab's new governing structure, and he was more relaxed and cheerful than I'd seen him in over a year. "I've been thinking a lot lately about my legacy," he said, laughing heartily. "Well, I guess legacy's not the right word. . . . It's still an *odyssey*."

The psychological landscape at F5 Labs came more and more to resemble a Midwestern plain in summer, swept by one sudden thunder-and-lightning storm after another. The company seemed to find failure and frustration wherever it turned, whether toward code, sales, present-day tasks, dreams of the future, or investors.

Mike Almquist had run out of patience both with his former friend Avi Bar-Zeev and with company cofounder Jeff Hussey. Bar-Zeev he considered a traitor, and Hussey an "idiot," a "fool," a "neurotic fuck," and a "*wee* little man!" More and more, as he told "incredibly humorous," "quite amusing," "quite hilarious" stories about Hussey—all of them more or less grim and bizarre—Almquist would punctuate them with, "He's a *wee* little man! A *wee* little man!"

Hussey, for his part, kept trying, with no success and with mounting frustration, to find the key that he believed could somehow unlock Almquist and make him miraculously finish BIG/ip. He was convinced that F5's problems were not caused by organizational chaos or lack of developers but by Almquist's lack of discipline. He peppered Almquist constantly with questions about his hours, work habits, tasks, lack of focus, and plan of attack. He decided to institute mandatory eight A.M. daily meetings of the core leadership of F5—himself, sales VP Lynn Luukinen, CFO Brian Dixon, and Almquist—as a way of improving Almquist's work habits and making him more "businesslike." The move, of course, was counterproductive: Since Almquist preferred working late into the night to working in the early-morning hours, the meetings made him only more tired and less efficient, and his resentment toward Hussey grew into an even greater distraction than it already was. All of this seemed lost on Hussey, who could never be persuaded that his company's sole working programmer was more productive writing code than sitting in meetings.

Every time Almquist left the office, he found Hussey waiting at F5's door when he returned, anxious to grill him on his whereabouts. And whenever he was sitting at his terminal working, Hussey interrupted him almost constantly with questions. He also fell to calling Almquist at home late at night and on weekends, and to showing up unannounced at his house. Almquist installed a second telephone line in his house, kept the number from Hussey, and hooked an answering machine up to the first telephone so that he could screen his calls and avoid talking with his CEO as much as possible. He and Joey King fell to joking that Hussey was a "stalker," and they loved retelling the story about listening over and over again to a recorded diatribe Hussey had left on their answering machine, then looking out their window and screaming in terror when they saw Hussey approaching the front door.

Almquist delighted in silencing Hussey in mid-diatribe with humiliating questions. Whenever Hussey attacked him for not having finished BIG/ip, for being absent from the office, for making some change in his schedule or in the list of features in their product, Almquist would ask, "Where's the placement document, Jeff?" or "Hire any new developers yet?" Since the answer to both questions was no, and since Almquist was always careful to ensure that someone else heard the questions, Hussey would fall immediately silent and flee.

Questions about the placement document were particularly humiliating partly because Hussey by his own admission (to me, at least) found writing difficult, partly because he had a hard time concentrating on a single task for long stretches of time, and partly because by now the F5 story had become a story full of red flags to potential investors. Hussey had intended to finish the document and begin raising money before the end of 1996. Now, well into February 1997, and with F5 down to its last $200,000—loaned to F5 by a friend of Hussey's, it figured to last only sixty days—he had written only a few disorganized pages and made no progress for two or three weeks. His frustration and panic made him turn more and more often in anger toward Almquist, who reacted with condescending amusement. Every day featured at least one exchange like this:

"Where were you, Squish? You've been gone for more than an hour!"

"Lunch. Where's my money, Jeff?"

"It's not *your* money, Squish!"

"Where's *our* money, then?"

Hussey then would turn on his heel and stalk off, while Almquist stood making faces at whoever remained in the room.

Meetings and status reports almost always were punctuated by shouts from Hussey and ripostes from Almquist. The arguments generally started over a Hussey-imposed deadline that Almquist missed. "The eighteen to-do items on my list turned into a hundred, and I've finished eighty," Almquist said one day, triggering a typical argument.

"Squish, you failed me," interrupted Hussey.

"Fuck you, Jeff! Where's the placement document? Where are all the developers you're supposed to hire? Where are all the sales and strategic partnerships you're supposed to be getting?"

The rest of the company began to fear not only any group meeting, but any moment that found Hussey and Almquist in the same room. Whenever Almquist updated Hussey on his lack of progress, an argument would ensue. Going over a list of tasks and features one morning, Almquist was interrupted by Hussey: "No, Squish! Wrong wrong wrong!"

"Okay, *you* code it, then."

"Don't give me that 'you code it' bullshit!"

When not fulminating at or about Almquist, Hussey was sputtering over the behavior of Avi Bar-Zeev, who continued his informal strike by spending his days lying on the couch in the office he shared with Almquist. Finally, Hussey drafted a "probation letter" for Bar-Zeev, holding him to productivity goals that, if unmet, would result in Bar-Zeev's being fired.

Bar-Zeev resumed sitting at his desk, but still resolutely avoided real work. Instead, he complained to Almquist and to me about not being allowed to work on real VR, as Almquist had promised when the two had discussed Bar-Zeev's moving from Disney to F5. "Squish thinks we can do version 2.0 in three months," he said to me, clearly skeptical. "But I need to be doing VR *soon*. And what does 'soon' mean around here?"

Things came to a head for Bar-Zeev when Hussey insisted that everyone show up exactly on time for ten o'clock Monday-morning company meetings. Bar-Zeev showed up an hour late for the first one, was excoriated by Hussey in front of the other programmers, and stormed out of the conference room. Five minutes later, he came back and said quietly, "I just can't work under these conditions anymore. If things don't change, I'm going to have to quit."

"All right, Avi," Hussey answered, "I accept your resignation."

"Well, I don't mean that I *want* to quit. . . . I was just staying—"

"As far as I'm concerned, Avi, you've quit, and that's fine."

"Well, I'm not quitting. . . . You're *making* me quit! I don't want to quit!"

Later, talking with me, he enumerated the ways in which he felt deceived and betrayed by Almquist. Much of his frustration, he explained, was caused by his fear that if he did not get started soon on developing VR tools and applications, someone, somewhere, would beat him to the next huge market in personal computing. The longer he was mired in the mess at F5, he believed, the more disadvantageous would be his position in the emerging VR market.

Bar-Zeev spent his last two weeks at F5 nailing down a new job at Zombie, cleaning out his desk, and alternately (and, for that matter, incongruously) trying to talk Almquist and Joey King into leaving F5 and starting a new company with him. King was both contemptuous and incredulous—how could Bar-Zeev, he kept asking himself, think that he, King, would turn his back on his close friend and take off with someone he couldn't stand? Almquist was amused and encouraged. "Avi's terrified of having to compete with me," he said gleefully.

Almquist was also encouraged by Bar-Zeev's frustration and anxiety to get started with a VR tools and applications company because he saw it as corroboration of his own vision. With the continued rapid growth in speed and power of PCs, and with the rapid enhancement of the Internet by technology like that being developed by F5, the day was drawing ever closer when it would be possible to produce compelling and inexpensive immersive VR applications for everyday use. Almquist wrote often, in the journal he was keeping of his F5 adventure, of his anxiety to get his VR company off and running. "I keep feeling," he wrote in January, "like I'm about to miss the boat."

He was, of course, stuck with getting his interim Internet vision off the ground before he could even think of boarding the VR-industry boat. And his chances of getting free of F5—which he had seen a year ago as a quick, six-month adventure—now looked more remote than ever. The company, shrinking steadily almost from the day it was launched, now had a single software developer—Almquist—and a CEO who seemed to think the company didn't need any more engineers. Whether he realized it or not, Almquist had long since lost interest in finishing BIG/ip and overseeing production of the rest of the BIG product line. Now, his sole concern was burnishing F5's image in the eyes of investors and potential purchasers so he could sell the company and get out from under the yoke he had fashioned for himself. And who, he kept asking Hussey, would want to buy or invest in a company that had only one software engineer? "We need to get like twenty developers in here," he said, "so we'll have something to *sell*."

Hussey invariably retorted that the problem was not lack of engineers, but lack of discipline on Almquist's part. Finish a salable version of BIG/ip, he said constantly, and all our troubles will be over.

When it came time for the February 1997 board meeting, however, Hussey found a less than sympathetic jury. When he began making his case for raising more money, the board started peppering him with hard questions. "What valuation are you hoping to put on the company?" someone asked.

"Ten million," Hussey answered.

"Well," came the answer, "in order to get that valuation, you have to have 'critical mass.' You have to show that the company is growing. Critical mass means lots of employees and a product on back order, so you can say, 'See, we have to grow to meet the pent-up demand for our product.' But it looks instead like you're *shrinking* instead of growing."

Almquist saw an opening. "I agree," he said. "I've been begging for more developers for months now."

Hussey, fuming, fell silent, and the board began asking more questions about various business and infrastructure matters that the board felt fell under the aegis of the CEO. "Where's the placement document?" one member asked. "You said it would be done by now."

Hussey, hemming and hawing, was interrupted. "We expect development to slip. *Development always slips.* But what makes development companies succeed is the business side keeping to its goals and deadlines. It's the business support that makes or breaks a company."

Outside the conference room, a visibly shaken Hussey took Almquist aside. "I don't ever want to have another board meeting like that again," he said.

After that, Hussey grew fixated on me, apparently deciding that BIG/ip was slipping because I had become too much of a distraction to Almquist, and that my interest in him had swelled the developer's head. Whenever I showed up at F5, Hussey would shout, "It's the Heisenberg Principle! The Heisenberg Principle!"—particularly if he found me talking with Almquist. I assumed he meant the Heisenberg Uncertainty Principle, which states that in the quantum mechanical world it is impossible to accurately measure both the momentum and position of a subatomic particle because every attempt to take a measurement disturbs the particle's environment, thereby altering the phenomenon being measured. King and Almquist, who were enormously entertained by these outbursts and kept trying to get me to come by their offices just so they could set one off, believed that Hussey had confused "Heisenberg" with "Hawthorn," and meant to invoke the Hawthorn Effect—a sociological term for the beneficent effect any change in a working environment has on the workers there. Increase the lighting in a warehouse, for example, and productivity goes up. Decrease it, and productivity goes up again.

Neither interpretation, it seemed to me, quite made sense, and I kept intending to ask Hussey what exactly he meant. But then he sent me e-mail asking me to stay out of the F5 offices during business hours. "I noticed that you and Mike were away from the office for quite a while yesterday," he wrote. "I'm sorry to say this, but we have gotten ourselves into a position where I can't afford that kind of distraction. The Heisenberg principal [sic] is looming its ugly head."

Thus was I banished from F5, reduced to taking in its travails through the eager filters of King and Almquist, who were as anxious for me to know what lay in store as Hussey was anxious for me not to know.

When Zombie first procured the Disney contract for work on the DisneyQuest virtual roller-coaster project, Mark Long and Joanna Alexander had hired Peter Oppenheimer, a longtime HIT lab artist and scientist, to head up the project's technical team. Oppenheimer, a mathematician, software engineer, and multimedia artist, was the lone William Bricken protégé still at the lab, and he was unpredictable, mischievous, and mystical. I did not expect him to survive for long in a business environment—even one as unconventional as Zombie's—because of his penchant for wackiness and his disdain for meetings, written documents, deadlines, and supervisors.

Enthusiastic as they were about Oppenheimer, Long and Alexander had their doubts as well, and they decided to hedge their bets by hiring Bar-Zeev. Long, in particular, remembered "lab types" all too well from his days at Sarnoff, and he was worried about keeping Oppenheimer's mind and imagination on track and on schedule for an extended period of time. "I've been around guys like Peter before," he said. "They're arty, they're unpredictable; they can get it together just enough to put together a demo. But developing a product is a whole different enterprise."

Among Bar-Zeev's other advantages over Oppenheimer were his history with Disney and his familiarity with the corporation's way of doing business and managing projects. "Man, did he drive a hard bargain!" Long said after Bar-Zeev and he had agreed to terms. Bar-Zeev had been well aware that Long desperately needed a skilled VR programmer, as the Disney project was on a tight deadline, and Bar-Zeev also brought with him familiarity with the Disney way of running projects. "He had us over a barrel, and he knew it," Long said ruefully.

While not disclosing the salary he was paying Bar-Zeev, he acknowledged that it set a new pay standard for Zombie. The only advantageous provision Long was able to wrest from Bar-Zeev was the way a large portion of the money would be doled out: Zombie would put bonus payments into an escrow account every time Bar-Zeev delivered a milestone on time, with all of the money to be turned over to him when the project was finished and accepted by Disney.

Given Zombie's investment in Bar-Zeev, and given Bar-Zeev's belief that he should be a team leader rather than a follower, it was only a matter of time before Oppenheimer was supplanted. The DisneyQuest team was moving with considerable panic and uncertainty toward its first milestone—delivery of a specifications document outlining the look and feel of the product and a detailed description of the hardware and software used both in building the attraction and playing it in the arcade—when Oppenheimer, who kept derailing team meetings with jokes and mysterious asides, fell into disfavor with Long within a month of his hiring. Bar-Zeev kept filling Long's ear with tales of near disaster and offers to step into the breach. Finally, when Oppenheimer's portion of the spec was finished, Long fired him, replacing him with Bar-Zeev.

Almquist and King found this more than mildly amusing. "You

watch," said Almquist. "The next thing he'll do is steal the Disney project away from Zombie."

In any event, Bar-Zeev took over the project with great enthusiasm, beginning by reconfiguring a portion of the Zombie offices for his Disney team. He built a prototype roller coaster seat in a tiny room, with a projector and screen, so the team could test its work on an arrangement similar to the arrangement users would confront in the motion pod. He put up new walls, sanding and painting them himself, oversaw the installation of the team's graphics engines and network, got down to work in earnest, and threw fits on the eve of Disney deadlines. "Man," said Long after Bar-Zeev had been there a month, "Avi's a really intense guy!"

By this time, I was beginning to wonder if there were any limits to Long's and Alexander's intensity. The two were managing a relationship with Disney on a VR project that in itself would be more than most single software companies could handle. In addition, they were fighting technical, bureaucratic, and commercial battles on two software games—SpecOps and Spearhead—that were complex struggles against computer technology and trends in gaming. A labor of love for Long, they were yet another attempt to come up with a game that was aesthetically satisfying, had a compelling narrative element, and that also would be a blockbuster for Zombie.

There was a lot of excitement building at the company over the two simulation games, and it was easy to see why Long was so much more interested in them than in the Disney project. VR adepts had seen everything the Disney attraction had to offer. The rendition of reality scrolling by, it was essentially the same old SGI trick done up a little bit faster and richer. "Technically, the risks are very low on that platform," Long said. "You just keep throwing more RAM at it." On the games' platform, however, his team was writing a new rendering engine from scratch, and now to see the engine delivering lavish three-dimensional environments with nearly the verisimilitude of a movie—all on a desktop PC—was to see the leading edge extended, new functions and capabilities invented for the desktop machine.

As both games got to the point where demos could be shown,

word began filtering out through the games community that Zombie was on to something big. *Edge* and *Next Generation* magazines, the two leading review organs in computer gaming, trekked out to Seattle to do features on Zombie's offerings. Both magazines were struck by the high level of realism in the games—a first for computer gaming. "Unlike *Doom*," wrote the reviewer in *Next Generation*, "where players become generic space marines with access to otherworldly weapons such as plasma guns, SpecOps puts the player in real-world environments. Players use real army-issue weapons, such as fully automatic M-16s, against real enemies, such as Afghanistan terrorists. The game's five missions are realistic and include hostage rescues and drug raids. What players won't find in SpecOps, and this is disconcerting to the wounded, are potions of healing around every other corner." *Edge* concurred, concluding that SpecOps "bears all the hallmarks of being a head-turner" and that Spearhead—which was being developed in collaboration with MAK Technologies, developer of network technology for the U.S. Army—had "the potential to be one of the most popular multiplayer networked games in the future." So remarkable was the realism in Spearhead's rendition of tactics, environment, point of view, and ambient sound that the U.S. Marine Corps enlisted as its first purchaser, signing up in advance to buy copies of the game for training Marine recruits.

Zombie had never before been so alive with the conviction that it was breaking out with a hit. The early interest in SpecOps and Spearhead served to legitimize the vision of Alexander and Long, and the company emerged from winter early in 1997 marked with that high energy you find wherever young people believe they are at work on something *really cool*. Visits by executives from BMG Interactive's San Francisco office grew markedly more frequent; the more the publisher saw of the game, and the more enthusiastic the advance reviews, the more BMG believed it had hit the jackpot when it bet on Zombie.

But as Long had constantly noted, the game publishing world was in turmoil, with publisher after publisher going under at the rate of what seemed like at least one a day. BMG Entertainment, the London-based parent company of BMG Interactive, had been growing disenchanted with the American computer game market, a chronic money loser with a customer base whose tastes were capricious and unpredictable. Now, just as Zombie was poised for takeoff, BMG Entertainment decided to get out of the American game market, and the ink on Zombie's ecstatic advance notices was not even dry when Long got word that BMG was shutting down its San Francisco office, disbanding BMG Interactive, and abandoning plans to publish and distribute SpecOps and Spearhead in the United States.

Although BMG promised at first to finish its contracts for the three Zombie projects—the third one a game, called Vox, just getting under way—it was extricating itself from the games business in a way that was potentially crippling for Zombie. BMG Entertainment wanted to keep the European publishing and distribution rights to all three games, relinquishing only the American market. Since foreign distribution now accounted for fully 50 percent of a game title's sales, this threatened to make it impossible for Long and Alexander to find an American publisher. No publisher would be willing to take on a game if it was shut out of half the game's potential market. Long and Alexander would have been better off, in their view, if BMG withdrew completely. Now, unless they could get BMG either to market the game in the United States or sell its foreign distribution rights to another publisher, they were more or less doomed to finish out their projects and watch them die without ever being given a chance to succeed in the marketplace.

It was a classic illustration of the pitfalls game developers encountered when dealing with conglomerates. Long sat tearing out his figurative hair over the absurdity of BMG's apparent determination to kill his projects through ignorance. The company, headquartered in London, was involved in an array of entertainment enterprises of which Zombie's games were a tiny, ignored, and misunderstood segment. BMG Entertainment knew or cared nothing about the computer gaming market, and was making decisions that had no discernible sense or rationale, from Long's perspective. In trying to figure out how to penetrate the vast and distant BMG bureaucracy, he and Alexander spent hours upon hours getting nowhere. "We're just a tiny line in some massive BMG budget somewhere," Long lamented.

In the meantime, the two had commenced a new initiative that grew out of Long's visit to the 1997 Sundance Film Festival. While at the festival, Long had fallen into conversation with Scott Rosenfelt of ShadowCatcher Entertainment, a production company based in Seattle. In full raconteur mode, Long began explaining that computer technology had advanced to the point where developers using desktop PCs could do a computer-generated movie—or, as Long kept calling it, an "all-CG movie"—like *Toy Story*, for considerably less than $4 million. If the movie were developed for the emerging DVD platform, Long went on, its creators could develop a movie and computer game simultaneously, then market both to the public, possibly on the same disc. The buyer then could either watch the movie on his or her DVD player or play a role in it by playing the game on computer.

The project would be another step in the gradual evolution of the computer game into a legitimate interactive fiction.

By the time Long had returned to Seattle, he and Rosenfelt had agreed to pursue funding for the project, to start signing up screenwriters, set designers, animators, and other production people, and to put together a treatment. Within weeks, the two had written a proposal for "Liberty: DVD Movie and Computer Game" and had signed up Nick Sagan, an established writer/director and the son of astronomer Carl Sagan, and Syd Mead, set designer for a number of futuristic and science-fiction films, including *Blade Runner*. ShadowCatcher then went off in search of funding, most of which was to be raised by "pre-selling" foreign distribution rights for both the game and the movie.

Liberty was in some ways the culmination of the vision that first had goaded Long and Alexander into starting Zombie. They had always been interested in advancing the narrative element in computer games to the point where they began taking on some of the relative sophistication of more established forms of fiction. Now Long was convinced that the computer platform had reached the point where the same data could be arranged variously for both an interactive game narrative and a passive movie narrative.

Once news of the initiative filtered out of Zombie's and ShadowCatcher's offices, the press was intrigued. Articles about the effort began appearing in various film-industry and computer-industry outlets. *Wired* magazine took note with an article posted in its Web edition at the end of June. "The dual approach sprang from Long's mulling the question of 'why all games based on movies suck,' " *Wired* recounted. "His answer is that 'it's a flawed concept' which can only be overcome by planning a project from the outset that can work in both formats."

For all of Long's excitement about *Liberty*, and for all the promise shown by the interest he generated in industry and press alike, he knew that it was a long shot and that the day was at least a year off when the project might find enough funding to get under way and bring in money to Zombie. In the meantime, he had to find a way to get his current games finished and distributed in the American market.

Distribution deal after distribution deal that Long managed to get started fell apart as soon as his prospective new publishers tried dealing with BMG. Long began wondering if his publisher was intent on killing Zombie rather than helping it survive without BMG's continued involvement. Unless he could find U.S. distribution for the BMG projects, he was destined to finish yet another set of games that no one would ever see or hear about.

His SpecOps team, meanwhile, went into round-the-clock mode as it headed toward its July deadline for the alpha versions of its game. Completion of the alpha—a version in which all of the game's core functions are complete and demonstrable while much of the environment and game play elements are yet to be finished—would bring a much-needed infusion of cash into the company. Bad as things were with BMG, the publisher at least was keeping Zombie alive for the next few months.

But then BMG rejected the alpha version of SpecOps—a decision that effectively doomed the project, and Zombie along with it. BMG representatives, who had insisted for months that Zombie scale back SpecOps so as to finish in time for a Christmas 1997 release, now suddenly reversed course, insisting that a variety of functions be added before they would be willing to move forward.

BMG's change of heart meant that SpecOps would not be finished until spring 1998, at the earliest—after BMG Interactive had shut its doors. More important, it meant that Zombie would not be receiving the much-needed infusion of cash it had been expecting upon completion of the alpha.

Long interpreted the BMG move as a maneuver toward somehow breaking its contract without giving Zombie the freedom to find a new publisher. "They can't just shut us down because they know they'll get sued," he said. "So they're coming up with these pretexts for not going forward. They're looking for a way out of our contract."

The closing down of BMG Interactive, of course, was part of the industry-wide consolidation Long had been anticipating. One of his employees, John Williamson—producer of Spearhead—sent mail around one day detailing the layoffs throughout the games industry since the beginning of 1997. Nine companies were on the list, having laid off anywhere from 10 percent to 100 percent of their workforces. Disney Interactive had laid off ninety employees—20 percent of its total—Sega had laid off nearly eighty, or 13 percent, Rabid Entertainment had cut back 28 percent, turning twenty-four engineers loose. . . . And now Long was facing the possibility that he would have to lay off employees for the first time in his company's three-year history.

Sitting one day over a sandwich at Zombie's conference table, Long looked for the first time since I'd met him as if he was running out of energy and optimism. "Music-industry lawyers, man," he said resignedly. "They never want to give anything up—even something they don't want themselves." Without the money due upon acceptance of the alpha, he continued, Zombie would find it hard to keep its doors open. "We only have about six weeks' worth of money left. I'm looking at a worst-case scenario here where we start laying people off, keep the Disney team going until we finish that project, then close our doors."

David Melville had moved on to Microvision determined to hope for the best. He hoped that by joining Willey and Rutkowski just as the two were putting their enterprise together, he might have a hand in shaping the company's culture and strategic direction. He had worked out an arrangement with his new employers in which he would be director of research, in charge of leading the quest for new advances in retinal display—particularly in developing successive-generation scanners—while a production staff took his current scanner and built first-generation products around it.

Almost from his first day there, though, he found himself puzzled and distressed at the way the company was taking form and at the kind of work he was being made to do. Matters were not helped when Willey and Rutkowski refused to hire Mike Tidwell—a decision that Melville felt cost the company at least six months' worth of progress, as he now would have to find and train a new optical engineer rather than hire the only one in the world with expertise in retinal-scanning optics. "This is just a disaster," he said to me during the last conversation we were able to manage once he had gone to work directly for Rutkowski and Willey. "This is going to cost us tremendous amounts of time—and time is something we really don't have."

Melville was worried about time not only because he wanted to start selling retinal-display products before Microvision ran out of money, but also because he was worried about competitors beating him to the nascent scanning market. He didn't know directly of anyone else working on this technology, but he was convinced there were companies out there developing competing retinal scanners. Every day Microvision lagged, he believed, was a day lost to some more able competitor.

His fears were considerably heightened by the way Microvision directed its efforts and spent its money during his first months there. Instead of hiring engineers and buying laboratory equipment, they hired a CFO, several more marketing employees, and a director of communications. This all took two or three months, during which Melville sat listlessly in an office waiting with mounting impatience to set up his lab, start tinkering, and get some engineers working productively under him.

Melville had been at Microvision for no more than two months before he started confessing his doubts to Johnston and Tidwell.

The two greeted this news with far more delight than anger.

They were gleeful less out of malice, though, than out of self-interest. Johnston, now at Information Optics, and Tidwell, who had gone to work for Advanced Marine Technology after Virtual i/O went bankrupt, both wanted Melville to come work with them at their new companies. Their motives were fourfold: they terribly missed working with Melville, who was brilliant and companionable; they both were working on extremely difficult scientific problems that they felt Melville could make great progress toward solving; they felt obligated to rescue Melville from Microvision; and both of them wanted to stick it to Willey and Rutkowski.

Melville's unhappiness mounted as the months went by, and he found himself spending more and more time doing boring things that did nothing, as far as he could see, toward moving his beloved technology forward. He found himself writing technical papers—something he loathed doing—traveling to conferences and making speeches, and spending countless hours at a desk writing reports and doing management tasks rather than sitting at a lab bench doing science.

It took four months before the company finally began hiring engineers, but even that hint of progress ultimately proved, in Melville's mind, to be disastrous. One of the first engineers he hired took one look at Melville's mechanical resonant scanner and decided there must be a more efficient way to scan images on the retina. Melville, who is not given to forcing his will on people, felt he had no choice but to let the newcomer find his own way, so he waited patiently while the new hire busied himself researching and experimenting, for what turned out—much to Melville's chagrin—to be eight months.

Even worse than the span of time the research took was its result. After waiting eight months to see what his engineer came up with, Melville stared open-mouthed, breathless with shock, when the man said, "Well, it looks like your approach was best after all."

With that, Melville decided to leave the company, provided either Johnston or Tidwell could get their new employers to match his rather high Microvision salary. "I'd take a job for less money," he told Johnson, "if I didn't have a daughter going to college in a year."

While Johnston and Tidwell lobbied with their new bosses to

break their banks and hire Melville, Tom Furness was preparing another blow for Willey and Rutkowski. For almost a full year now, Furness had wrestled with his conviction that Microvision's owners were cheating him out of shares in the company that were rightfully his. He had struggled, argued, prayed, consulted, and agonized over how aggressively to fight Rutkowski and Willey over the matter. Every time I met with him, he would bring the subject up, telling me alternately that he had all but decided to forget it or that he was resolved to sue. "What my heart is telling me is to forget it and move on," he said in the spring of 1997. "But my head is telling me, 'Wait a minute. This is something that you've put your heart into all these years, this is a manifestation of many years of your career, your family deserves to have the rewards from it so you can rise above the wages of a faculty member and reap the rewards that those guys are reaping down there as a result of your invention.' "

More to the point, his lawyer was assuring him that he had a strong case against Microvision—Furness had found, it turned out, company board minutes in which hundreds of thousands of shares of stock were promised to him, and he said that other former management figures expressed eagerness to testify on his behalf—and he felt more and more entitled to shares in the company equal to those of the founders and Willey and Rutkowski. "And so it boils down to standing up for what's right and fair. Not trying to get something for nothing—just standing up for what's fair."

Furness had spent months negotiating with Willey, intimating more and more strongly each time they met that he was inclined to sue if the company didn't give him what he felt was a fair share of their success. True to form, Willey kept putting him off, temporizing, waffling, until finally he told Furness flatly that he and Rutkowski had decided not to give him any more stock. "Now I have *nothing*," Furness said angrily. "I've spent seven grand on attorney's fees, and I don't have anything to show for that. You know, I would have hoped that those guys would be falling all over themselves to be fair, saying, 'He deserves this, and here it is,' rather than forcing me to hire an attorney. The hard part is that I just don't like contention! And I really want to love these guys! I really do! I mean, the model I had in my mind was that we'd walk off into the horizon together, with this perfect model of the university-industrial way to do things."

Instead, he was preparing to walk into a courtroom and do battle with his would-have-been allies. "I've resisted a lawsuit kind of thing because I've felt that it could come back to bite me in terms of my role as principal investigator for the university," he said. "But now I've decided to wait until after our contract runs out later this year, then sue them."

Nearing the end of its first year as a publicly held company, then, Microvision looked as if it was about to show its true colors to its stockholders. Not only was its best scientist preparing to bail out of the company, but the inventor of the technology it was trying to peddle was preparing to sue Microvision. Small wonder that Johnston and Tidwell were careful every day to check the company's stock price on the Internet, eagerly expecting each day to see it suddenly plummet.

The Sense of an Ending

> . . . for behold they did murmur many things against their
> father, because he was a visionary man, and had led them out
> of the land of Jerusalem, to leave the land of their inheritance,
> and their gold, and their silver, and their precious things, to
> perish in the wilderness. And this they said he had done
> because of the foolish imaginations of his heart.
>
> —*The Book of Mormon*, 2 Nephi 11

FEATURE BY FEATURE, Mike Almquist had built BIG/ip up in increments, beginning with a November 1996 version he called 0.9,
then following with 1.0, 1.1, 1.2, 1.3, 1.4, and now, in June 1997,
a nearly completed version 1.5. Each version incorporated a new
function that Hussey and F5's sales VP, Lynn Luukinen, insisted
that BIG/ip needed in order to be widely salable.

Yet Almquist couldn't help but notice that each time he added
a feature, Hussey and Luukinen insisted that BIG/ip needed yet
another one before they could sell it to customers and the company to investors. As far as Almquist could tell, the only part of the
company that was moving forward was the software. Sales and
fund-raising had gotten nowhere over the previous eight months,

while he had brought BIG/ip through six new iterations. So why did Hussey and Luukinen persist in blaming the only productive part of the company for its financial problems? Every day, it seemed, he heard the two blame him for F5's futility in the software and financial markets. If BIG/ip isn't selling as expected, Luukinen insisted in company meetings, it is because of failings in the product. And if we haven't found new investors yet, Hussey kept saying, it is because you—Almquist—keep missing deadlines and slipping into undisciplined, sloppy work that the rest of us have to suffer for.

This only added to the co-founders' mutual loathing, which generally took the form of Hussey screaming at Almquist for doing poor or slow work and Almquist taunting him over his failure to raise money. Things finally came to a head in mid-June, when Almquist reported on a Friday that he would need five more days before he felt confident that version 1.5 would be ready to ship to customers. Hussey blew yet another gasket and stormed out of the office.

When he returned, he triumphantly told Almquist that he had set up a meeting between Almquist and the two leading F5 board members, Kent Johnson (Hussey's former boss at A.H. Capital) and Al Higginson (former vice-president of Sierra On-line). But Almquist, rather than feeling fearful, felt astounded at his unbelievable luck: Hussey had handed him the opportunity to tell his side of the F5 story to board members without Hussey's being there to argue against him. So on the appointed afternoon, Almquist eagerly trooped over to A.H. Capital. He walked into a small conference room and spent fifteen minutes listening to a furious Johnson recite the list of his crimes. Almquist waited patiently, recognizing all of Hussey's drearily familiar complaints about F5 not being a "research lab," about Almquist's inability to adhere to time lines, about his lack of "professionalism," and about his tendency to foment mischief and act out of "spite."

"Then," Almquist recounted later, "I came out punching. And I gave them the whole story. And the deal is, history is written by the victors. And the history of F5 Labs was being written by Jeff and Lynn. And that history was completely *wrong*. So when I had my chance to 'educate' Al and Kent, I had a different spin on history. And the most interesting thing is that there is lots and lots of corroborating evidence." Almquist pointed Johnson and Higginson to board minutes going back to the previous October, in which it was recorded that F5 had a finished product that was shipped to Tower Records—one of the busiest mission-critical web sites on the Internet. The BIG/ip installed there, he added, was still working, and Tower was thrilled. He showed them ecstatic reviews of BIG/ip— many of which they had seen before—from publications, customers, and potential vendors. He showed them e-mail from a Microsoft networking manager, Richard Maring, who wrote that BIG/ip was "far better" than any competing products he'd tested. In other words, Almquist pointed out, we have the best product on the market, but we can't get customers or investors to buy into it. What does that tell you?

Almquist also impressed on his inquisitors the real dimensions of the crisis facing F5 Labs. Not only was the company losing sales and investment because of Hussey and Luukinen, it also was facing a window of opportunity that was about to be slammed shut. The F5 shareholders' only hope of cashing in on their investment was to sell F5 to a bigger company with a compatible product line and established marketing force, and soon. The idea of growing F5 into a company that could compete on its own was no longer workable. Almquist told the board directors that Joey King had recently visited Microsoft with a group of researchers, and had been allowed to see one of the company's secret projects—a load-balancing function that was being added to its BackOffice suite. "It was essentially BIG/ip," King reported to Almquist, "and they're going to give it away for *free*." Now, Almquist said, Microsoft would have its load balancer, available at no cost, on the market in a year, which meant that unless someone at F5 could broker a merger with a big, established networking company soon, F5 would be dead. "Give me three to five months with some more resources," he said, "and we can create the most amazing, tastiest fish and sell the sucker." He then insisted that the board replace Hussey and Luukinen. "Right now," he said, "the message is very difficult to get out and that's basically because Lynn still doesn't know what the product is. And Jeff is constantly distracted, can't get anything done, and is ruining the morale of the company."

Johnson and Higginson sat as if shell-shocked when Almquist was finished. Then they promised to take immediate action.

Almquist and King spent the next few days cataloguing, with great amusement, the signs at F5 that the board was closing in. Suddenly no one was criticizing Almquist anymore, and he sat through company meetings as a spectator watching Luukinen, Hussey, and Brian Dixon, the CFO, attack one another. Almquist positively relished talking about these meetings, which he described as "most amusing," filled with "Jeff's neurotic babbleage," and "big, monstrous fights" in which his F5 fellows were "beating the shit out of each other" while he and King "had to work really hard to keep from giggling out loud."

In order to determine how to change F5, its board brought in an engineer/investment banker named George Futas to interview F5's principals and make recommendations to the board on how the company could be saved. Futas spent two weeks looking over F5's product, sales, expenditures, and history, then had long conversations with Almquist, King, Hussey, and the rest of the company's surviving workforce. He began attending company meetings and acting, in Almquist's point of view, as if *he* were the new CEO.

Almquist was excited at the arrival of Futas, whom he viewed as a fellow engineer capable of understanding his—Almquist's—predicament. With advanced degrees in both finance and engineering, Futas had a long history of success in brokering IPOs, strategic alliances, acquisitions, and venture capital deals. In the course of a thirty-year career, he had been a project engineer at Westinghouse, a manager at General Electric's Computer Division, a manager at Logicon—a 1980s high-tech start-up—and in the late 1980s had launched a technology business unit for Johnson Controls that had grown within five years into a $30-million enterprise. He moved into management and finance in the early 1990s, serving as CEO, president, or vice president of various technology start-ups. Then he had come to A.H. Capital to help the banking firm turn around troubled companies.

Futas was scheduled to present his report to the F5 board at its

July meeting. He was preceded by Hussey, who announced that a Silicon Valley firm, Vantage Point Venture Partners, had offered to invest $300,000 immediately in F5 and an additional $300,000 over the following six months, with the understanding that Vantage would try to broker an acquisition of F5 by a larger company for between $20 million and $40 million before the end of 1997. Although they did not like the financial terms of the proposed investment, Almquist and the board were excited by the offer because they interpreted Vantage Point's belief that it could secure a buyout as a sign that someone out there was interested in acquiring F5. So the board meeting, Almquist said later, was "kind of upbeat and interesting."

Then it came time for Futas to present his report, and Almquist and Hussey were told to leave the room. They were to come in afterward to be briefed on what the board decided, but when Futas was finished, everyone left without telling Hussey and Almquist anything.

Almquist spent an anxious night waiting for the next morning's meeting, at which Futas finally explained how F5 was to be restructured. Almquist, he said, was to remain in charge of development. Hussey was to relinquish the authority and responsibility of his CEO position (although he would keep his title) in order to devote his time exclusively to seeking out strategic alliances, money, and other business deals. Hussey, Luukinen, and Almquist were to report to Brian Dixon, who was to consult with Futas, who in turn would report to the board.

From then on, Almquist watched eagerly for signs that Hussey would be fired. He believed that the Vantage Point Venture deal was a litmus test for Hussey. "The board is waiting for Jeff to land this VC deal on decent terms or for him to fuck it up," he said. "For the past eight, nine months, this deal is the only thing he can point to. We've heard from way too many people that Jeff offends and alienates everyone he meets. I think his ass is toast."

It was always hard for me to tell which was more interesting— the events at F5 or the panache and style with which Almquist recounted them. His delight in telling these stories, as measured by his language, served as a barometer for his substantial *schaden-*

freude. Thus Almquist told me about his coworkers' swan song—the last meeting before the board's forced changes began taking effect—in this fashion:

> Lynn, Brian, Jeff and I had an executive meeting, and there were three amusing events: Lynn went on about how we shipped the product to Bear Stearns and how it doesn't work and how the problem was hardware-related. To which Brian was going on and on and on, "Its not hardware-related, we don't know what the problem is, but Andre and I built the machine and we can't be at fault." To which Lynn started going on, "Did you test it?" "No." "Then it's your fault" . . . and back and forth and back and forth. I expected Lynn to jump over the table and start beating the shit out of everybody.
>
> Then it was on to projection of sales. They went on about projections, and Brian kind of felt *toasty,* so he started beating the shit out of Lynn, about how her projections are wrong, where are sales, where is the money, to which Lynn didn't have any answers and there was a fight going back and forth, back and forth. . . .
>
> And then when that died down, we look up, and the VP of sales candidate is waiting outside the door. We're going to bring him in and hire him as VP of sales, then we're going to move him into the COO role. And *that* started a huge fight, and for no purpose—they're just fighting.
>
> Now Lynn's a really nasty, mean fighter and a really nasty, mean person. And whenever she's cornered she takes shots that are mean and personal. So she kept saying this person would be hired as CEO, because she's aware of Al and Kent's dissatisfaction. So she kept going on, "We're going to hire him as CEO," to which Brian kept saying, "No, COO," to which Jeff kept saying, "No, VP of sales!" To which Lynn would go, "CEO!"
>
> I'm like, "This is too mad!" I said nothing during this meeting, I just sat and watched. Nobody's giving me any shit . . . the reason being that Kent and Al had said, "This kid's the only one doing anything, you guys get your act together."
>
> So then they went around in circles for a long time, they fi-

nally stopped, they said, "We're going to bring him in here and we're going to think about this guy being hired as VP of sales. But since there's no consensus, let's bring him in and see where he kind of walks."

The most amusing part . . . when the music started, Jeff went to the head of the conference table and there wasn't a chair there. There were other chairs around the table, but none at the head. So he left the room and dragged a chair in so he could sit at the head of the table. He's an extraordinarily amusing little man.

The F5 board had found the waiting candidate, thirty-seven-year-old Steve Goldman, through a headhunter, and it was clear from Goldman's background that the board had made up its mind about Hussey's abilities and about the future of F5. Goldman had been hired by the board to impose organizational order on F5, put sales and technical support teams in place, hire thirty or more new people in less than two months, move into the CEO position six to nine months down the road, and help orchestrate the sale of F5 to an established networking company. Goldman's previous two positions had been as head or second-in-command of companies that were, as he put it, "sold to the competition." With a background in mergers and acquisitions and a relish for the deal—"I really enjoyed those two experiences," he said—he had been brought in to make F5 acquisition worthy. "They were interested in me because I helped drive two mergers over the last three years," Goldman told me.

His arrival not only signaled the board's intentions to Almquist and others at F5, it also signaled the company's potential worth, for here was an experienced, businesslike, rational human being who saw tremendous potential in the company. He expected within a matter of months to sell F5 for somewhere between $25 million and $30 million. "They have a solid product—a technology that solves a real *business need*," he said. "They just need management structure. Jeff and Squish both lack management background, and enjoy the vision a lot more than the execution. I looked at what they had, what they'd gone through, and decided that the fact they had overcome all their turmoil was a really good sign."

Within three months of his arrival, Goldman had accepted Luukinen's resignation, put nine sales and support people in place around the country, planned to add twenty more over the next sixty days, had hired enough new programmers and other technicians to necessitate a move to larger quarters, had lured a new VP of engineering away from industry giant U.S. Robotics, and had thoroughly energized F5. "I certainly didn't join the company to eke out an existence as a quaint little computer company in the five-million-dollar range," he liked to say.

Almquist could scarcely contain his excitement. In little more than a month, he had gone from thinking he was about to go out of business for the third time in his life to thinking he was about to become a multimillionaire. "He's the one who's going to make it happen!" he said of Goldman. "We might end up being successful in spite of ourselves!"

He was not alone in his newfound confidence. On August 15, when the company was down to just enough money to make one more payroll and with the board still leery of the Vantage Point offer, Joey King lined up $250,000 from connections in Texas, the EnCompass Group promised to put in an additional $300,000, and Goldman secured a $250,000 line of credit. The new money would prove to be more than enough to tide F5 over until its sales took off and started bringing in thousands per month. "By the end of the year," Goldman predicted, "we'll be at five million in sales."

The sudden surge upward in his company's fortunes had Almquist reflecting on the bizarre ups and downs of the past year. "This is a way freakin' weird deal," he said. "If I'd known how easy it was to raise money, I never would have had to get involved with Jeff. But I didn't know anything! I didn't know what a CEO was, what a VP of engineering was, what they were supposed to do. All of my experience had been in research labs. I didn't even know what a product cycle was! I didn't know how to get the damned thing out the door! I have great intuition for a lot of these things, but I didn't *know*. And learning at the HIT lab taught you everything but how to be successful."

He recalled a particularly memorable conversation with Futas, who had observed that people are essentially the sum total of their previous experience, and that it was obvious from Almquist's rather high tolerance for trouble that he previously had worked at an extremely disorganized place. "Then we talked about the dysfunctionality of the HIT lab," Almquist said. "It had thickened my skin to the point that it may have been *too* thick. That may be appropriate for a research lab, but to create successful companies I have to learn to scream and holler a lot sooner. Boy, Joey and I have learned a lot of lessons that we regret learning."

He didn't know when he said that last sentence that he had more—and more regrettable—lessons yet to learn.

One of Virtual i/O's more memorable promotional items was a picture reproduced on innumerable flyers, magazine ads, and posters. It was a lavish, full-color depiction of a glamorous young couple in bed. The woman was asleep and the man was wearing Virtual i/O's i-Glasses!

The flyer, sent out by the James G. Murphy, Inc., Commercial/Industrial Auctioneers, had this picture printed on its front cover, with the words "PUBLIC AUCTION By Order Secured Creditor" superimposed over the fantasy. The auction was scheduled to take place at Virtual i/O's headquarters on June 10 and 11, 1997, with the day before set aside for prospective bidders to tour the auction site and look over the merchandise.

I walked over to Virtual i/O on the preview day and joined a large crowd making its way through the door at street level and queuing up at the building's single elevator. When it reached the sixth floor, the elevator opened into Virtual i/O's foyer.

The foyer was transformed. Three James G. Murphy employees stood at the receptionist's station, taking names of those who wanted to register for the auction and giving them a bidder's paddle and list of items. Others were setting up tables, adding machines, calculators, and computers for collecting payment from winning bidders over the next two days. One of the people signing in visitors explained to me that the items were sorted more or less by type, with each room dedicated to specific genres of equipment: One room had computers and printers, another scanners, another luggage, and so on.

I started off toward a room filled with headsets and various other electronic equipment, and was greeted as I came through the door by a long laugh, coming from behind a partition. I walked into the cubicle and found a young man there staring down at a table on which were arranged twenty-three cellular telephones. Looking up at me, still laughing, he said, "I'm laughing at all the cell phones. It looks like the bottom of Linden's shoe closet!"

The rest of the room was packed with all manner of electronic and video equipment, from the historic near miss to the baffling. There was one never-released Sega VR headset, in its promotional packaging ("The 360° gaming experience"), memorializing the aborted deal between Virtual i/O and Sega. There were stacks nearly to the ceiling of five-disc CD changers, video CD players, VCRs, scanners, card readers, and televisions. One table held five satellite-dish TV receivers.

I asked the laughing visitor, who turned out to be an ex–Virtual i/O employee, about the dishes. "It was one of Amadon's fantasies," he said, shaking his head. "He wanted to link i-Glasses! with every new technology, and he wanted to have working proof. So like three days before COMDEX or something, you'd suddenly get the order: 'I want a working satellite dish in the middle of the convention center floor!' "

The preview was heavily attended by former Virtual i/O employees who wandered among the rooms reminiscing, laughing, gloating, and indulging their curiosity. "Look," said one when he and his group entered a large room filled with computers and printers, "there's Greg's laptop!" A NEC Versa 6010H, outfitted with Microsoft's Leonardo Office 97 software suite, it was a high-end machine that retailed for $3,800. The group descended on it and began roaming through its files, looking for entertainment.

I passed through the computer room, walked past a five-hundred-gallon aquarium surrounded by laughing Virtual i/O expatriates—"Nothing of value," one of them was saying, to general laughter, "never was!"—moved through an array of scanners and other peripherals, passed through a gigantic room full of heavy equipment, web servers, and other industrial-strength hardware, walked past Linden Rhoads's old office, and was making my way through a roomful of office furniture when I came upon Rhoads herself, holding court in one corner of the room. She was talking nonstop to a group of acquaintances and passing out her new business card, on which was emblazoned: "Rhoads and Associates . . . Assisting New Technology Ventures."

I returned next morning to a positively packed house, a sea of familiar faces. The HIT lab was heavily represented, as was Microvision, Deep Bile, Advanced Marine Technology, and nearly every other VR or VR-related start-up in Seattle. Friendships were renewed, memories exchanged, bid lists gone over. Earnest bidders tested computers, VCRs, and disc players, and pawed through headsets trying to determine their condition.

By the time the auctioneer had set up his stand and taken his position, there was scarcely room to move. And once the bidding started, there followed a frenzy of competition and confusion.

The first items up for auction were printers and fax machines that proved to sell, after a flurry of bidding, for more than their retail value. These transactions had savvy bidders in the room looking around at one another in disbelief, their shock turning to anger as item after item went for many times what they might be expected to fetch. Eventually, headsets started selling for $400 each, with sets lacking electronics going for as high as $200. "Remind me to have an auction next time instead of a garage sale," said one chagrined bidder.

The proceedings droned on, over two days, with little in the way of entertainment. Joey King waited nearly a whole day to bid on some "cheesy Japanese posters" promoting the i-Glasses!, and HIT lab representatives made off with as many headsets as their meager budget allowed them to buy. Mike Tidwell was disappointed when he was outbid for the never-marketed Sega VR headset, and I heard one ex–Virtual i/O employee express mock outrage at the disappearance before the auction of the company's collection of "3D porn."

It was not until late in the afternoon of the second day that the auction provided a moment of high entertainment. The auctioneer had made his way from room to room, his energy unflagging, coming at last to Rhoads's office, in which sat, tagged and ready to be auctioned off, her lavish oversized desk. As the crowd gathered round, an ex–Virtual i/O engineer named Walt Web sidled up to Rhoads and sneered, "I'm gonna get your desk!"

The bidding began. After the first few rounds, there were only two bidders left: Web and Rhoads. They went head to head for several minutes, until finally Web—in what must in retrospect have seemed a pyrrhic victory at best—won.

"Walt won," Deep Bile reported later, "he got the satisfaction of beating her, but he had to pay more."

The end of summer 1997 found both Rich Johnston and Mike Tidwell courting David Melville with renewed energy and higher hopes. Johnston's employer, Information Optics, and Tidwell's, Advanced Marine Technology, had both secured new rounds of funding and now could afford Melville's high price. And Johnston and Tidwell both knew that as Melville neared the end of his first year at Microvision, he would finally have lost the last of his patience and hope.

Melville's disenchantment had grown steadily from the day he first went over to Microvision, and now it had reached intolerable levels. He was particularly disappointed in the engineers Microvision hired to manage the VRD project and to supervise him. One, Douglas Stoll, had looked promising at first, as he came to Microvision after sixteen years of work with TRW's Space and Defense Section. But Stoll proved an unimaginative manager—"the kind of guy," Melville said one day, "who would be a great manager for something like the B-1 bomber project, but who can't manage something that involves invention."

Melville was particularly vexed over the way the company was using him. He spent his days writing memos, tracking projects on his computer, and being interrupted constantly by people with questions. "By the time I get home," he said, "I'm too tired to think about problems." He yearned for a return to the university environment, where he could define a problem and work on it for as long as it took to find a solution, and where he was surrounded by fellow thinkers instead of businesspeople and profiteers.

"I told them when I came to work for them," he said, "that I was interested in one thing only: developing the technology and moving it forward. But I don't think they're interested in that." Every day he spent there fooling around with his managerial responsibilities was another day wasted. "I'm like a Swiss Army knife," he continued. "I have a corkscrew, I have a knife blade, I have some scissors . . . none of them are *particularly good*, but I've got all of them. I'm an *integrator*. But they're using me as a hammer—and I'm a *lousy* hammer."

The breaking point finally came when Microvision issued its first annual report. Melville read the document with a deepening sense of shock, then promptly called Tidwell and told him he would accept the job offer from Advanced Marine Technology.

From his point of view, the report was filled with red flags. A paragraph in the Commitments and Contingencies section detailing the likelihood that Furness would sue Microvision was particularly alarming, as Melville had known nothing about the dispute until reading the report. Characterizing Furness as an unnamed "consultant to the company," the report stated that, "if the consultant were to commence legal action against the Company, there is no assurance that he would not prevail on some or all of his claims."

Melville was no less alarmed by the Price Waterhouse Report of Independent Accountants, appended to the report. "The Company does not expect to have any significant revenues until late 1997 at the earliest," read the Price Waterhouse appendix. "Revenues in late 1997, if any, are expected to be derived from cooperative development projects. Revenues from sales of products may not occur until substantially later, if at all. . . . There can be no assurance that the Company will ever be able to generate revenues or achieve or sustain profitability."

If Melville's decision to leave was any indication, Price Waterhouse was predicting nothing but trouble in Microvision's future. "Additionally," the auditors wrote, "the Company must be able to attract, retain and motivate qualified technical and management personnel. . . ."

The report was the subject of countless discussions among employees at Microvision, many of whom were disappointed, if not shocked. When Melville left, he had the impression that several other engineers would be leaving as well, and there was a great deal of gruesome speculation among employees with stock options over the impending plunge of Microvision's stock price.

The market, however, had ideas of its own. Having started out in July, just after the report was issued, trading at $6 per share, Microvision stock bounced around between $5 and $6 all month long. Then it shot up in mid-August to $12, and climbed to $19 in September.

Negotiations between Zombie and BMG reached a point at the end of August 1997 where it looked like Zombie might have some hope of survival. BMG agreed to continue financing Spearhead and SpecOps until they were finished, in December 1997 and February 1998 respectively. The company wanted to cancel its third Zombie project—Vox—however, and Long was trying to negotiate a cash settlement in return for dropping the game. "It's a big commitment they're trying to get out of," he said, "and we wouldn't be able to keep operating without that money."

Long and Alexander estimated that they had a "50–50" chance of getting what they wanted from BMG. "We're not sleeping very well at night," Alexander said.

Still, the company was pressing ahead on several new fronts. Long had flown down to Los Angeles to negotiate joint projects with Wildstorm Comics, creators of the enormously successful "Wetworks" series. Long wanted to do a series of games using comic-book artists and art directors, based on archetypal superheroines—highly sexed, underdressed, dominatrix forces of law and order. "Comics have been dominated by the superbabe or bazooka babe for years," Long said. "These sexy, aggressive characters," he was convinced, would appeal to the hard-core computer gamer. He had put together a plan to do a series of games that could be "cross-marketed" with comics, some of the games based on existing comic-book characters, others on the exploits of a new, Zombie-created superbabe named Lace. In all, Long was discussing four separate comic-art/game projects. "We're pretty excited about all that," he said.

In addition, Long and Alexander were on the verge of closing a deal for Zombie to develop a game in the enormously popular MechWarrior series—a game that was almost guaranteed to be a best-seller, as MechWarriors 1 and 2 had sold more than half a million copies each.

Since none of these deals had been formally signed, however, Long and Alexander still were nervous about their company's future. "We've got a million irons in the fire," Long said, "but it always takes more time than you have to close these deals. Timing's our real enemy now. By January, we may have more titles than we can do—or we may be out of business."

One thing Long had in common with Furness was an odd kind of irrepressible exuberance in the face of constant frustration, setbacks, and the ever-present danger that he would be put out of commission. Just as Furness tirelessly pursued new initiatives even as all his old ones were turning into blind alleys, so did Long seem able to come up with ten new schemes for every one that had disappointed him.

Thus the just-concluded August SIGGRAPH, held in Los Angeles, had been a series of meetings for Long with various potential partners and financial backers for various game and movie ventures. Long had devoted a good part of his SIGGRAPH trip to trying to line up financing for his *Liberty* movie project—the DVD movie/game composition that was to be entirely computer-generated, with no live actors. His partners at ShadowCatcher had arranged some meetings for him, and he accordingly found himself one night walking down a Los Angeles street for a rendezvous at a restaurant.

He arrived at the appointed place to find that the restaurant was closed. Long stood leaning against the wall for fifteen minutes or so, wondering what to do, when a black luxury-model BMW with black-tinted windows pulled up to the curb in front of him.

The rear passenger window rolled down, and Long found himself face-to-face with rock musician/actress Courtney Love.

"Is the restaurant closed?" she asked.

"Yes, it is," Long answered.

Love rolled her window back up, and the car drove off.

Minutes later, a man came running breathlessly up to Long.

"Are you Joe Cassini?" Long asked.

"No!" shouted the man. "Has Courtney Love been here?"

"Just a minute ago."

"What'd you tell her?"

"I told her that the restaurant was closed."

"Why the hell did you tell her that?"

"Well . . . because it was *closed*."

The man ran off, cursing. Long was just coming to the realization that he was a producer or screenwriter who had gotten a rare chance to get five minutes of Love's time, pitching a script to her, then had missed his chance, when the man Long was supposed to meet came walking up to him.

"We went off to some other restaurant," Long recalled later. "This guy was wearing a baseball cap that he had sewn a *really bad* toupee to the inside of. I guess he just wanted to able to pick up his hat and hair and put it on all at once when he went running out the door or something. Anyway, we're sitting in this restaurant, and this guy keeps saying, 'I've got a hundred million just sitting there,' and he keeps taking his hat and hair on and off, and I'm trying to talk to him, and trying to pay attention to what he's saying, but I just can't stop staring at this guy, and I'm trying to figure out how Zombie ever got me to the point where I'm talking to a guy with his hair sewn into his hat and I'm thinking, 'My God! Is everyone in LA psychotic?' "

Telling me the story days later, sitting at his desk, he reached over and pulled out an immense pile of printed forms. "I guess we really are talking to somebody, though," he said. "They sent me a bunch of paperwork to fill out."

It had now been two months or more since I last had seen Furness, and I trekked up to the HIT lab with some trepidation, expecting to find that he had grown even more dispirited and desperate. The lab, after all, was marching ever closer to the end of its biggest contracts, there was no new money on the horizon, and his "life's work"—the VRD—was still in the hands of malevolent clowns who appeared to be killing it off for the sake of short-term profit.

As I walked up to the door of his office, my head was filled with old-movie clichés: "Mayday! Mayday! We're coming in on a wing and a prayer!"

Thus I was considerably unprepared for the happy storm of a greeting the director gave me. Furness came bounding around his table, with his arms extended, shouting his classic and energetic, "Why, hello there, young man!" He took my hand and pumped it ecstatically, his other hand whacking my shoulder. "Come on in!"

Before I had a chance to return his greeting, he started filling me in on all the "wonderful things" I'd missed, on his "amazing" new students, on the array of new initiatives he had going on various fronts. . . . "You oughta come with us down to the Museum of Flight," he said at last. "We've been talking with the folks there about doing a spaceflight museum, a 'virtual Starfleet Academy,' and it looks like it's going to happen. I'm doing a presentation to their staff next Friday."

It turned out that the Museum of Flight (a lavish museum on the Boeing grounds, underwritten in large part by Boeing family members) had begun talking with the HIT lab some months before about building a relatively simple kiosk on spaceflight. As is typical of any Furness project, though, the thing grew into a multimillion-dollar monster of ambition, stretching both the museum's budget and the limits of computer technology. Furness proposed that the museum build a Starfleet Academy, in which visitors wearing VR headsets would sit at flight controls in a mockup of the flight deck of the starship *Enterprise* and navigate through a virtual outer spacescape. Visitors would have this experience in groups—flight crews—all of them networked on a Silicon Graphics system that would render the surrounding universe in real time while allowing the crew to communicate with one another and with a "ground control" back on virtual Earth.

I kept trying to picture the dreamy Furness spinning this fantasy

to the nuts-and-bolts Boeing world, and decided this was a performance not to be missed. So I showed up at the Museum of Flight
at the appointed time early one morning, and waited for Furness
to arrive.

The museum is a gleaming, opulent, glass-and-steel structure
on the Boeing corporate campus in south Seattle. It sits among
Boeing administrative offices that are housed in some of the company's oldest buildings—small, red, wooden, barnlike hangars from
the company's earliest days, back in the 1920s. The museum is
filled with airplanes of every description, from all over the world.
It positively reeks of money, and it was easy to picture Furness's
gimme glands swelling magnificently when he first set eyes on the
place.

The museum board room, which was elegantly furnished with
a massive inlaid cherry-wood table, looked out through a row of
picture windows on the Boeing Field runways. It was outfitted
with all the accoutrements of the modern corporate wealth Furness was forever trying to access: indirect lighting, flawless climate
control, high-backed leather conference chairs, an elaborate sound
system, state-of-the-art projectors, screens, and oversized video
monitors.

The overall impression was of a place with pretty much an unlimited budget.

Furness arrived with an entourage of six staffers and students,
all carrying computers, audiovisual equipment, posters, or hand-
outs. The director was wearing a dark suit—an unusually formal
touch for him—and a wide tie depicting Winnie-the-Pooh gazing
Winnieingly up at the stars. He greeted the museum staffers with
great good cheer, pumping hands and smiling broadly as if *never* in
his *wildest dreams* had he expected to meet such *wonderful* folks.

While his audience—now large enough to take up all twenty-
two seats at the table and many of those along the walls—settled
in, and while the students in his group looked open-mouthed
around the room, Furness set up his laptop, plugged a tape into the
videotape player and turned it on, strung cords linking everything
together, miked himself, and tested the functionality of his equipment—all in a matter of a few minutes. Then, after a brief intro-

duction by the museum's director of exhibits and programs, Joan Piper, he started in, his folksy twang and rural North Carolina accent, I thought, turned up just a notch.

"Well, we're just really excited," he began. "We've been chomping at the bit for a long time to come play with you guys."

Furness always begins his presentations with a nonchalant allusion to his air force career—" 'black' airplanes and fighter cockpits and things like that," as he characterized his work to the Boeing audience—before moving on to the VR portion of his program. "What we want to build here," he said, "is a six-degrees-of-freedom museum."

On the oversized video screen off to one side was playing an animation showing an astronaut on a spacewalk making repairs to his spacecraft. On the screen behind Furness, a series of slides stored on his laptop were being displayed: a rocket, an air force VR helmet, a picture from deep space taken by the Hubble Telescope. . . .

Now Furness was going through a long, homespun story about the boyhood he spent dreaming of flight and space travel, building homemade rockets—"I came up with this fuel mix that burns real fast—matter of fact, it burns so fast it sort of *explodes*"—leading his listeners through the story of his science fair awards, his week with the navy, his meeting with the Mercury astronauts, his acceptance into the Air Force Academy, and his being turned away at the door to his dreams because of poor eyesight.

"And lemme tell ya," he said, "I was *heartbroken*."

Now he began a story from late in his air force career, when he had traveled down to NASA in Texas to help implement a head-up display for landing the space shuttle. While there, he revisited another of his creations—a VR system with a stereographic helmet-mounted display that was being used to train astronauts for future repair missions in outer space. It was called the Manned Maneuvering Unit. Trainees would don a spacesuit and the helmet with its virtual display, then navigate through a virtual outer space, repairing a virtual spacecraft.

This was the system being displayed on his video monitor, and Furness, pointing now at the space-suited avatar floating on the screen, described his own experience in the Manned Maneuvering

Unit as the belated realization of his boyhood dream. He made it sound as if his entire air force career had been a long, circuitous way of inventing a form of virtual flight to compensate him for the crushing disappointment delivered him by Nature.

"They let me put this on, do a walk in virtual space," he said, pointing at the figure in the video. Then, in a softened voice: "It was just a joy to finally get a chance to fly."

Furness paused for a second, as if giving his listeners a chance to compose themselves, before launching the description of his plans for the museum project. "We want to build a Starship Center," he said energetically, "a virtual learning environment for future leaders and explorers of the universe." Kids taking part in the starship project, he continued, would sign on through the Internet to a project web site, do preparatory lessons on science and spaceflight, then subsequently come to the museum. There, they would undergo a brief orientation, go on a mission into deep space, and upon their return would be "debriefed"—report on what they had learned. The lessons would continue indefinitely, again over the Internet, as the students would continue their studies and their relationship with the museum through the World Wide Web.

Furness's presentation included a description of the project, its costs, how it would be implemented, and how it would work; an argument for using an immersive VR approach in education; an enumeration of the ways such a project would benefit the museum; and a presentation of some of the visuals the starship visitors might see through their headsets. Thus his laptop was broadcasting an array of slides up on the screen: now some charts showing the components, time lines, and costs of building the starship; now a breathtaking, full-color picture of a star being born; now a view of Earth from outer space; now a schematic diagram of the school's Internet connection, or "virtual schoolhouse," the flight deck of the starship *Enterprise*, the debriefing room, and the post-flight, Internet-mediated revisitations to the starship; now the landscape of Mars, now a field of stars; now figures showing that television viewership among children had declined in the post-video-game age. "Studies show kids prefer interactive entertainment. . . . Kids are getting bored with traditional ways of education. . . ."

Although Furness, who never raises his voice, eschews the shouts and dramatic exclamations of garden-variety orators and evangelists, he nevertheless communicates powerful passion and conviction when he speaks. His language is rich, and the range of his intonations wide and deep. He has the odd ability to project his voice across a packed room in a way that makes it sound as if he is standing next to you, talking quietly and persuasively to you alone.

His presentations always have woven into them an ardent argument for the virtual-world interface. "Computers are still *outside in.* . . . You can't *go to a place.* . . . Building a virtual world leads to building a much more robust mental model. . . . We want to present a circumambience of visual information, we want to build a high-bandwidth interface with the mind."

Lest his dreamer recruits fear that his visions were outlandish, he offered, by way of reassurance, his own long experience. "VR isn't new—I started working on it in 1966," he said. "After twenty-three years, a hundred and fifty million dollars . . . now it's beginning to appear in commercial markets."

Now the presentation was building to something of a crescendo, with the understated rhetorical flourishes and the images on the wall coming thicker and faster, richer and more colorful. Furness was offering the museum an opportunity to *change the world*, to *shift the paradigm* of education, to "open the portal between information and the mind." With the system he envisioned, "if you want to, you can crank it up to a hundred Gs and juggle on Jupiter." Even after more than thirty years of work on this interface, he still was reduced to an awestruck kid whenever he thought about its potential: "Y'know, I was thinking to myself, 'Gosh . . .' "

Not only did the museum have a chance to join him in unlocking the human mind and changing the face of education, it also could set humans free from the prison the PC age was slowly building around them. "Computers are basically symbol processors," Furness said. "And to use them, we've had to act like computers. The only innovation in interface in the last twenty years is the mouse—and that's about it."

Moreover, the museum could do this at relatively low cost—could, in fact, work the spatial equivalent of the miracle of the loaves and fishes: "The beauty of this is that your real estate is *unlimited*. The cost per square foot of virtual real estate is *infinitesimal*—because you can *roam the universe*. The only limit on where you can go is your imagination."

By now, Furness's listeners looked like kids in Disneyland. They sat stock-still, their eyes riveted on him, their mouths agape, as he segued from the dream portion of his speech to the practicalities of realizing the dream in the museum. "Previsit, from at home or at school, over the Internet, students will log in to the 'Starbase.' " They would download reading material, video clips, and software that would help prepare for their visit to the museum. With those lessons absorbed, they would come to the museum for a "starbase training session, their flight experience on the starship, and a starbase debriefing." There could be no end to the activities and learning experiences that could be built into their spaceflight. "They will work in small groups, in immersive worlds, performing tasks that help them learn. We can put them into a space where they can do EVA. We want to *imbed* them into this fun activity." Their immersion would change the way they took in instructional materials forever afterward. "When you come back to Earth, as it were, you look at a screen, it has a different meaning because you had this immersive experience."

Furness detailed the "scalable, modular system" he wanted to build—one that would allow the museum to plug in or remove computer modules as software and hardware advanced, so that the system—one that "might be a real precedent in the world"—could be kept constantly state of the art. He could get started, he said, with "an R-O-M—Rough Order of Magnitude—of $1.4 million," which would get the starship and its support system "through construction." He would like to get started as soon as possible, he added, "because we have several projects that are ramping down."

I sat through the presentation alternately swept up in the soft whirlwind of Furness's speech and mindful of the intimidating technical obstacles that stood between the museum and its virtual

Jupiter—obstacles, come to think of it, that approached those of a spaceflight to the *real* Jupiter. I started thinking of the enormous difficulties of getting a network of SGI reality engines to render the real-time, rich, collaborative environment that Furness was describing. I wondered how he would maintain and repair the Virtual i/O headsets he wanted to use without the support of the manufacturer, which had gone out of business. I wondered how the system could stand up to the punishment sure to be inflicted on it by kids with no experience using VR equipment, and by museum employees who could be taught to deal with its interface but who would lack the expertise to tweak broken or misbehaving hardware and software. And I realized that Furness was promising to deliver something no one—from his own, impecunious laboratory to the infinitely wealthy Walt Disney Imagineering—had ever managed to deliver.

And most frightening of all—Furness actually believed he could pull this off. I realized that the key to his success, his energy, his inability to be kept down for long by disappointment and failure, was an amazing ability to keep seeing the desired as the actual, the vision as the reality. As Rich Johnston had told me a year before, he had no idea how to get from the imperfect here to the perfect there, but he knew in his heart that he could somehow get there. If it was good and useful and something humankind desperately needed—and Furness was convinced that his virtual-world interface was all of those things, and more—then it was as if he had already found the way there and had only to pull the less imaginative up into his paradise.

There came time for questions from the museum staff, whose members made a strenuous, if futile, effort to shake off the effects of Furness's hypnosis and ask some skeptical questions. "I have a question about maintenance and support long term after you move on to other projects," said Joan Piper. "I'm particularly worried about custom software that only Joe Blow from God-Knows-Where knows how to use and fix. And what about the life cycle of something like this . . . in this world of rapidly changing technology?"

Not to worry. Furness promised full support and maintenance

for as long as the museum exhibit existed. "Once you buy off on this, you're hangin' on to the roller coaster," he said, smiling.

With that, the museum was sold. The staffers all but jumped up and joined Furness in a celebratory song and dance à la the citizens of River City under the spell of Harold Hill. "It's so exciting to be talking about the Internet," exclaimed one of the staffers. "To think of kids at home, dialing in to this station, instead of playing Donkey Kong or whatever they do. . . ."

After a few more encomiums, Piper stood and brought the program to a close. "My goodness," she said. "We didn't realize that you were going to come down here with bells and whistles and dancing girls!"

"Great presentation!" someone else chimed in. "Very good!"

"An *outstanding* presentation!" added Mark Kirschner, the museum board chairman.

When I left, the entire group had moved to the front of the room and was standing clustered around Furness, still feeding greedily on his charisma.

I hitched a ride back to downtown Seattle with Peter Oppenheimer, now back at the HIT lab after his brief stint at Zombie. Although he had seen hundreds of Furness presentations, he was nevertheless visibly impressed by this one. "Man," he said, chuckling, "when Tom told that NASA story, there wasn't a dry eye in the house."

I ran into Furness two days later, and mentioned how powerful I had found his presentation and how obviously moved his audience had been.

"Well, muh heart was really in that one," he said.

POSTPARTUM

Shoot the Inventor

DURING ONE OF MY CONVERSATIONS with Mike Almquist, I found myself hearing him say—in the midst of one of his bleakest monologues—"And ultimately, I think F5 is going to be incredibly successful." Given that at the time he and his business were self-destructing spectacularly, and that he seemed unlikely to emerge psychologically intact from the impending disaster, I thought at first that he had gone as mad as Furness.

But then he went on to offer various definitions of success: "And that can be anything from all the press it's generated, the reputation it's generated, or just eventually the possibility of selling the solution and making the solution available extremely cheap. *Which will make an extraordinary ripple in the force.*" Nowhere in that definition could I find any mention of the survival of his company in the marketplace or the millions he stood to make if F5 Labs were to be sold for $25 million or more.

It had never occurred to me until then that success in the technological arena could be anything other than financial success, or that the story I was following was the story of a new technology exploiting people for the sake of its own advance rather than of people exploiting new technology for the sake of their own enrichment. But after taking in Almquist's astonishing statement, I remembered something I had been told nearly a year before by VRD project manager Rich Johnston: "The technology has a life of its own. It's going to move forward. . . . There may be some specific things that never get invented, because these are some guy's dreams, but in general invention will continue. The problems are going to get solved."

Until Almquist, in recasting his fate for me, forced me to reexamine the territory I had covered while following him and his fellow prospectors around, I had seen the struggles of these people as another in a long series of failed promises, broken dreams, and the inability of people to deliver on their visions. But when I turned my attention away from the people and toward the fruits of their labors, I saw a microcosmic example of progress marching slowly but steadily onward.

Most striking in this regard was the reemergence from bankruptcy of the technology of two Seattle companies—Virtual Vision and Virtual i/O—that had struggled to find a market for the head-mounted display. Virtual Vision was purchased out of bankruptcy in the summer of 1995 by Telxon Corporation, a wireless mobile communications company, and by mid-1997 was marketing augmented reality displays for use by engineers on construction sites and in factories. (Although the company would not release sales figures, I did see its product in use at Boeing.) And Virtual i/O no sooner ceased operations than a California display company, Ilixco, announced that it had purchased enough Virtual i/O equipment and hired enough Virtual i/O engineering talent to release an improved version of the company's head-mounted display for video viewing by autumn 1997.

In both cases, then, the technology had survived the failed vision of its progenitors and was starting over again, with new humans, at a stage further along in its evolutionary advance.

And while Tom Furness was personally disappointed, if not devastated, by the way his invention was handled and brought to the threshold of the market by his sponsor, Microvision, there was no question that virtual-retinal-display technology itself had made remarkable advances into the public consciousness and possibly into the marketplace. When I first visited Furness in 1993 and first saw the VRD prototype, there were no retinal-display products or prototypes anywhere in the commercial arena. By the time David Melville left Microvision, he had found four other companies working on retinal-display technology, and Microvision—for all of its failings—had signed a research contract with Fujitsu Research (the two companies at long last had reached agreement on a Fujitsu research project into the uses of the VRD for the vision-impaired). Microvision also had signed agreements with Boeing and Saab to develop VRD prototypes for use in fighter pilots' helmet-mounted displays. While the company itself did not figure to survive (delivery of their first prototypes to Saab, for example, had what was described to me as an extremely "low yield" of working scanners), understanding of its technology had clearly spread from Furness's lab, through media and Microvision, out into the mainstream industrial world. It was now one of those problems that "a whole pile full of people," in Rich Johnston's words, were working on.

Similarly, Long and Alexander had brought immersive environments—once the stuff of science fiction—ever closer to reality through their work on three-dimensional computing environments for games and other entertainments. During my year with them, I had seen their company, Zombie, move from the fringes of the computer-games world into large-scale development efforts with Disney Imagineering and the film production company ShadowCatcher. Although Long and Alexander still saw themselves as struggling to survive—indeed, even as they were pursuing and completing these initiatives, they were laying employees off in anticipation of closing their doors for good after the Disney and SpecOps projects were finished—the arena of their struggle had changed substantially. By way of Zombie, they had moved from the exotic, orphaned research laboratory kept alive by the fading military-industrial complex to the mainstream software world fed and sustained by the surging entertainment-industrial complex. SpecOps, with its cinematic realism, breakthrough game engine, and astonishing production values, would debut in February 1998, distributed in Europe by BMG Interactive and in the United States by Panasonic's Ripcord Publishers, with a first U.S. pressing of eighty thousand copies. Zombie, then, was either poised on the brink of survival through a megahit or about to go out of business in a blaze of aesthetic glory.

Mike Almquist and Joey King, meanwhile, had created in F5 Labs the beginning of a possibility that the Internet could be transformed into an arena of large-scale, immersive, collaborative environments—the dream of every VR adept from the days of Ivan Sutherland and ROTC lieutenant Tom Furness. BIG/ip was infiltrating the Internet in a big way: Not only were several large established Internet companies negotiating to buy F5 Labs and make BIG/ip part of their product lines, but Microsoft had begun to buy BIG/ip packages for use in its own internal and external web sites. In January 1998, Microsoft bought ten BIG/ip's, and Almquist was doing demonstrations and presentations to ten other Microsoft product groups. The Microsoft sale had Compaq Computer looking into the possibility of bundling BIG/ip in its Proliant Series servers, which were among the market leaders in server sales. Sales of BIG/ip had crossed the $6-million mark and were still rising, with Microsoft closing another $1-million order as I was writing this.

The entry of BIG/ip into the networking environment, along with the coming battle between BIG/ip and load-balancing solutions from more established competitors, signaled the near readiness of the networked communications world for Almquist and King's next company—one that was getting off the ground even as F5 was just establishing itself.

By early 1998, King and Almquist had completed detailed plans for Indaba Communications, Inc. (Indaba is the Zulu word for "interact" or "a meeting of wise people"), a company that would develop interface tools and system software for a new computing machine. A combination computer and video telephone, it would be a platform serving large-scale virtual environments for communication and collaboration. The two envisioned a company employing nearly a hundred people that would be a kind of VR Microsoft, developing an operating system for hardware and applications software to be made by others that would allow dis-

parate people connected over the Internet to inhabit and collaborate in virtual environments. Gus Caballero, an executive at
Hughes with thirty-five years' experience in large high-tech projects, strategic planning and alliances, organizational development,
corporate policy making, and engineering, agreed to become Indaba's president and CEO. King and Almquist—who was negotiating Almquist's complex release from F5—were to devote the
spring to raising money for Indaba, an enterprise made all the easier by the arrival of someone with Caballero's credentials.

Thus I came away from my sojourn among Seattle's digital
prospectors with the conviction that I had witnessed a latter-day
version of some 1960s slice of the computer-engineering world,
where hardware and software engineers, at work on the first tentative advances in the new science of transistor technology, were
building the tiny gateways to the PC revolution that was to come
twenty years later. Just as that revolution had built upon advances
made in mainframes and minicomputers, so this modern com-
puter-interface effort was building upon the hardware and software advances of its predecessor, the PC revolution.

It seemed to me then that the virtual-world interface, like the
Great Pyramids of Egypt or the great cathedrals of Europe—those
massive projects whose planning and construction spanned countless generations—was destined someday to emerge as the end result of the combined dreams and suffering and effort of thousands,
from all over the world, hard at work—like Furness and his willing
and unwilling collaborators—on the preoccupations and obsessions of their age. From outside, and from a suitable temporal distance, the result will look spectacular and instantaneous. From
inside, from the perspective of the individual engineers and dreamers working on their particular problems, the enterprise looks futile and halting.

We live in an age when the popular image of success is comprised exclusively of the sensational happy ending. A successful industrialist, engineer, or scientist is considered to have dreamed up
a new device, then invented, developed, and turned it into a lucrative product all on his or her own. But the classic breakthrough of
modern American myth is a fiction. We look at the success of a Bill

Gates or an Andrew Grove out of context, willfully ignorant of the efforts of thousands of people, for hundreds and sometimes thousands of years, that preceded and attended it. The grand successes of our titans of industry generally are functions as much of luck and timing as of ingenuity and strategy. The spectacular success of a pivotal industrialist or businessman is built upon the foundation of thousands of tiny individual victories in battles against the laws of physics, the limitations of materials, and the purblindness of the human imagination.

As if to confirm my view of the HIT lab and its entrepreneurial planets as a successful collective enterprise, Furness and King came back from a week-long trip to Japan late in 1997 to report that they had signed up four new Virtual Worlds Consortium members—including Advanced Telecommunications Research, Mitsubishi, Omron, and SSI—and eight more solid prospects: Canon, Toshiba, Olympus, Seiko, Epson, Sanyo, Shimadzu, Sony, and Matsushita. The trip amounted to a hearty endorsement of the HIT lab and its work from the top echelons of the Japanese electronics industry. In addition to the money the new memberships would bring to the lab, King told me, Japanese industry would be investing heavily in other funded research—particularly into the safety of head-mounted displays. Sony now had on the Japanese market three different versions of its Glasstron—one of which included head tracking—and was selling five thousand headsets per month there. Sony would introduce the Glasstron in the U.S. market in September 1998, and other Japanese companies were jumping on the head-mounted-display bandwagon. "They're prototyping over there like crazy," King said. "And they want to spend one million a year on safety research."

When I look at the Glasstron, I see the Japanese realization of an American dream first conjured up thirty years ago by Sutherland and Furness in their subsidized laboratories. In the way Dr. Masahiro Kawahata had described to me two years before, the Japanese had taken a great American idea and turned it into a great Japanese product. Now King saw the Japanese move into the consumer electronics market with the Glasstron and other head-mounted displays as a classic Japanese leg up for the American dreamer. He regarded the move as good news not only for the lab, but for the American VR industry in general. With cheap, safe, credible, and widely available head-mounted displays in American electronics stores, the hunger for applications and machines making use of the headsets figured to grow ever greater. King and Furness had come back from their Japanese trip convinced that VR at long last was on its way out of the lab and into the mass market.

As the F5 chapter of Almquist's life drew to a stormy close, I was to see the relationship between investors and inventors in an ever-harsher light. I came to understand that investors are more like hard-headed professional gamblers than soft-hearted supporters of an inventor's cause. They bet on inventors the way gamblers bet on horses, using up the beasts' potential to win, then sending them off to be shot.

In the fall of 1997, when it was clear that F5 Labs would soon be racking up millions in sales, venture capitalist Jeff Hussey grew increasingly belligerent and threatening toward his inventor partner, Mike Almquist. While Almquist—who thought his troubles with Hussey and the F5 board were over after the examination conducted by A.H. Capital's George Futas—was hard at work upgrading successive versions of BIG/ip, Hussey was relentlessly insisting to board members that F5 Labs was imperiled by Almquist's wackiness and unreliability. Finally, he garnered enough votes to have Almquist removed from the company board, and he began uttering ever more vociferous, dark threats to fire Almquist and seize all of his stock. In shock at the apparent turnaround in the board's attitude toward him, and uncertain as to how much ability Hussey had to deliver on his threats, Almquist hired a lawyer.

There followed a period of enforced discovery, in which Hussey and the F5 board had to turn over to Almquist's attorney, Jon Kroman, all of the documents relating to the founding of F5 Labs and any agreements Almquist had signed with Hussey and the company. It turned out that Almquist—who had not consulted an attorney and who took what little legal advice he had from F5's at-

torney, Bill Carlton—had signed away control of all of his intellectual property for the rest of his life to Hussey and F5 Labs. He also
had given Hussey the right to fire him at will and seize all of his F5
stock. "You see this kind of thing all the time," Kroman said, "where
a naïve inventor back in the 'We all love each other' phase of a
start-up signs all kinds of stuff with business types, VCs, without
understanding what he's signing."

Almquist was hardly calmed by the news that these agreements
would not stand up in court. Kroman assured him that if he sued
for his freedom and his stock, he would win. "But it will take years
and cost you around four hundred thousand dollars."

In the days immediately following this revelation, Almquist was
to come as close to giving in to depression as I was ever to see him
come. He was both shell-shocked and thoroughly unsurprised, berating himself over and over for having allowed himself to be
duped when he should have known better. It was painfully obvious to him now that Hussey's plan from the beginning had been to
manipulate him into developing BIG/ip on the promise that they
would both get rich, then seize all the resulting wealth for himself.
"They wanted to squeeze everything out of him they could," Kroman said, "then throw him away."

Watching Almquist cope with his depression as he entered into
protracted and difficult negotiations with Hussey, A.H. Capital,
and Bill Carlton, I realized that I was watching the culmination of
a theme that had eluded me throughout my work on this book. It
first was raised to me by Furness, when he was talking about his
travails with Microvision: "I know they have to shoot the inventor,"
he said, "I know they have to do that! At some point, you have to
get the inventor out of the process. But this is just too much."
David Melville said much the same thing when he left Microvision: "They always have to shoot the inventor." Joey King had
watched his first employer make millions off Digital DJ while paying him next to nothing for his work. And nearly every engineer I
had studied over the past two years had either been fired by his
paymasters or found himself maneuvered out of stock made salable on the strength of his work. The VRD development team had
lost out to Microvision's managers; legions of engineers at Virtual

i/O had gone down in flames; and now Almquist was fighting both for the coming fruits of his invention and for his freedom to profit from future inventions. Everywhere I looked, I saw inventors being manipulated out of their stock by people who controlled their access to the money they needed to turn their ideas into something real and profitable. It looked to me as if the American engineer trying to survive in a business world inhabited and controlled by venture capitalists is essentially a child who has been lured into a car by a pedophile with a handful of candy.

There is, of course, tremendous unease in the American soul over the worth of the American dreamer/engineer. We simultaneously romanticize these peculiar men and women, profit off them, try to starve them out, and kill them off. Investors, as if furious at their dependence on visionaries, subject them to painful rituals of accounting and screaming and begging by doling out cash to them in increments too small ever to get them from "here to there," to quote Rich Johnston yet again. It is as if investors, distrustful of their own ability to tell the difference between an American Dream and an American Pipe Dream, hedge their bets by holding visionaries to budgets and time lines that are just short of adequate.

This contrived adversity, however, may be the key ingredient in the mix of conditions that helps the visionary succeed. If American science and engineering is indeed a unique laboratory for the realization of dreams, it likely is due no more to the quality of the visions themselves than to the punishing nurture visited upon the visionary by his or her banker. I asked Joey King once why he kept coming back to the HIT lab and to F5 Labs, where he was starved for cash and respect, when he had lucrative and prestigious jobs for life awaiting him in Japan, at the Advanced Telecommunications Research Institute, and at any one among dozens of well-funded, long-established American research laboratories. "It's true that I could go over to ATR and sit at a desk and stare thoughtfully out the window for a living," King said. "But I keep coming back here because I do my best work under adverse conditions."

ACKNOWLEDGMENTS

It would have been impossible to complete this project without the astonishing openness, honesty, and trust accorded me by Dr. Thomas A. Furness III. Others in the HIT Lab—most notably Suzanne Weghorst and Toni Emerson—gave me invaluable assistance, insight, information, and encouragement. The lab's Ann Elias played Beatrice to my ersatz Dante as I tried to plumb the historical, psychological, and technical mysteries of her domain. Had it not been for her perspective and good humor, I would neither have finished nor survived this exercise. Hunter Hoffman, Mark Draper, and Jerry Prothero were kind enough to experiment on me deviously and at great length.

I am tremendously fortunate to live in a community that supports and encourages its writers and that understands the vagaries (most of them financial) of my trade. Friends, acquaintances, and others, sometimes unwittingly, provided me with much-needed assistance and inspiration. I am particularly indebted to Jane Sutherland of Bainbridge Island's American Marine Bank; to the Bennett Memorial Committee of the Bremerton, Washington, Kiwanis Club; and to Glen and Jean Moehring, Kathy and Rick Countryman, Cadet Samuel Hudson (USCGA), Richard Holt, Sally

Hewett, and Jim Bromley. Leanne Preble also stepped in at a critical moment to provide timely and invaluable support.

Thanks also to David Brewster for giving me the time to research and write this book, to Van Conner and the rest of the Screaming Trees for their accompaniment, to Pat "Loose Cannon" Moody, and to the estimable Nat Sobel, surely the world's hardest-working (and hardest-bitten) agent.

Finally, I would like to thank Kevin Gammill and Nicole Mitskog for inspiration beyond wo

INDEX

ABOUT THE AUTHOR

FRED MOODY has held a variety of jobs, the most interesting being cowhide curer at Friese Hide and Tallow in Bellingham, Washington, and the longest-standing being staff writer at the *Seattle Weekly*. He grew up in the Pacific Northwest and has traveled elsewhere as little as possible. He was educated at Fairhaven College and the University of Michigan. He writes on technology, sports, graphic arts, rock and roll, beer, and business, and his writing has won a variety of awards too few and too undistinguished to bear mentioning. He lives in an offshore exurb of Seattle with his wife, children, burdensome debts, and infuriating household pets.